I Don't Want *to* Talk About Home

www.penguin.co.uk

I Don't Want *to* Talk About Home

Suad Aldarra

doubleday

TRANSWORLD IRELAND
Penguin Random House Ireland, Morrison Chambers,
32 Nassau Street, Dublin 2, Ireland
www.transworldireland.ie

Transworld Ireland is part of the Penguin Random House group of companies
whose addresses can be found at global.penguinrandomhouse.com

First published in the UK and Ireland in 2022
by Doubleday
an imprint of Transworld Publishers

This book is a work of non-fiction based on the life, experiences and recollections
of the author. In some cases names of people, places, dates, sequences and
the detail of events have been changed to protect the privacy of others.

I Don't Want to Talk About Home receives financial assistance from the Arts Council.

A CIP catalogue record for this book
is available from the British Library.

ISBN 9781781620625

Typeset in 11.5/15.75pt Minion Pro by Jouve (UK), Milton Keynes
Printed and bound in Great Britain by Clays Ltd, Elcograf S.p.A.

The authorized representative in the EEA is Penguin Random House Ireland,
Morrison Chambers, 32 Nassau Street, Dublin D02 YH68.

Penguin Random House is committed to a sustainable
future for our business, our readers and our planet. This book
is made from Forest Stewardship Council® certified paper.

For Housam and Keenan

'The wound is the place where the light enters.'

Rumi

Contents

CONTENTS

Prologue

WE ALL COME FROM somewhere.

However, when someone asks where I come from, I pause, for longer than I should, before I answer. And every time I say I am from Syria, I feel like I'm standing at a funeral while Syria lies in an open casket and mourners tell me how sorry they are for my loss.

When I'm asked what I miss most about home, my mind bustles with a thousand memories from the vibrant streets of Damascus. I picture what I left behind: my sweet grandmother, my fluffy black-and-white cat, my pile of books. But more than all of this, the thing I miss most is myself. I was a different person then; my thoughts, my words, my outfits and my friends were all different. Everything about me now has changed – whether for better or for worse isn't yet clear – but the earlier version of me is still trapped inside. Some might call this integration. I call it an identity crisis.

I may have stopped trying to explain the love I hold for Syria, but I have never let go of it. I carry my troubled homeland within me; I hide it like a crime. After nine years of forced separation and living in other countries, I am still not sure if I should move on, stop counting the years and settle for a new home.

Sometimes, I try to define home in my mind, in order to try to

1

recreate it. I always fail and end up even more disappointed than I was before.

What, after all, is home? It is the smell of a traditional home-cooked meal that greets you as you walk through the front door after a long day. A warm hug from a grandmother who always treats you like a special guest. Hysterical laughter with an old friend at a favourite coffee shop where they know your usual order. A loud family gathering you secretly wish to escape to avoid the endless prying questions. Your native language on the street signs and on the radio. Familiar faces, and the roads you know like the back of your hand. It is all the little things that can't be written down or described to those who haven't been there. It is the hole inside your soul that can't be filled by any other place.

A few years ago, I discovered a term for what I feel when I think of home. A Portuguese word: *saudade*. Defined in the *Dictionary of Untranslatables*, *saudade* is deep nostalgia, the longing for something that is no longer there.

This feeling, *saudade*, sometimes hits me out of the blue. I might notice an Arabic word, or a colleague tells me about their trip to Syria back in the day. A song that I used to play back home pops up on shuffle, or an old photo from my archive appears on my computer screen. It hits sudden and hard, like a car crash. As if I've just woken up from a coma, I can't recognize the world around me. *What am I doing here? Why is everyone speaking in English rather than Arabic?* Everyone becomes a stranger.

I become a stranger.

Chapter 0

Goodbye, Home

Damascus, Syria – 3 December 2012

I DON'T KNOW WHAT exactly is waiting for me on the other side, but I know what I am leaving behind. And that, for now, is enough to keep me going.

The car barely moves through the busy streets of Damascus while I sit in the back seat, trying to stare at the crowds instead of overthinking what we are about to do. My cousin Samer drives, while Housam, who became my husband three days ago, sits beside him in the passenger seat. We are quiet, but the noise of traffic surrounds us. It has always been packed in Damascus, but the newly installed checkpoints on every major street have suffocated the city. The ramifications of recent events are reflected in the faces of the people walking by. No one knows what is going to happen next. People go through their daily routine, hoping for the best, hoping they don't get killed or arrested on the way. I can't remember who said 'Homeland is not a hotel that you leave when the service goes bad', but that is all I can think right now.

I didn't want to leave, not at the beginning. I love it here. I've accepted this bad service for almost two years: the lack of electricity and gas, the explosions, the threatening security checks and, finally, the collapse of the currency. I wanted to stay and help. I was on the waiting list to join the Red Crescent emergency team. A sudden missile explosion takes me out of my thoughts, falling somewhere too far to be seen but close enough to be heard. My heart races; these missiles don't seem to be stopping any time soon. If anything, they are getting more frequent. I can't bear to hear that whistle any more. I can't keep wondering if we will be the next target.

I need to leave Syria. I need to leave this country of unanswered prayers.

This traffic seems to be holding us back deliberately, refusing to let us leave the city. I've already said my farewells to the friends who haven't yet left, but who will probably say their own goodbyes soon. I hugged Lara, my closest friend, who held her big supportive smile right until the last minute. I kissed my grandmother, who walked unsteadily to the front door of her house to say goodbye and wish me luck. I said farewell to my fluffy cat, my precious books and my home. I took a total of forty kilograms of my belongings in two suitcases and stored the rest. I covered my furniture with old sheets and closed the wooden shutters. As I switched off the electricity and stood in the now dark house, I could hear the sounds of our former normal life: summer visitors, morning radio, evening news reports on the TV, my beginner piano practice, the waves of laughter and endless arguments with my family. The darkness swallowed all the noise. I left the house before the ghosts of the past could follow me, and locked the main door and the backyard gate, not sure when – or if – I would be back.

'Yes, we are on our way to the airport now.' Housam is talking on his mobile phone. 'I just wanted to thank you for . . .'

I am not sure what the travel agent has said, but I see the look on Housam's face change.

'What? When did this happen?'

I move to the edge of my seat, trying to understand what is going on.

'No, we weren't notified. OK . . . I see . . . We will figure it out. Thanks.'

Housam hangs up and sighs. I look at him desperately, dying to know what has just happened, but at the same time afraid to hear it.

'Our flight to Egypt has been cancelled.'

My heart skips a beat.

'Looks like the conflict around the airport has spiked today: our plane couldn't land and had to return. They've shut down the airport completely.'

'What about leaving through Lebanon?' Samer asks.

'I guess that's our only option now.' Housam smiles with left-over hope. 'We will have to rebook another flight from Beirut.'

I collapse back in my seat without saying a word, leaving Samer and Housam to figure out how to hire a car to drive us to Beirut. A tear slips down my cheek. I close my eyes tight, trying to hold back sobs, until Samer notices me in the rear-view mirror.

'Hey, hey! You will make it out, don't worry!' Samer tries to cheer me up while Housam remains silent, feeling helpless and guilty for breaking the bad news.

'I know.' I look at the road to avoid any eye contact. 'I know it's for the best. I know we might have been killed if we'd continued driving to the airport.' My voice trembles as I try to stay composed. 'I am just . . . tired . . . of all this.'

The last sentence breaks the dam of tears I have held back through the past stressful months. I have pretended to be strong through every explosion, every farewell and every heartbreak,

reminding myself that it will all be over soon. I have been anticipating this moment, the moment we would finally get on a plane
and leave this hell behind. And now it's not going to happen – not
today, at least – and I am exhausted. I cry it all out as Samer takes
the next exit, returning to Damascus, the city that we never left.

Tomorrow is another day.

The staff at the hotel are surprised to see us return after checking
out earlier in the day. I am numb and out of words, so I stand
behind Housam and let him deal with the woman at reception.
She hands him a key for a new room. We are no longer newlyweds now. It doesn't matter where we spend the night or in which
bed we lie next to each other. We head to our new room, and we
scatter our disappointment on the tidy bed.

'Now what?' I say, lying down and staring at the ceiling.

'Now nothing,' Housam says. 'It is already too late to do anything
today. I will deal with it first thing tomorrow.' He grabs his phone as
it vibrates, then adds, 'Ahmad says that he is coming with the rest
of the group to check on us. Are you OK to meet up with them?'

'Whatever.'

'Get up and wash your face. Let's go for a walk around the hotel.'

My body doesn't respond until I feel Housam's fingers pressing gently on my shoulder as if to wake me. *How is he still holding
up?* It feels easier to lie on the bed and watch the ceiling than to
go out and meet other people, but I find a ray of hope in Housam's
eyes and I hang on tight to it.

The company of our good friends changes the rhythm of the
day. The jokes start being cracked as soon as we meet and last
until the end of the night in the relative safety of the hotel's ter-
raced restaurant. A dark sense of humour has been a powerful

survival tool for the Syrian people over many decades. I feel lighter, surrounded by our friends, as the weight of the unfortunate events begins to lift. We laugh contagiously, dine together, and for once it doesn't seem such a bad idea to stay one or two more nights in Syria.

It's softly raining in the morning when Housam leaves to book another flight and deal with another dilemma. Because he is a Palestinian refugee, he requires a security permit to enter Lebanon, obtained through a bureaucratic procedure that consumes time and patience, especially during such a difficult period. Housam's father accompanies him for support, and he manages to convince the arrogant employee at the General Authority for Palestinian Arab Refugees to issue the permit on the same day.

While I wait, I decide to check on my cat at his new home. Beso rushes towards me and meows nervously while he circles my feet and rubs against them, as if saying, 'Where have you been?' His new owner tells me that he hasn't been eating for the past three days. 'But he'll be fine. He probably just misses you.' I want to cry, but I am out of tears.

I am breaking, quietly, into thousands of pieces inside. I bend down and pass my fingers through Beso's thick white-and-black fur, not sure what to say. He will never understand why I left him or why I came back, so what's the point of staying? I get up at that thought and thank the new owner for letting me see him for the last time. I turn my back on Beso and march towards the door of the house without looking back. His meows get louder as I close the door behind me. I merge with the noisy streets of Damascus; I can still hear my abandoned cat calling for me. I am gone.

*

Housam and I reunite at the hotel in the afternoon. His face is lit up and he holds the travel permit in his hand.

'I can't believe my father managed to convince the man, just as I was about to punch him in the face!'

Housam's enthusiasm sends hope through my veins as I realize that things are back on track. He shows me our new tickets to Cairo, this time from Beirut instead of Damascus.

'I've booked a taxi driver for nine a.m. tomorrow,' Housam adds. 'He's an expert in checkpoints and border control, and does this journey all the time, so everything should go smoothly.'

I notice the time of our flight's departure is 7 p.m. Although the trip usually takes less than two hours, Housam wants to beat the odds and be prepared for any surprises. Something impossible to do during these times, but one can only try.

The yellow taxi arrives right on time. The driver takes our luggage from the hotel entrance and places it in the boot. Housam's parents show up at the hotel to say goodbye. I wait in the car to give them a moment alone and watch them hug for the last time, thinking of my own far-away parents. I block the memory and look away. Housam joins me after a few minutes and sits in the passenger seat, avoiding eye contact. I rub his shoulder from the back seat and whisper, 'Don't worry, honey, they will be fine.'

Our plan-B escape out of Syria is now on. We reach the border before noon – the driver managing to fulfil his promise – and breeze through the security checkpoint. The knot between my shoulders relaxes as we leave Syria, knowing that the worst part is over, but the tension sneaks back up my spine as soon as we hit the Lebanese border and I catch sight of the long line of cars ahead of us.

The driver parks on the side of the road and turns his face to us.

'There is not much I can do here,' he explains in a serious tone. 'Each of you should take your passport and stand in the specified line in the passport control building, and I will do the same myself.'

He points at the lines ahead of us: one for women and one for men. There are two extra sub-lines for Palestinian-Syrian women and men. They are always treated with extra 'care', given the infamous history of Palestinian military operations in Lebanon.

'Whoever finishes first should come back and wait here by the car.'

We get out of the car, holding our passports, and part, heading to our specified lines.

The passport control area contains a three-storey, faded yellow-brick building with a sign featuring Lebanon's famous cedar tree. Due to the large number of travellers, the lines stretch outside the building and into the cold open air.

Alarmed, I take my position at the end of the women's queue, which is full of raised voices. The women standing around me are dressed in dark-coloured *jalabiyas* – traditional loose-fitting dresses – and headscarves. They are shouting at the officers while young children are playing and babies crying. I recognize their suburban dialect, and remember that there was a massive conflict in a town near the Syrian border, forcing many families to leave their homes. That explains the long queue, but I have no idea why they are so angry.

I can barely hear my thoughts. I feel trapped in the middle of a fight, being pushed from the back and the front, as more women join the scene and stand behind me in line. As the crowd sways, it becomes more of a wave than a line. I am out of breath. I rise to the tips of my toes to look around.

Why isn't this damn queue moving?

I have been here for about ten minutes now, and I am still standing, or struggling to stand, in the same place in line. I look towards the window where the officer in charge is supposed to be checking passports and realize what's going on. The officer is just standing there, away from his desk, along with three colleagues. They're looking out at the angry women from their booth and not doing anything. *They don't want to work!*

Lebanese people have a long history of struggle with the Syrian government and the continuous abuse of power by the army. This moment is their chance to finally get back at Syria. We are all victims of political corruption, but instead of facing the people in power, they are attacking powerless people like us.

I stare in disbelief. I catch a glimpse of their eyes through the crowds, and I see cruel enjoyment on their smirking faces. The Lebanese passport control officers are taking pleasure in watching desperate women pushing each other in line, shouting and cursing. To them, it's like watching a wrestling game, knowing they have the power to end it.

This is sick.

Between the shouting women and the heartless officers, I am stuck here in the middle, helpless – and quiet. My yells won't change anything; they will just give the officers more joy. I let a storm of rage seethe within me. There is nothing to do but wait for a miracle to happen. The women are getting angrier by the minute. We all feel the shared humiliation of having to wait for a low-grade officer to let us pass through into the country that is now our only exit out of Syria. Suddenly, he points to one of the women standing in line to come forward. She moves a few steps, and we instantly see the difference between her and the rest of the crowd. She is a young, modern, stylish blonde girl who is clearly wealthy. The officer takes her passport, stamps it in seconds and allows her to pass without a word. As soon as he does that, the women get furious and start cursing the girl and the officer.

'You like sluts, huh? Well, excuse us for being covered up in hijabs, you animal.'

The modern girl takes her passport and forces her way between the others, impervious to their insults. The officer returns to his regular watch, cursing back at the women, satisfied with the unnecessary rage he's caused.

I am exhausted. I know if I fall apart now I will drown in the sea of angry women. *What am I going to do? What if Housam is waiting for me?* I look around, and my desperate glance crosses with the officer's. I don't know what he sees in my eyes, but he points at me to come towards the window in front of him. I leave my spot in the queue and pass the others, rushing forwards. The officer takes my passport and stamps it. I am torn between thanking him and spitting in his face for humiliating us all, but I know it's hopeless trying to change anything. I leave, a coward, as the crowd turns on me. The woman who was standing behind me in line hurls insults. It's the last straw. 'I was fucking standing in front of you!' I yell, defending myself. 'You saw I didn't do or say anything, so just shut up!'

The woman is surprised by my reaction, and the others are quiet for a second. She turns away and starts murmuring while I run towards the car, shaking.

This war is changing me. It is bringing out the worst in all of us.

Away from passport control, I breathe the freezing December air and look around for Housam. I spot the taxi driver walking towards me.

'Your husband is still stuck inside,' he updates me. 'His line is not moving. It is the worst one! Come and sit in the taxi. It's too cold out here.'

The driver unlocks the car, and I slide inside to rest and get some warmth, keeping my eyes fixed on the exit, hoping to see Housam show up any minute.

The wintry sun starts to disappear behind the passport control building, announcing the end of a restless day. I check my watch for the millionth time. It's 5 p.m. Almost five hours since I split up from Housam. A knock on the window of the taxi startles me. Housam's troubled face appears. He joins us in the car without saying a word, but with a stamped passport. The taxi driver is the only one with energy left.

'We can still catch the plane, don't worry.'

He starts the engine and wakes up the cold car. It is now a race against time.

We fly down the road leading to the airport with less than two hours left to catch our salvation flight and sixty-seven kilometres still to go. My soul is aching. I feel the urge to vomit the whole experience out of my body. I close my eyes and lie back, but December creeps under my woollen jacket. I shiver as I feel the car jumping on the bumpy road, but can't find the energy to open my eyes. I think of my favourite hot milky drink, *sahlab*, with cinnamon sprinkled on top. I think of how its warmth spreads through my hands when holding the cup, and then down my throat when I take the first sip. My head is heavy, and my stomach is unhappy. I am lost somewhere between consciousness and dreaming. I hear the mixed voices of my husband and the driver, but can't understand what they are talking about. *Did they just say 'snowstorm'?*

I am not sure how much time has passed before I open my eyes. I realize we are not moving any more, but one look around tells me we haven't reached the airport yet.

'What happened? Where are we?' I try to speak up, but my voice comes out low.

Housam turns back to me and gives me another desperate smile.

'A snowstorm has blocked the road. We are waiting for the snowplough over there to clear the way.'

I feel a punch in my stomach. I look at my watch, then to Housam, and then to the road.

'But ... the flight ...' I try to articulate my words, but they vanish.

'You guys have the worst luck,' the driver says. 'I am really sorry, but this is the worst weather I have ever seen.' His voice is flat now. He was beaming with enthusiasm when we met him this morning. Now he can barely talk. We did this to him.

I look through the windshield and see the giant snowplough working slowly through the white mounds. The yellow street lights make the snow look gloomy in the dark. I used to love snow back in Syria, but now I can't look at it any more.

In *The Alchemist*, Paulo Coelho wrote, 'When you want something, all the universe conspires in helping you to achieve it.' What a pretty lie! *Why does it feel like the whole universe is conspiring to sabotage our attempt to leave?*

We are so close to Beirut's airport, but still too far to reach it on foot. There is nothing we can do but sit and wait in the cold, listening to the thunder of the snowplough. As the noise dies down, we take it as a sign that the road is now clear. The driver restarts the engine and gets us back to the road, a sliver of hope still remaining. We're at full speed, trying to race time, but I wonder if we can reverse it.

We arrive ten minutes before our scheduled flight.

We know we won't be admitted, but the driver keeps us hanging on to the last thread of hope. Maybe the flight has been delayed. Maybe they are still waiting for us. Housam hands me the passports and urges me to run to the check-in counter while he brings the luggage. I push my fragile body through the airport and rush towards the Egyptian Airlines counter, but I don't see anyone. I nervously ask around, but no one has a clear answer. Minutes later, an employee saunters towards the desk. I explain our urgent situation, but he barely looks at me.

'I am sorry you missed your flight.'

He isn't sorry. I can see it in his face. I turn around to see Housam rushing from the airport entrance with our luggage. I shake my head, and he slows down to catch his breath. When he reaches me, I tell him what happened, but he insists on talking to the airline's agent.

'I am aware you missed your flight, and there is nothing we can do,' the agent replies in his arrogant tone.

'OK, when is the next flight, then?' Housam asks.

'It is tomorrow at seven a.m.'

'Can you change our booking and put us on it, please?'

'I am afraid I can't do that. It is fully booked.'

'Isn't there a waiting list that you could put us on?'

'No. Come back again around check-in time. If two of the confirmed passengers don't show up, then we can give you their seats.'

'But . . . we need a clear answer or we'll have to find another solution.'

'I can't help you. There are many others in the same situation as you. Go help your people who are sleeping on *our* streets.'

The terrible Lebanese revenge is still going on.

We stand at Rafic Hariri Airport with our big suitcases, not sure what to do next: we have no phone coverage or Wi-Fi, and we don't know anyone in Beirut. We conclude we'll have to spend the night at the airport. The taxi driver has already left. There's no going back.

My stomach growls, and we realize we haven't eaten anything since we left Syria this morning. Housam leaves me with the luggage to grab some food, but there is only one restaurant left open at this late hour, with an expensive menu. Housam brings back a variety of mezzes, and spreads out the small plates on the metal seat we're resting on. Over the food, he tells me how he dealt with the passport officer who was determined not to allow anyone entry on his shift. After waiting for hours, Housam had to explain to everyone in line ahead of him that he was about to miss his flight. Although everyone sympathized and let him go first, it wasn't until another Lebanese officer intervened that Housam managed to get his passport stamped.

I look at Housam miserably, feeling guilty that while I was resting in the taxi, he was going through another level of humiliation.

We wander around the airport until we find a PC with an internet connection and send our friends and family a short email updating them on our current situation. We pick a bank of seats as our bed for the night, and I lie down on the hard metal, while Housam stays up to guard me and the luggage. It is cold, even inside the airport. I keep turning, failing to find a comfortable position. The airport announcements continue to broadcast. Nobody cares if it is late; nobody expects us to be sleeping here. I didn't expect that either. I close my eyes and pretend to be asleep, pretend to be in a better place, pretend to be dead – anything to get through this night.

I manage to sleep for an hour or two before the check-in counter opens again. The arrogant airline employee still stands between us and our chance to leave this miserable place. I wait in my seat while Housam is trying to get us tickets on the next flight. He goes back and forth between me and the counter as the employee keeps asking him to wait for longer. An hour passes slowly. We are nervous about missing the second flight and spending another day at the airport as we notice crowds of passengers waiting ahead of us. I can see Housam's veins throbbing as he struggles to control his rage. Finally, he comes back with tickets in his hand.

'Come on, let's go. We are leaving this place,' Housam announces.

I jump up with a sudden charge of energy. 'What happened?'

'I upgraded our tickets to first class with some of the money I was saving for our trip. That asshole completely changed his tone with me when he realized I had money.'

Housam takes our luggage to the check-in counter. At this moment he looks heroic to me. We head together to the designated gate to make our third attempt to leave.

I never thought that the first time I flew first class, it would be a one-way ticket, from war to the unknown.

Chapter 1

A Girl with a Typewriter

MY NAME IS SUAD. It should actually be spelled Sua'ad, but my mother couldn't bear to break a grammatical rule and have three consecutive vowels, so she dropped the *a*', which stands for an Arabic letter that has no equivalent in English. My mother never broke any rules, except once, but it is still too early to talk about that.

I was named after my paternal grandmother, and my elder brother, Walid, was named after my grandfather. My mother had wanted to call me Sally, but my father controlled names, as he did everything else in our lives.

My father was a proud Syrian from Al-Kanawat, a district that existed inside Damascus's ancient walls long before the city grew beyond them. These walls had ceased to exist over a thousand years ago, but he occasionally joked about my mother's inferior origins in the conservative neighbourhood of Al-Midan, technically on the outskirts. My father expressed his love for the city by despising everyone who wasn't from there. His xenophobia was a side effect of his Syrian patriotism, his feelings for the country he remained in love with even after leaving it. His father's death at a young age pushed him to take a job in Riyadh to build a decent life and support his family. My mother left for different reasons. Around the time she became the first woman in her family to graduate from university, a wave of troubles started in Damascus. In 1980, a failed attempt by the Muslim Brotherhood to assassinate the then president, Hafez al-Assad, led to arbitrary arrests of conservative Muslim men. My mother wanted to help her brother escape the tension, so she accepted a teaching job in Saudi Arabia where the rules stated she should be accompanied by a male guardian. My mother's plan was to get her brother settled in Riyadh and go back to Damascus, but after meeting my father, she was married in 1982 at the age of twenty-six and uprooted for ever.

'It was raining heavily that night, and you couldn't wait to be born in the streets of Riyadh,' my mother would say, smiling, in her calm voice. 'We were worried you would pop out in the car before reaching the hospital.' After a complicated delivery with Walid three years previously, thankfully my birth was easy. She always laughed afterwards, before adding, 'But later you sure made my life harder due to your stubbornness!'

My father's abiding memory is rather different. 'When I held you for the first time, I realized you had dark skin!' His eyes would widen in shock. 'I accepted this and thanked God, but after they gave you a warm bath, you turned out to be a blonde girl!' He grinned. 'I was over the moon!'

When I was younger, I didn't realize that my father was a racist. I didn't understand why he frowned when he smelled the incense spreading out from our Sudanese neighbours next door, or why he mocked our Palestinian neighbours' dialect when he overheard them talking to my mother. I was brought up to believe that the Damascene people were superior to any others, our food, culture and ancestors the very best.

Sami was my younger brother. He came along in the year

following my birth, and together, we gave my parents the busiest year of their lives. As we grew, we spent all our time either playing together or plotting against Walid. Sometimes I would change my strategy and plot with Walid against Sami, but they were never allowed to plot against me. My father constantly reminded them to look after me. His overprotective love made me invincible. I could risk getting into trouble because I knew he would always have my back.

Whenever my father was asked about us, he would say, 'I have two girls and a boy,' referring to me as the boy. I was louder, more active, more destructive and more curious than my brothers. I loved to hear him say that. It was his way of being proud of me.

'He called you girls!'

I would tease my brothers and burst into laughter, as if being a girl was an insult. Little did I know how sexist my father's compliment was. Although I was my father's favourite then, that was to change a lot over the years.

I inherited from my father more than just his looks; I also got his explosive rage and tender heart – two characteristics that I have struggled to control through most of my life. My father blamed his diabetes for his extreme mood swings, while my mother blamed his troubled family history and his first marriage, which was deemed unsuccessful after less than a year. His disease did not stop him from eating sugar-loaded sweets, a habit that sparked many arguments between my parents, on top of the many differences triggered by their twelve-year age gap. I don't think they loved each other – I don't think any married couple I knew loved each other – but they still cared. She looked after his diet and medicines, and he would put out a protective arm in front of her whenever he braked suddenly while driving.

But most of the time, he was angry, she was anxious, and I was both.

We lived in a two-bedroom apartment located in a new residential complex in the old part of Riyadh, beside Deera Square – or 'Chop-Chop Square', because of the occasional Friday public executions. On other days, the spacious, palm-lined tiled square would be full of kids playing on their bikes or scooters, and shoppers wandering in the retail area – women wearing the black *abaya* and men in the white *thobe*. Children were mostly exempt from such traditions, so they added a vibrancy with their coloured clothes and bright laughs.

My father's job as an accountant at the Saudi Ministry of Electricity didn't impress me as a child, but it was, combined with my mother's salary, enough to provide a decent life for our middle-class family. It was my mother's job as an English teacher that fuelled my youthful curiosity. I still remember the echo of the typewriter whenever she brought it back from school to type up an exam paper. I used to drop everything I was doing and rush to sit next to her, and try to touch the keys.

'I will let you use it when I am done; just don't touch anything and let me focus,' my mother would promise. I would hold my breath, following the dance of the type bars with my eyes as she clicked on the keys, the letters appearing on the paper like magic. Each time she grabbed the lever on the side of the typewriter to start a new line, I would ask, 'Mama, are you done now?' until she finally pulled out her paper from the roller and blew on it to dry the ink. That was when I knew it was my turn to be the writer. She would slide a new sheet of paper into the typewriter or reuse the back of one she had made a mistake on. My chubby face would gleam with excitement as I started pushing keys – in a rush at first, but then more slowly, trying to see the exact moment the ink was transferred to the page. Sometimes, I would end up getting my little fingers stuck in the void between the keys, or one of the letters would jam. At that point, my mother would say, 'OK, that's enough for today,' and pack the typewriter away in its case. I knew it was the school's property and not ours to keep, so I didn't argue. Instead, I reminded myself that one day I too would be a teacher. I would have my own typewriter, and no one would stop my words.

The typewriter wasn't the only fascinating thing that my mother brought back from school. Before the beginning of every semester, she brought a pile of new English books along with a couple of black markers.

'The books are from Western countries, and they contain inappropriate images,' she explained, pointing to several pictures of women wearing short dresses or swimsuits. I used to watch her go through each page and black out the same images and words in every book, hiding Christmas, which we didn't celebrate.

Part of my mother's job was to make sure such ideas were kept well away from the curriculum and the students' minds. All the schools in Saudi Arabia followed a similar approach in order to make sure that the education system was in line with Islamic customs and teachings. Whenever I felt bored in class, I used to play a game, trying to guess what lay behind the black strokes.

Is it Santa?

Is it wine?

Is it a woman?

Is it a pig?

Similarly, video games were also censored in Saudi Arabia. We would often buy games with the female character blacked out on the cover. My favourite game was *Tomb Raider*. Lara Croft was all black except her face, but I could still see her fully detailed, pixelated body when I played the game.

My mother didn't redact the books she got me outside school. When we went back home to Syria every summer, she would take me to Sayegh bookshop in Al-Salhiyah Street, where she used to buy her English literature books for college. My love of reading was born on those short, joyful trips, particularly when I discovered the English books with the red Ladybird logo in the corner. My mother didn't buy me dolls or teddy bears. Instead, she gifted me the magical world of words, which kept my imagination busy during my early years in Saudi Arabia. The best thing about those books was that they were never marked with black.

My father also used to take me to his favourite Arabic bookshop, Al-Noori, the oldest and biggest bookshop in the heart of Damascus. There I bought Arabic children's stories and, later, coming-of-age novels. My father was fond of novels and political books, but he didn't try to influence my taste. He bought his books, and I bought mine, and we never talked about it.

Another summer ritual was going to the shore of Latakia on the Syrian Mediterranean coast. Swimming with my father and brothers was the best part, as I got to show off my skills in front of my brothers and try to copy my father's moves. Beach days were rare moments when my father smiled more and worried less. His face was brighter in Syria than in Saudi Arabia, and the sun would hide behind his body as he stood tall in the middle of the water. I would swim with him for as long as I could, stretching out those brief moments of happiness, even after my brothers withdrew from the water and went to change.

My mother never joined us in the sea. She would sit on a tall bench on the beach under a parasol, wearing her long skirt over thick nylon tights, a loose blouse under a navy ankle-length coat called a *manteau*, and a white hijab covering her hair, all in the flaming August heat. I knew she couldn't join us, so I didn't try to convince her. Mothers didn't swim. They just sat in the shade, sweating and waiting for their children to finish having a good time with their fathers so they could help them shower and get dressed.

I don't want to be a mother in the shade when I grow up.

Every time I glanced at my mother from the water, I had that thought in my mind. It was more intimidating than the vast blue sea surrounding me.

The education system in the Middle East consisted of three levels: primary, intermediate and secondary, which lasted for six, three and three years respectively. I attended the prestigious private all-girls school where my mother had recently started teaching English to the older girls. My brothers attended a public all-boys school. From Saturday to Thursday, I wore a uniform of an olive-green, full-length pinafore dress and a pale-yellow, long-sleeved shirt. My brothers wore white *thobes*.

My parents wouldn't have been able to afford the private school fees, but the special discount for teachers granted me a place among the daughters of wealthy Saudi families. It also meant I was on the radar as a teacher's daughter who had to obey the rules before anyone else. That didn't bother me at first; my teachers liked me, and it was easy at that age to make friends. No one cared where I came from or what my parents did for a living and I would regularly get invited to birthday parties in massive villas or mansions that looked like a Disney world on the inside. The goody bags at those parties were usually more expensive than the humble gift I had brought.

What used to embarrass me was having to bring my brother, Sami, to those parties. My parents felt better having us together in a stranger's house, but I didn't like being the only one arriving with a brother in tow. Though I complained about my brother's company, there were times when I was grateful for it, especially when he found me after I ended up getting lost in one of the vast party mansions. I felt safer with him, but I never admitted it, and he never complained. Sami was sweet and obedient, but I was too competitive to appreciate him outwardly. I wanted to be the strongest and smartest, and always the winner. That's why I enrolled in every competition held in my school, and why I always won.

Reciting the Quran was the most important of these school competitions. Participants had to memorize a specific chapter of the Holy Book throughout the year, then deliver it in front of a judging committee and a theatre full of students and teachers. For me, this was just another competition, but seeing my parents' proud looks every time they asked me to recite parts of the Quran in front of their friends and relatives made me enrol year after year.

Besides learning the basics of reading, writing, science and maths, we also studied Islam, which was broken down into five subject areas, one a day: the Quran, Hadith (the stories and sayings of the Prophet), Jurisprudence, Monotheism, and Quran Interpretation. The textbooks were all written in antiquated language, too complicated for our little minds. It was as if someone had forgotten to update them. We were asked to consider what would be the right portion of *zakat* to donate to the poor in terms of assets we didn't have, like sheep, camels and cows, or our equally non-existent gold and silver. I would daydream and imagine commuting to school on a camel instead of in my father's old Mazda, or wonder how many snacks I could buy with a gold coin. We memorized the definitions of terms like 'devotion', and were told that God was always watching us. We also learnt to be wary of befriending non-Muslims, copying their lifestyle or celebrating their holidays. There were hardly any non-Muslims around me, so I didn't pay that rule much attention.

Although I was top of the class at school, my mother didn't appreciate my lack of contribution to the chores at home. While I wanted to spend the weekends immersed in my favourite books, she wanted me to dust and clean. As well as her full-time job, she was also responsible for looking after a house with three kids and an unhelpful husband. My brothers had chores of their own, but there was always an expectation for me to do more and offer to help without being asked. My mother and I argued about this constantly until she eventually invoked the ultimate sanction. No more books.

Why did she take me to bookshops and make me fall in love with books just to take it all away from me? Her sanction only made me want to read more, and I decided to look for an alternative source. The school library didn't have a good selection, so I looked to borrow books from the girls in my class. I used any opportunity to ask about their reading interests, and that's how I met Raya.

Raya was funny, smart and my first Saudi best friend. Her nationality didn't matter at that time, but it did later. I met Raya at the age of nine. She owned the latest book from an Egyptian series that I loved but couldn't afford, and she gladly offered to lend it to me. That was the first time we spoke and we connected straight away. We made sure to sit next to each other in class, and seemed never to run out of words. We were competitive academically, while having fun commenting on everything at school, like the teacher who wore the same outfit for two days in a row or repeated the same word more than fifteen times during one class. Our relationship extended beyond school over long phone calls to discuss homework and lots more besides. Although Raya wasn't Damascene, her high grades and impeccable manners were good enough for my parents to allow our friendship.

We continued to exchange books, but Raya had a much bigger library than mine. She introduced me to a new world of classic foreign literature translated into Arabic: *Les Misérables*, *A Tale of Two Cities*, *The Three Musketeers*, *Jane Eyre* and many more. She also introduced me to the dazzling world of music through her cassettes and CDs. She had a crush on Nick from Backstreet Boys and couldn't stop talking about him. I didn't like him, nor did I understand what a crush was, but I loved listening to the band's songs on my red cassette player, despite my mother's disapproval. I relished being 'cool' in a conservative Middle Eastern Muslim house, although I couldn't get rid of the guilt that sneaked up on me every time I played a song.

Music was frowned upon in Saudi Arabia, and listening to it was haram, a sin. The religious police were always distributing poorly designed brochures in the streets, warning people against listening to music and listing the punishments offenders would receive in the afterlife. Although music cassettes were displayed in the supermarkets, they'd be quickly covered when the religious police invaded the place for an inspection.

Only faces of men appeared on those cassettes. There were no melodies to be heard in shops and restaurants, unlike in Syria, where music was everywhere. *Why is music haram in Saudi Arabia but halal in Syria?* I couldn't understand. My mother was fond of Fairouz, the Lebanese musical icon whose songs had become a morning ritual in most houses in the Middle East. My mother looked so bright and joyful whenever she heard them that I was sure that Fairouz's songs were halal and Backstreet Boys were haram.

Weekends in Riyadh were always similar in our house: one day for the park, and one day for grocery shopping and preparing for the next week. Several of my parents' relatives lived in the city, but we were closest to my mother's cousin, Aunt Wafaa, her two daughters and her son, Samer.

When we met up with them, my mother and Aunt Wafaa would spend most of the day preparing food we would later eat on a mat in the park, while our fathers sat on two folding chairs and discussed work and politics in Syria. Falafel sandwiches, marble cakes, fruits and nuts, and hot and cold drinks were always part of our picnic.

My brothers and Samer played football and I would join them without thinking twice, leaving behind the girls talking about pop artists and nail polish. I found joy in competing against Samer. He was smart and confident and always received compliments from his mother, while I received complaints from mine. I wanted to be like him – better, even. I kept score of our football matches and I compared our grades at school, but as soon as I officially became a woman, I started losing the lead.

That was when my punishment began, for a crime I didn't commit.

Chapter 2

Girls Not Allowed

'MAMA, WHAT DOES *FUCK* mean?'

Various reactions flickered across my mother's face before she quickly put on a stern expression.

'Where did you hear this word?'

'It was painted on a chair in the art class. What does it mean?'

'I don't know.' My mother looked away and grabbed a dirty plate from the sink, pretending to be busy. I left her in the kitchen and went to the living room to check the brown bookcase in the corner. I looked on the shelf where she kept her English books, and I picked up the Oxford dictionary. I flipped the pages, as she'd taught me to do when looking for a word, and stopped at the one starting with the letter F. I passed my finger over the bolded words, but I couldn't find my f-word, not even in the biggest dictionary on the shelf. I had known it was a bad word when my teacher became furious and the girls tried to hide their giggles, but I didn't know what it meant.

At the age of ten, I started noticing whispers about a secret topic that no one openly talked about. Our religion teacher briefly explained the verses in the Quran that talked about the relationship between a husband and a wife and how they *connect*. Some girls in my class were now using a napkin to turn the pages of the Quran. The teacher said that we should never touch the Quran during the menstrual period because we were considered *unclean*. She told a tale about a woman who loved flowers and always had a vase full of them in her house, but once every month her flowers died when she touched them. That story left us astonished as we realized the wisdom of such a rule.

'Wash your body after menstruation; pray five times a day, or you will pray in hell; commit to a full hijab; lower your voice in the presence of men.' The religion teacher went on, listing all the new rules of puberty. 'You are now responsible for your actions in front of God.' She also spoke vaguely about wives' *duties* and how angels curse those who fail to obey their husbands. *Is that why my mother is always apologizing to my father even if she didn't do anything wrong?*

When we studied our physical development and the new changes that we should expect, it was described in terms that I couldn't correlate with my body.

'Did you know this class is different at the boys' schools? I saw it, I swear!' a girl whispered after class. She also mentioned that their books had fewer pages, 'because boys are stupid'.

I realized why she'd said this after I went home and flipped through the pages of my brothers' books, in shock. Their books talked about boys' puberty in the same vague language that I struggled to comprehend. Science, history and other topics were explained with fewer words and extra images.

Are boys really stupid? Why should I study harder than my brothers? My mother explained that in Saudi Arabia, boys and girls had separate education ministries that issued their own rules, curriculums and exams. We also had some extra subjects; boys studied geology and nationalism, while we girls studied sewing and housekeeping.

It was as if we lived in two separate countries, and that was only the tip of the iceberg.

At the end of primary school, I was introduced to my first *abaya*, as was mandatory in school. The *abaya* was like a black robe that covered my body. I had a hijab – a black scarf – with it, but I was allowed to leave this hanging on my shoulders due to my young age. The *abaya* was only to be worn in the presence of non-*mahram* men. *Mahram* is a male family member who's not allowed to marry the girl, like her father or brother. Teachers and students took off their *abayas* and hijabs as soon as they entered the gate of the female-only school campus, which was guarded from the outside by a man and a high fence, and only wore them again upon leaving. However, public schools had stricter rules and enforced full black coverage, including girls' faces upon entering and leaving the school.

It was also obligatory for women and adolescent girls to wear *abayas* and hijabs in public. The religious-police officers made sure the rule was followed by raiding public places like shopping centres and yelling at women who dared to show their hair or face. There was no particular age to start wearing this clothing in public; some conservative families covered their girls at a very young age, while some waited until the girls' first periods or until their bodies became 'tempting', whichever occurred first.

When my mother took me to buy my first *abaya* from a shop next to our house, there was only the basic over-the-head *abaya* model on display, with its full blackness and extra-loose design to make the woman's body as discreet as possible. We asked to see other styles, so the shop owner told us to wait a minute, peeked his head outside, then went into a back room to get the other models. These were designed like a robe, with some small floral embroidery or beading around the sleeves and on the front. They were also not as long, and some had a tighter waist to make them look like a dress. Those models weren't approved by the religious police but many women wore them anyway, especially upper-class Saudis or non-Saudis risking some angry yells.

During school hours, which started from around 7 a.m. and stretched for six hours, we had two breaks: one for breakfast and a shorter one for praying. We laid large carpets provided by the school in the hallways between the classrooms while a religion teacher repeated 'Allahu Akbar', to announce prayer time. We weren't forced to pray, but it was expected unless we were impure, since Islam excused women from praying or fasting during menstruation. Some girls abused that excuse to avoid reading the Quran in class or praying during the break, but I was embarrassed to use it.

The first rule I learnt about my period was 'hide everything': the underwear, the sanitary pads and, most importantly, the pain. Even during Ramadan, when Islam allows women to break the fast during their periods, I used to take a quick bite of a sandwich secretly in the kitchen, worrying that my brothers could walk in and figure out that I was on my period. Shame was always implied when it came to women's menstrual cycle.

Every month I accepted my fate as an impure creature. I hid my pads, took painkillers, pretended to be OK and washed afterwards as described in detail in my religion textbook. When I was in doubt once about a sentence written in old Arabic and tried to ask my mother about it, to make sure I was washing correctly, she sternly told me not to discuss this matter again. 'Stop asking questions. It is all described in your book; go read it.'

Shame. I felt it.

*

As I moved to the intermediate level of school, another wave of changes hit me. In the first week, the student administrator interrupted our maths class. After she'd checked attendance, she asked the foreign students to raise their hands.

'Suad, why aren't you raising your hand?' the administrator asked with an encouraging smile.

I looked at her as if she had spoken in a language I didn't comprehend. *Why should I?* She repeated her question.

'I am . . . I am not a foreigner.' I hesitated, thinking of Miss Louise, our American English teacher. She was a foreigner; I was not.

'Well, are you Saudi?' she asked in a firm tone, as if stating the obvious.

'No?' I replied, feeling the burning stares of my classmates around me.

'Then you *are* a foreigner.'

The supervisor wrote my name down with the others and left me with a new realization. *I am a foreigner. I am not like everybody else.*

I soon learnt what 'Saudization' meant. A new government policy was introduced to favour Saudi natives over foreign workers in an attempt to improve the soaring unemployment rates. As a result, my father was replaced with a Saudi employee whom he had to train before leaving. My mother gained a younger Saudi supervisor.

Saudization didn't only affect adults. Raya also replaced me with a Saudi friend. She carelessly told me her mother had suggested she was better off with a Saudi friend now. My religion teacher was also replaced. The rules were less strict for other subjects, but religion was a sensitive topic that shouldn't be left for foreign teachers who might corrupt students' pure faith. Only Sunni Saudis would know the right Islam. I later found out that, although I'd won the school Quran competition, I was not shortlisted for the national one where girls from all over the country competed. It was only open to Saudis.

My little world had suddenly changed, with a jobless father, a stressed mother and no best friend. A dark cloud floated over our house. My father seemed ready to explode at any minute, and he did so on several occasions for little or no reason. As soon as we heard his keys rattling in the front door, we dropped everything and sat down to do our homework. Eventually, he found a new job in a private company that didn't have to adhere to the Saudization rule, but he never liked it. I told myself that it was the loss of his job that caused his sudden change towards me, his verbal aggression. But every night when I lay in bed, I couldn't escape the feeling that it must have been me.

The only good thing I remember from that time was the new addition to our family – my youngest brother, Majid. I woke up one day and saw my school uniform hanging over my chest of drawers, clean and ironed, but my mum was not around. My father told me he had taken her to the hospital when her waters broke but she had insisted on preparing my uniform before they left.

Majid, my new little brother, brought joy to our house. My parents were happy around him all the time. I couldn't stop looking at him or offering to help. Everyone changed around him, but not like the way they changed around me. I made them stress, while Majid made them smile.

My parents had new set of rules for me. 'No laughing out loud, no running, no questions or objections. Your brothers are your guardians now.' The bookshop visits were halted, and swimming in the sea wasn't allowed, either. I ended up sitting beside my mother on the bench in the shade, watching my brothers in the water with my father, who seemed to forget all about me. I was a better swimmer, but that wasn't a good enough excuse to wear a swimsuit any more.

'No' was the most common word in our house. My father treated me as a suspect, questioning the occasional girls-only parties with my friends. At some point, I stopped asking to go out to avoid another argument, especially since I needed my father to drive me everywhere. With the limitations of the Saudi public transportation system and taxis considered unsafe for women, I had no other option. No one expected women to go out on their own.

The party invitations became less frequent, as if my classmates had suddenly discovered the ugly truth that we weren't the same species. I did not live in a mansion, nor did I have a personal driver with a luxurious car. My father didn't own a company or manage one, and my mother worked instead of staying at home or enjoying social events. On the rare occasions when I got invited and my father agreed to drop me off, he would spend the entire drive lecturing me.

'I am not your chauffeur!' he would yell while I sat in silence in his car with its broken air conditioning. I always arrived at the party sweating guilt and shame. Once there, I felt like I didn't belong. I couldn't add much to my classmates' conversations about music or TV shows since my parents didn't allow satellite TV in the house. We only had two censored local TV channels – one in Arabic and one in English – so I didn't know any of the popular shows. Slowly, I became silent.

A sense of solitude started to strangle me, but just as I started to withdraw from Saudi social life, a new group appeared in my path. They promised serenity for my soul, lost in a worthless materialistic world that didn't matter to the merciful God.

Thus began my long journey of atonement for being a girl.

Chapter 3

Covered Up

DURING MY INTERMEDIATE-LEVEL YEARS, I was becoming lonely at school and at home. My conversations with my mother had shrunk to a list of household chores. I noticed how she hardly listened when I spoke any more. I often got interrupted by the oven timer, by my father calling after her, or by the evening news report that never said anything new. Over time, my sentences got shorter and shorter until they became nods, shrugs or door slams.

Nora approached me at the school library, during one of my reading escapes, to tell me about a group of friends meeting at her place on Thursday to read the Quran. I was around twelve; Nora was a few years older than me, and one of my mother's favourite students at secondary level. My mother encouraged me to go – and, eager to be part of any group and hoping to find comfort in my indignant teenage years, I said yes. She convinced my father, who couldn't say no to furthering my religious education, especially as Nora was from a well-known Syrian family.

The scattered pairs of shoes in front of the inner door gave me a hint of how many people had already arrived. The door opened, and Nora welcomed me inside her villa with her bright smile. Although she was in the privacy of her home, and there were no men, she kept her hair covered, as we all did during this meeting.

'How many pages have you memorized for today?' Nora asked.

'Two ... Actually, one – I need to practise the second a bit more,' I said hesitantly.

'Don't worry,' Nora said with an encouraging smile, 'you can do that here!'

I nodded, blushing, ashamed of my humble achievement. Nora had already memorized the whole of the Quran and had an official certificate in a golden frame hanging in her stylish living room, which looked nothing like our modest home.

'*As-salamu alaykum*,' I greeted the girls in the room. Some replied in a low voice to avoid disturbing the girls already reciting the Quran. I picked up a copy from the pile placed carefully on the table and settled in an empty spot on the carpet to practise the part I had memorized for that day. I closed my eyes and started murmuring the verses under my breath. Nervous, as Nora kept checking to see if I was ready, I finally gave up and decided to be tested.

I handed my Quran to Nora and began reciting to her, while she followed along with the text. She corrected my intonation every now and then, and gently reminded me whenever I faltered. After my two pages were over, Nora smiled and gave me back the Quran.

'Well done; you just need to practise this verse here.' She pointed to where I had stumbled over words. She wrote down my progress in a notebook, and I returned the Quran to the table, feeling relieved. Nora always made me feel relaxed and welcomed. She was calm and pure. I wished I were more like her.

Maybe one day when I grow up; maybe when I finish memorizing the Quran.

'Has everyone finished reciting their parts for the day?' Nora asked, and all the girls nodded politely. It was time for the lesson. We sat in a circle around the three-seater couch in the middle of the room, where Teacher Safiya sat. I never asked why we sat on a lower level to her.

Teacher Safiya was a witty, petite middle-aged woman who led our group of young girls, who were mostly non-Saudis. I liked the way she joked with us as if we were friends. Her speeches were always fun and exciting to listen to, especially compared to the boring religion class at school.

Instead of preaching whenever we did something wrong, she would tell us indirect stories to make us subtly aware. She once told us a story about a girl who was annoyed by the rough texture of jeans, how it was affecting her femininity and making her act like a boy, so she decided to switch to skirts instead. I felt embarrassed in my jeans and tried to cover them with my *abaya*, and never wore them to the group meetings again. She told another story about a girl who used to swim in her pool at home and started feeling terrible because the tight and revealing bathing suit made her lose her modesty, so she decided to give up swimming to be closer to God. I didn't have a pool, and I knew I wasn't allowed to swim in the sea any more, so I felt good that I ticked that box on the description of a good Muslim girl. Teacher Safiya also told us that we shouldn't be completely naked in the bathroom: the *jinn* could always see us and possess us.

'Where is Arwa? I can't see her.' Teacher Safiya looked at Nora.

'Arwa is not going to make it today. She fell and broke her hand this morning,' Nora said sadly.

'Oh, the poor girl!' Teacher Safiya then turned her head towards us and added in a different tone, 'I wonder if she read the morning *azkar* when she woke up. See, girls, the importance of prayers?'

I panicked. I never read the *azkar*; I never liked them. I preferred to address God with my own words instead of formal generic prayers, but after that meeting I read them every day.

After the lesson, Nora distributed a couple of *dafs* – frame drums – and all the girls started chanting an Islamic *nasheed*. I remembered some of the words from the last time, so I tried to sing along with the group. The next song was familiar, but I didn't know why. I tried to remember, and then I realized that it was a popular song by a Lebanese artist, but the lyrics had been changed completely; it was now about God and Islam instead of love and lust. It was challenging not to think of the original lyrics, but I tried to fight my inner demons.

After singing, we did the evening prayer together and had a light meal before we went home, thinking of how we could fix ourselves, and others around us, so we could all be better Muslims.

At first, the meetups made me feel less angry and lonely.

Apart from school, this religious group was my only escape from home. And, unlike my classmates' parties, it didn't require long arguments with my parents, nor did anyone care about my social status. No one asked me about the latest episode of *Kassandra* or the new album by Backstreet Boys. No one judged my non-branded shoes or outfit, which were always covered by my *abaya*. My religious knowledge was growing, too. I was good at memorizing the Quran, and was progressing quickly. During my period, when I couldn't touch the Holy Book, I would read and memorize the Hadith, the sayings of the Prophet Muhammad, which was treated as a regular resource book and was OK for me to touch. Every time I finished memorizing a chapter of the Quran, I would be given something symbolic like a small hand-made paper figure of the Kaaba, the great mosque of Mecca. Bringing them back to my parents and seeing their faces light up for a change was the best reward.

Sometimes other girls in the group would host the meeting, but I never could: my house was far from everyone else's and too small. Even religious people had fancy houses.

At the end of every academic year, the group held a big cere-mony in Teacher Safiya's home, the biggest house of all. The living room, one of many, was huge, with high ceilings that had several chandeliers hanging over almost a hundred girls. I hadn't realized that other groups just like ours existed in different areas of the city. They were all invited to that ceremony. It was a big network of religious groups, each with their own Nora and Teacher Safiya.

The ceremony was to mark the end of a year of hard work and achievements before we parted for the summer holidays. There was a schedule of events prepared by several groups to run over the course of an exciting day. A small stage and a microphone stand were set up, and a senior girl around Nora's age started the ceremony by reading some verses of the Quran. Afterwards, there was a keynote speech by an older woman who I later learnt was the leader of all the groups. This was followed by a play writ-ten and performed by some of the girls: funny, but always with an important moral lesson on how to be an obedient Muslim girl who chose the path of God. The day was packed with Islamic chants, and quizzes with prizes. Everything was done with laughter and joy to ensure a fun time, but also with an Islamic flavour – responsible fun.

The last part of the ceremony was the most significant. A senior girl went onstage holding a list of names of those who had managed to finish memorizing the entire Quran. It was the greatest honour, and as I stood at the back, I felt so small for not having my name mentioned. Each girl on the list went up to receive a certificate with her name on it while the crowd cheered, '*Allahu Akbar.*' There was no clapping; that was how the infidels used to worship their gods in Mecca before Islam.

Another celebrated achievement was committing to wearing the hijab. At that point, I only wore it loosely in public in Saudi Arabia as it was compulsory, and I also wore it during the religious group lessons. Still, I didn't wear it when we had my parents' friends and relatives at our house, or back in Syria. During the celebration, a girl got inspired by the majesty of the moment and decided to announce her hijab commitment. She shed tears while the crowd of women and girls cheered louder for her.

I was sitting on the ground with my group when Nora rushed towards me and asked if I wanted to announce my hijab commitment, too. My heart was thumping as I became nervous and shy, not sure what to reply.

'Come on, Suad, just say yes! You are already wearing it, so why not take the full reward from God?' Nora kept insisting, and I kept sweating while my eyes watched more girls go onstage.

'Come on, Suad, come on!!!'

She was right. I was already wearing – loosely – a hijab in public, so I'd only need also to wear it indoors when we had visitors.

I felt jealous of the other girls. I wouldn't mind being in the spot-light, especially with the lack of attention I was getting from my stretched-too-thin parents. Plus, this was another good-Muslim box I could tick.

I nodded, and Nora jumped up and down, grabbed my hand and rushed me through the crowds all the way to the stage. She whispered my blessed decision to the woman with the mic, and seconds later, my name echoed in the hall along with the excited shouts of '*Allahu Akbar*'.

With everyone's eyes on me, I took a few proud steps and joined the rest of the girls onstage.

I was now officially wearing the hijab.

~

I stood in front of the large mirror in my grandparents' house in the old neighbourhood of Al-Midan in south Damascus, trying for what felt like the hundredth time to wrap my white silk hijab around my head. I looked at my reflection in the mirror, fighting back tears while my body was crying from the heat under my blouse and skirt.

'Come on, we are late!' my mother yelled from the front door. She had promised to wait for me when everyone else left so I could get a few extra minutes to wrap my hijab.

'I can't get it on! I look ridiculous!' I yelled back with tears in my voice as I walked towards her.

'You look just fine!'

I hadn't realized the size of the commitment I had made until I travelled to Syria for my summer holidays. In Riyadh, I was already wearing the mandatory black *abaya* and hijab, and I only went out to go to school, where I was allowed to take them off as soon as I entered. Things hadn't changed much after I'd announced my commitment to the hijab, but the first time we went to the park with my cousins, I was nervous about greeting Samer without shaking his hand – I now wasn't allowed to touch the hands of non-*mahram* men. I avoided him and pretended to be busy helping my mother or chatting with his sisters. A week after that, he got the message and stopped trying to say hi or ask if I wanted to play football. I didn't realize that I was getting shy and anxious around men, trying to disappear by lowering my voice and hiding in the blackness of my *abaya*. Apart from those awkward moments with Samer and having to cover up when we had visitors, my life in Saudi didn't feel much more restricted.

But in Syria, I began to notice the cultural differences between the two countries. Women in Damascus wore dark-coloured *manteaux* while young girls, like me, wore loose skirts and shirts with white hijabs. When I made the decision to commit to the hijab it was the nineties. No one cared about fashion for teenagers. Clothes shops in Syria had three sections: men, women and kids. A few shops had a tiny section for what they labelled 'The Confusing Age', which was an accurate definition of how I felt about adolescence. My mother and I spent most of that summer invading those shops, trying to find something suitable that we both agreed on. It was not an easy task for her; having moved to Riyadh, she no longer knew Damascus well. She didn't know how other confusing-age girls dressed. Eventually, we found an oversized skirt and a shirt, along with a white hijab to go with it. The hijab scarves in Syria were also made from different materials and colours, and wrapped differently and secured with pins in a way I couldn't master easily, unlike the black scarf that I could just throw around my head. My body rejected the new style like a failed organ transplant. I felt out of place and couldn't recognize myself in the mirror.

Hijab styles were not the only differences between Saudi Arabia and Syria. Women in general had more freedom in Syria; they didn't seem to need a man to chaperone every breath they took. Syrian women drove cars and used public transportation. They walked down the streets and sat in cafes without the need to hide themselves in the darkness of the *abaya*. Of course, the male-guardian prerogative still existed in most parts of the country, but the gap in freedom was significant enough for me to realize the difference, and to start dreading going back to Saudi Arabia, where I could see Samer and my brothers resuming their lives normally while I had to act like a responsible adult.

At the end of each summer, I would leave my heart in Damascus and go back to our quiet apartment in Saudi Arabia where no one laughed, and no music played.

It took me a couple of years to realize I was not happy at the religious group. I never admitted how relieved I felt whenever I had my period, just because I had an excuse to skip a meeting. I avoided phone calls from Nora and her suggestions to read the Hadith instead of the Quran. The knot inside my heart kept getting tighter with questions. *Why do we have to stay covered even though there are no men around? Why do we have to sit on the floor while the leader sits on the couch? And what's wrong with trousers? They're more comfortable! And isn't it mentioned in the Quran that God looks at our hearts, not at our appearance?*

Although all those questions had answers, they were no longer convincing enough for me.

I realized the irony of running away from the judgement of my Saudi classmates only to become judged by another group. Here, I wasn't judged for not wearing branded clothes, but for wearing jeans. I wasn't judged for not knowing the latest songs, but for not listening to religious tapes.

The judging never stopped. It just took a different shape.

I remember coming back from one of the summer ceremonies feeling the weight of the world on my chest. I stayed in bed the next day and avoided talking to my family. I couldn't understand why I was feeling distressed in a place that was meant to make me feel better. No matter how much praying I did or how much of the Quran I read, no matter how wide my skirt was or how thick my stockings were, every time I came back from a group meeting, I felt like a sinner.

Sobbing, I told my mother that I didn't want to go there any more.

She didn't argue. And I never went back.

Chapter 4

The Fire Starter

WEEKENDS IN RIYADH WEREN'T the same after Samer and his family moved back to Syria. We never went to the park again and we rarely had any visitors at our house. Although we had other relatives in the city, we didn't seem to have that same close connection. Despite not having been able to play football with Samer or interact much with him in the past years, I still missed the warm family vibes we had shared every weekend. Now, that was all gone.

After Walid finished secondary school and I started it, he also moved to Syria to study finance, following in my father's footsteps. We met him twice a year, but I missed him. I was jealous of the life he got to live in Syria. It felt like watching my cellmate walk free while leaving me behind. My parents worried about letting him go on his own to a more open world than the one he'd grown up in, but as Saudi's public universities were exclusively for Saudi nationals, and with the lack of private universities, Syria was their only option. To ease their concerns, they made him stay with my grandparents, who were thrilled to have someone in the house again. Walid loved his new life and I counted down the days to when I could share it with him.

I escaped my life in Saudi Arabia through Syrian TV dramas. My parents finally gave in and bought a satellite TV when my father realized he could watch the news twenty-four hours a day. I walked with the actors around Damascus's neighbourhoods, and learnt more about my people's culture. I wept secretly after the end of each series, frustrated that I wasn't in Syria like my brother. I could not walk in the rain, or sleep at my grandparents' house; I could not ride a bus on my own or listen to music on the radio.

My parents didn't share my feelings. Whenever we were in Syria, they couldn't wait for the summer to be over. Over the years, they'd got so accustomed to their lives in Saudi Arabia that they felt too foreign for Syria. Or perhaps Syria was too foreign for them. The places they'd loved were not there any more, and the streets seemed crowded and chaotic compared to the new, organized ones in modern Riyadh. Even the healthcare system and government services were comparatively better in Saudi. While they looked forward to returning to their routine, I started to resent the life they'd chosen for me and failed to understand their choice of diaspora.

Syrian dramas weren't the only thing I watched. Shows like *Friends*, *Gilmore Girls* and *Oprah* gave me access to the Western world. The shows were broadcast on a privately owned Saudi channel. Unlike the heavily censored public channels, these ones showed brief hugs and kisses that made me feel conflicted, but most importantly, they showed freedom. Those channels were gates to enigmatic worlds beyond my reach.

I knew I didn't belong in Saudi Arabia. What's more, the people around me didn't want me to belong either. In school I was bullied for my Syrian dialect, unbranded shoes and high grades. Every morning when my father dropped my mother and me at school, our car would be squeezed between a BMW and a GMC SUV, or other luxurious brands I didn't recognize.

'Look, that girl in the Ligzags is looking at you – is she your friend?' my father said one day, grinning.

'It's LEXUS, Baba. LEX-US!' I pronounced it with an exaggerated American accent, like how the other girls at school talked in English. I rolled my eyes and sank deep into the back seat, avoiding being seen. 'And stop looking at her!' My father giggled and enjoyed repeating the word several times in his humble English. When he was in a rare good mood, he loved to tease us. He couldn't care less about brands or how he looked. My father knew from the start that he belonged to a different world, and he took pride in that, not shame.

Having my mother as a teacher in the same school also didn't help with the bullying, especially when she was assigned to teach my class. I was reluctant to raise my hand in class to avoid being in the spotlight, while many girls assumed I had access to the exams and quizzes that she wrote at home. When one student asked me on the day of the English exam if the questions were easy or tough, I answered, 'I don't know.' *How would I?* The girl just walked past me and whispered, 'Liar.'

At the age of fourteen, the world seemed to push me to the edge. I didn't want to be a good girl; I didn't want to do chores. I arrived late for class and didn't treat homework as if my life depended on it. I stopped doing up the top button of my shirt, started rolling my sleeves up to my elbow and wearing perfume – forbidden for women in public, as it could lead to the seduction of men. That was the limit of how far I could push things, but it was far enough for my parents. I argued with teachers when I didn't agree with them and my mother received lots of complaints, which only led to more tension between me and her. My attitude was also welcomed by the cool girls I was desperate to befriend, even if it meant bullying my peers to divert the bullying away from me. I laughed when the mean girls made cruel jokes about other girls. I even made some jokes myself. This behaviour followed me home, where I took it out on my brothers and made them feel less worthy. It's something I can never take back, but now I fully understand how poisonous bullying can be.

No matter how good or bad I acted, I was still lonely. My family thought my classmates had made me too snobby, and my classmates thought I was too poor. I was never enough.

Searching for an outlet for my emotional baggage, I fell in love with basketball, which was offered in the wide, fully equipped private gym on the school campus. For forty minutes each week, I was allowed to run and jump and sweat; I was allowed to feel alive. It was a privilege, as girls in public schools weren't allowed to practise sports.

During the rest of the week, I found myself expressing my suppressed emotions by writing. Everything I had read and absorbed over the years, everything I was feeling started flowing on to paper. Literature helped me as a rebellious teenager to calm down a bit and find pleasure in being alone. It also helped me escape my father's anger that never seemed to rest. With time, I learnt how to avoid him. It wasn't hard, as he spent most of his time in his room, lying in bed and watching TV. He only left for work, or to pray at the mosque five times a day, never missing a single prayer. My brothers and I got used to hearing his angry arguments with my mother through the bedroom door. We knew better than to knock or open it, but I couldn't help feeling bad for my mother.

He wasn't physically violent, but his rage would shake the house. And the more my mother defended him, the more furious I got. Her helplessness fed my anger and hatred towards my father. I tried to ignore it, like Walid and Sami did, but on bad days my father and I exploded like oil meeting fire. My brothers would watch the flames while my mother got burnt trying to control the disaster.

Despite his temper, he only hit me once. I was nine or ten years old. I overheard my parents complaining about the dried grass in the neglected backyard of our house in Syria.

'Why don't you burn it?' Aunt Razan suggested. 'It won't cost you money or extra work. Just one match and the fire will do the rest.'

My parents appeared to be considering that option, so I decided to do a trial for them, as they never seemed to make a decision. I waited until they had their noon nap and sneaked out to the backyard with Sami. I took out the matchbox that I'd got from the kitchen and looked at my brother. 'I will just burn one match, and you have to put out the fire with this blanket.' I gave out my orders, and Sami nodded.

I lit the match. My adrenaline level spiked as I threw it on the ground and let it eat a small portion of the dry grass before Sami managed quickly to put it out. The thrill of success made me risk a second match, then a third. I didn't know that dry grass catches fire easily, and before I knew it, the flames were eating more than I intended and Sami had left his blanket to burn after he couldn't control it any more. My mother woke up to the smell of smoke. I knew I was in trouble when I heard her wake up my father. I hid in my room and watched him from behind the curtains of my window as he extinguished the flames. When he came back inside, I knew he was coming to me. The thought was enough to shake me to the bone. When he opened the door of my bedroom, I stood and apologized as he took giant steps towards me.

'I know you are sorry and that you know you made a mistake, but I am going to hit you to make sure you remember this and never repeat it.' He sounded sincere. When he left the room, I felt ashamed of what I had done but never blamed him. I understood his actions to be completely justified.

My father never hit me again after that, but my body ached from his insults. I tried to talk to my mother about the things he said but she would defend him, always suggesting it was said in the heat of the moment and dragging me to apologize. Any incident with my father always ended with me apologizing.

Things never improved after those apologies. My father still snapped at me, and I still hated him, and my mother kept pretending that we were a normal family and that my father was a good man who prayed five times a day and provided for us. She believed I was the problem; that it was me sparking the conflict, not my hot-tempered father. It was easier to blame me and try to change me than to do the same with him. But I never changed. For them, I was always the fire starter.

Chapter 5

Online and Far Away

I USED TO STAND in front of the living-room window, watching life go by on the busy streets of Riyadh. Our apartment building was shielded by a giant cement wall with rectangular holes in front of the windows to add an extra layer of privacy and a hint of prison.

The entire country was designed with women's privacy in mind, privacy that came out of shame, not respect – forced privacy. Although Saudi Arabia imported most of the modern Western world, it managed to leave Saudi fingerprints all over it. People lived in high towers, fancy apartments and posh villas, but if you looked carefully at the architecture, you would notice that they were all missing balconies.

American fast-food diners with the classic red booth seating were popular among the Saudis, but they created two separate seating areas with different entrances: one for men and the other for families, with extra partition walls to separate the booths. The waiter had to announce himself before approaching any closed booth. There weren't any waitresses.

The fanciest cars were imported, but the windows were blacked out to prevent the prying gazes of strangers. Drivers from developing countries were brought in to chauffeur women in those cars to shopping malls packed with famous and expensive brands but no changing rooms. There were designated hours and different entrances for men and families to avoid any ill-advised mix-ups. The separation was, most of the time, for men versus families, not men versus women, because women were not supposed to be wandering on their own without a male guardian, except for specified places such as mosques, schools or public toilets.

One luxurious shopping mall took privacy to the next level and created a whole floor entirely for women. The elevator inside the mall was secured by a guard who made sure only women accessed the female world on the top floor. The shops only had female staff, and women were allowed to drop their hijabs and *abayas* and dress casually. It was the only shopping area in Saudi Arabia where women could work in the retail business.

Even in Mecca, women were not allowed to pray directly in front of the Kaaba, the most important building for Muslims. Instead, we had to pray in a closed area in the Great Mosque of Mecca, hidden away from men so they could 'enjoy' their privacy. My mother was angry when we reached Mecca and she realized this. She ignored the female religious police and spread her praying mat on the white ceramic floor of the open space in front of the Kaaba.

'So only men are allowed to see the Kaaba? I also want to be able to face it while praying!'

I joined her rare rebellious act and started praying next to her before we were yelled at and moved to the separate female area. Although women were allowed to perform the *tawaf* and circle around the Kaaba along with the men, when it came to praying, the house of God felt like a place for men only.

Women's privacy was not limited to their appearance and visibility. It included any reference to them as well. Apart from official documents, a woman's name was hidden in the community and replaced by the name of her father, husband or son. She was a daughter, a wife, a mother of a man, but never mentioned as an independent entity, as a way to always remind her that she could never break free of men's authority; she would always remain dependent on a man, a burden. Even at events such as weddings, some invitation cards would list the groom's name and only reference the bride as the daughter of someone. The only time a woman's name would be mentioned explicitly in the community was in her obituary. Knowing the names of female family members was a dangerous weapon that could be used to shame a man. To talk about a man in relation to a female – for example, 'the son of Sarah' – was emasculating and a huge slight in Middle Eastern culture. My father learnt to call my mother by my brother Walid's name in public so this wouldn't happen to him. Later, he also replaced my mother's name and mine on his mobile phone with the same name. I was 'Walid2'.

Even my name was shameful.

Apart from their mothers, sisters, aunts and wives, most of the men in the city spent their lives without seeing a woman. The women were hidden away behind *abayas*, burqas or walls, where conservative cultural traditions made sure they stayed quiet and obedient. The woman became an enigmatic creature; even her shadow or the thought of her passing by was intriguing for some men. This meant staring and harassment were common, punished by a short spell in jail or some quick lashes from the religious police, depending on the severity. A typical approach for Saudi men was writing their phone number on a piece of paper and throwing it to her or sliding it through her car window. She could be covered in black from head to toe, but her costume would be enough to consider her a female worthy of hunting.

As I stood in front of the window, I could see an invisible line dividing the city, ensuring women and men did not have to meet at all. That line started to shake when the internet reached Saudi.

It took me years of persuading my parents and collecting ads from the newspaper before they finally agreed to get a computer. It was in early 2000, just after people thought computers would crash at midnight on 31 December 1999. Although there were many rules from my mother, and we didn't yet have internet, I still managed to spend many hours exploring it. My curiosity grew wilder with each click, until the computer felt like it had become a vital organ of my body.

When I learnt about the internet, I used my persistence and negotiation skills to convince my parents to allow it in our house. They reluctantly agreed to try a prepaid internet connection card. When the dial-up modem in my computer started making that iconic noise, my heart beat like a thousand drums. I was now connected to the world. It was as if a hole had opened in my prison cell after years of scratching the walls with a nail. I could finally feel the sun on my skin.

The internet in Saudi Arabia had its detractors, like every other invention that broke through into the life of traditional conservative people. Religious men had always tried to use their power to turn locals against radio, satellite TVs and even cars. They all, in their opinion, were created by the Western world or the Devil, and they all led to sin.

My parents insisted on having the computer in the living room. They did sudden checks and stared at my screen more than they should have, but it didn't matter. A click of a button allowed me to travel, without the need for my father's permission or his car. Saudi Arabia suddenly became less lonely.

My beginning was with Maktoob (later acquired by Yahoo), the Arabic portal that provided email, blogs and discussion forums. The world of anonymous writers suited me. I started writing and posting some of my thoughts under a pseudonym. It was no longer only my literature teacher who was reading my words. One day, I received a message from a writer I admired. At the end of it he said: 'Take care of yourself'.

As simple as that line was, it made my juvenile heart tremble. It was the first time someone told me to take care of myself; someone cared about 'myself'. I had never heard that sentence addressed to me, not even from my parents. I knew better than to reply to such a personal message, but that line was the first time I felt my heart beat differently. After some time online, my curiosity became stronger than my fear.

Now and then, my father would storm angrily into the house and unplug the cable from the computer. Either because he was trying to use the phone and found the line busy, or, worse, he had heard a story about an online scandal. A guy tricked a girl online into coming to his place, took advantage of her and recorded it to blackmail her for more. This was the most common internet story in Saudi Arabia. There was even an internet-awareness brochure made by a religious group, which advised guilty, shameless women not to talk to men online. These brochures were never aimed at men. On several occasions, my father cut the internet cable using a kitchen knife, but he would replace it a few days later when he calmed down.

A gloomy feeling led me to do an online search for the words 'longing for homeland or Syria'. I ended up in a forum that had a hint of Syria: the title, the usernames, the topics and the design. I was drawn to a post that poetically described how much it hurt missing home while living in Riyadh, and that home was Syria; my Syria. Did someone miss it as much as I did?

~

As I progressed to secondary level, I started finding a steady path. I stopped trying to impress the wrong people or change my accent. I made friends with a group of girls from mixed backgrounds: Arabs and Saudis. I began to understand the Saudi community better, and that Saudis themselves faced discrimination based on their family's origins.

It was still hard to be me; it was hard not to notice my friends' Nike sneakers while I was wearing cheap shoes, their fancy cars parked in front of the school gate while I got in our faded Mazda. Still, I tried to find joy in bonding with some of the smartest and kindest girls at school, whether it was over basketball or a difficult assignment.

I knew my ticket out of Saudi Arabia was college, so I focused more on my grades and managed to get them back on track. Although Saudi's public universities were exclusively for Saudi nationals, there was an exception made for the top ten students nationwide. My parents hoped for me to be one of those students so I could stay under their thumb, but I secretly wished I wouldn't make the list, yearning to be set free in my beloved Damascus.

I wasn't sure what I wanted to study, but I was sure I wanted to leave. I was torn between the two things that I loved: English literature and computers. My father didn't much care what I chose, but my mother voted for literature, as she saw my passion for it and knew how well I did in English classes. She also felt the hidden pleasure of her daughter following in her footsteps. On the other hand, it made sense to follow a scientific path worthy of my high grades.

My aunts and my mother's friends were also encouraging me to study English Literature, but for the wrong reasons. Unlike Computer Engineering, which they thought suited boys more, English didn't require attendance or hard work, which made it the perfect degree for a girl in Syria looking to get married during the early years of her course and still be able to handle a demanding husband and higher education. That reason itself made me feel furious, and finding a husband was far from my goals. Girls can be engineers; girls *are* engineers.

I was expected to study day and night, but I didn't. I learnt enough in school and revised before exams. I spent my time at home stealing some moments on the internet to read, write and be myself. I developed an interest in building websites and understanding how they worked. I decided to learn by creating a website for my school using Microsoft FrontPage – a software that no longer exists. With no tutorials or tech books available to me, I taught myself by randomly clicking and trying to understand the resulting code. I didn't share the final results with anyone in school, but it was a breathtaking experiment that made me realize how much I was drawn to writing code and building websites. It was probably then that I decided to pursue a career in computer engineering.

The dark cloud of the final exams approached slowly. This was it – the moment of truth. I stayed up for long nights and woke up early in the mornings to study hard.

The pressure of making my parents proud was the only thing on my mind as we waited impatiently after the end of my exams for the results. The top ten students got to know their scores before everyone else, as the list was published online and in newspapers. The stress was unbearable as my parents and I squeezed in front of the square computer screen, checking the results website that was overloaded with clicks and taking longer than usual to open. When the top-ten list finally appeared, my parents and I scanned it in hunger and realized my name was not there.

My father went back to his room without saying a word, while my mother kept repeating in disbelief, 'Your name is not there! Why is your name not there?'

I was sad and confused, relieved and happy. I was thrilled not to be eligible to enrol in the Saudi university, but at the same time my ego was shattered.

A few hours later, I got a call from a friend who had used her connections in the Education Ministry to get some of the scores, including mine. My hand was sweating as I waited for my results while my mother breathed down my neck. To my surprise, my score was only one mark away from being on the list.

The detailed list of grades that came later through my school showed that the few marks I had lost were mostly in the religion subjects – ones that would be disregarded as non-core modules when applying to Syrian universities. My high-school score was the perfect crime.

Before I left Saudi Arabia, my friends gathered in a cafe at the women's section of the mall to say goodbye. I was leaving for Syria to start my new life as a Computer Engineering student at Damascus University. They handed me souvenirs one after the other, telling me how much they would miss me. I'd never thought anyone would miss me. I was so focused on leaving that I hadn't noticed the real friendships I'd managed to find.

After my family went to sleep, I stayed up online, reading stories from Damascus for the last time before I started living there. And I couldn't wait. I wanted to put it all behind me: my stressed-out parents, the crowded apartment with its cement wall in front of the windows, the black *abaya*, the harassing eyes of men, the censored books and music, the shops that closed five times a day for prayer, the long commute on overcrowded highways, and our car that barely fitted us.

As I sat in the dark in front of the bright computer screen, I realized.

Tomorrow I am not going to be here any more.

It hit me, and the blood rushed faster through my veins. *Why am I dreading this step that I longed for?* My parents hadn't prepared me for leaving. We never spoke about our emotions. We hid them under the rug in every room of that awkward place we called home.

My father bought me my first mobile phone. Just as he'd bought one for Walid when he left home. Happy that I finally owned that piece of technology like all the rest of my friends, I failed to realize it was his way of keeping track of me.

My mother didn't say much. She took it personally that I'd chosen Syria over staying with her; she blamed me for my intentional negligence and not-good-enough grades that resulted in losing the Saudi scholarship. She wanted me to stay close to her, while she stayed close to my father, while he stayed alone in his room.

I turned off the computer and wept as I disappeared in the darkness of the empty living room.

Chapter 6

Damascus, My Love

AFTER WALID BECAME COMFORTABLE enough with life in Syria, he moved out of my grandparents' house. The two of us lived together in our family house in the Al-Mazzeh neighbourhood, at the bottom of Mount Mazzeh, which was covered with so many buildings that it was hardly a mountain any more. On the very top existed a randomly built area that looked like a child's Lego sculpture. Called Mazzeh 86, it was originally a military base and later developed into a residential area. It was known by the locals to be inhabited predominantly by Alawites, members of a minority sect of Islam that was associated with the Syrian regime. I always heard stories about the dodgy area but never dared set foot in it.

My family's home was a two-bedroom ground-floor apartment with a yard surrounding all the rooms. My father didn't like the neighbourhood and its proximity to Mazzeh 86, so he never made any efforts to make it look better. He'd bought the apartment through a government housing scheme, so he didn't get to choose the specifics. Every summer, he and my mother would try to find a better house, but house prices kept getting higher than their savings. They would return to Saudi Arabia to make more money, hoping to buy their dream house the following summer and settle back in Syria, but they never did. This cycle had trapped many migrants before. Despite their comfortable life in Saudi, they knew that once their contracts ended, they would have to leave the country. They would never be able to stay there for ever or get citizenship. As I saw my parents pack and unpack their bags over the years, I vowed to never leave Syria again; never live in a suitcase; never forget the roads; never miss family weddings or funerals. I vowed never to be a foreigner.

I didn't know what I was getting myself into when I registered in the summer of 2003 to study Computer Engineering for five years. The Computer Engineering department was located in the city centre, sharing a building with the Law College. When the department was established in 1999, supported by Bashar al-Assad, who was named 'The Patron of Informatics', nothing was ready for the opening; there was no building, no curriculum, no staff. The committee in charge borrowed a few classrooms from the Law department and squeezed the first batch of students into them. The university promised that this solution was only temporary, but the new building wasn't ready until after I graduated in 2008. As for the curriculum and staff, they were borrowed from other departments like Maths and Physics, and the Syrian Scientific Studies and Research Center.

My engineering class consisted of around a hundred students all sharing the frustration at the department's chaos, the lack of qualified staff and the overload of assignments. It brought us together to talk and make fun of it all. That was the Syrian way of doing anything. Go along with it, laugh at it, and try to make the best out of the worst situations.

Weeks into my new life in Syria, I started to get better at being on my own. I knew how to handle public transportation and the occasional harasser, how to go out without my brother, how to cook a meal and clean the house without accidents. I always carried a novel in my bag and enjoyed reading everywhere: in the streets of Damascus, on the bus, before lectures, in coffee shops. I learnt to come out of my cocoon. And it was all worth it.

Walking in Damascus became my favourite hobby. Older than the ones in Saudi Arabia, the streets seemed to have many stories to tell. When I was not reading a book, I watched the daily life story of the city: the merchants shouting about their products, the lovers walking holding hands, boys joking around and trying to get girls' attention. The streets were vibrant, loud and messy, but I loved them compared to Riyadh's silent, sanitized streets that I wasn't allowed to walk or drive on. The streets of Damascus weren't perfect, but they were mine.

As Syria had been ruled by various foreign powers in the past, I learnt which parts of Damascus were influenced by French architecture and which by the Soviet Union's. Some areas were elegant, while others were an eyesore. But my favourite part was the old Damascus, where life slowed down, lovers met and Fairouz could be heard singing all the time.

In Damascus, American brands and worldwide fast-food chains didn't exist. This was due to the government's vision, influenced by the USSR, to fight American imperialism. Syrians had to depend on their local industries, though some smuggled in goods from Lebanon. It was only after Bashar al-Assad took charge in 2000 that he gave the green light to imports from other countries, mainly China and Turkey. Credit cards didn't exist and ATMs only became available years after I moved to Syria, and then connected only to local banks. All that didn't stop people from creating alternatives to famous brands. We had Pizza Hot, Abibas, KataKit and many more.

After being paired up for a project, I got closer to a girl named Salma, who lived near my home, in the western part of Al-Mazzeh. Salma was fun and had mastered the satirical Syrian attitude towards life, spending her days making fun of everything and everyone, including me. When I first met Salma, I often found myself defending my taste in things, but over time I got used to ignoring her objections. She mocked my addiction to literature and I made fun of her horrible taste in music. Salma couldn't have cared less. She was the first person who taught me that it was OK to be different.

I felt intimidated that Salma didn't wear a hijab, but the girls who did wear one were harder for me to get along with. Most of them walked together like a flock of birds, wearing similar modest clothes and avoiding outsiders, particularly male ones. Whenever they passed by, I remembered Nora and the group I'd left in Saudi Arabia. Was this how my mother lived her college life? She used to brag about how she had finished four years at university without speaking to a single male student. She was very proud of an achievement that I couldn't understand.

She also couldn't understand when I complained about the university stress. She wasn't the only one, though. Whenever I met relatives at family gatherings and someone heard me complaining about university, they would still be surprised I hadn't changed my course yet. They could not comprehend why I would pick such a rugged path as a girl, and made sure to give their unasked-for opinion on every occasion. 'We told you to study English Literature. You would have been married by now.'

Marriage seemed to be a hot topic around me. I was on my

regular commute one day when a woman on the bus smiled and asked how old I was. I lifted my head out of the novel I was reading and looked at her.

'I am seventeen.' I smiled politely and turned my gaze back to my book in hope of ending the conversation.

'Are you married?' She ignored my lack of interest and looked deep into my eyes like she was about to fall in love with me.

'No.'

'So, you are a girl, then?' she asked while stealing a look at my body.

It was only after I answered 'Yes,' that I realized what she meant: a non-married woman in Syria was either widowed, divorced or a virgin – a girl, as she put it. She was looking for the latter. They all were.

'Are you in school?'

'Yes, I am studying engineering, and this is my stop.' I got up from my seat next to her and asked the driver to stop, leaving her and her rude questions behind.

My commute was sometimes interrupted by mothers like her who were looking for potential brides for their sons. Other times it was by sons who were looking for a casual flirt or an inappropriate fleeting touch. I quickly learnt how to scan the bus before choosing a safe seat to dive into my book with minimal disruption.

I didn't think of marriage. Especially not an arranged marriage. I didn't see myself doing chores for a man whose mother had chosen me, a man I had nothing in common with. I thought of engineering and books. I thought of friendship and love. I thought of all the years I'd missed out on in Damascus. I was falling for the city. I fell for the scent of jasmine leaking from the walls of the houses that I passed by during my walks. I fell for the daily chaos that magically calmed down at sunset. I felt that same umbilical cord the Syrian poet Nizar Qabbani described in his romantic poems about Damascus. This city was my biological home, not Riyadh.

Meeting new friends helped me feel that connection. It was Nadia who introduced me to her favourite parts of Damascus, the old and the new. Unlike Salma, we had similar taste in everything. Nadia belonged to the elite community of Al-Maliki and studied Political Science at a private university. She was one year older than me, and we used to chat online through the Syrian forum back when I felt stuck in Saudi Arabia. We met later in person in a coffee shop in what was Damascus's only tiny shopping mall back then. We clicked right away. Face to face, we were able to share personal details we wouldn't have shared online and realized that our mothers were friends from college. That helped my parents accept our weird relationship; they were not very enthusiastic about my meeting people I knew from online, or, as my father liked to call them, 'the ghosts'.

I learnt a lot from Nadia. She was a moderate, modern Muslim. She proudly wore her coloured hijab with bright, fashionable clothes and a bit of makeup with neat accessories. She didn't bother with thick stockings or extra-loose shirts that covered every inch of skin, like I did. She was content with herself as a good Muslim girl. She was comfortable chatting with the waiter or a shop owner while I was shy and formal, avoiding exchanging unnecessary smiles around strange men. I hid my laughter in public, while Nadia would release a loud and hearty laugh that made people around us stare. We went out for long walks and sat in her favourite cafes that then became my favourite cafes. We attended movies and musical events, and we prayed the *taraweeh* prayer together in Ramadan. When we weren't together, we were on the phone.

By the second semester, my mother had bought me my first laptop. It was grey and heavy, but the excitement of owning it made it lighter than a feather.

'Let's go to Al-Bahsa and get some programs installed,' Nadia said after I told her about my new companion.

'What is that?'

'It is computer heaven. You will love it.'

And I did. Al-Bahsa was one of Damascus's oldest neighbour-hoods and famous for tech shops. Since Syria was one of seven countries where the US had imposed technology sanctions, all American hardware, software and technical courses were inaccessible in Syria. However, that didn't stop Syrians from accessing them; it just made it more challenging.

Al-Bahsa was candy land for tech people. Shops proudly dis-played CDs of pirated versions of all known software. Some even took it to the next level and created their own mix CDs and DVDs of the latest versions of the best programs. A popular one called *The Giant* contained a huge collection of programs for every category imaginable. There were also educational materi-als, such as tutorials and courses in a range of subjects, technical or otherwise. This was before the existence of high-speed inter-net and Torrent Systems. Technical qualifications awarded by American companies such as Cisco or Oracle were available two hours from Damascus in authorized technical centres in Beirut. The Lebanese understood the game. They registered Syrians as residents in Lebanon, allowing them to sit the exams and get issued a certificate.

Some Google websites and services were also inaccessible, but Syrians found ways to overcome that too. They all became hackers by instinct. Even a kid would know how to manipulate the browser settings to change their location. This trick bypassed both American and governmental restrictions. As well as the US sanctions, some websites were blocked by the Syrian government for political reasons. Websites like Wikipedia and WordPress were blocked, usually after showing anti-regime content. More importantly, Hotmail, Yahoo and all the well-known email servers were also blocked because they were hard to monitor. This restriction forced me to let go of my old emails and open a new account at a not-very-popular domain that had not yet been noticed by the government.

I returned from Al-Bahsa with many CDs and a sense of pride that I was studying a field that was restricted in many ways.

~

The month of Ramadan was treated like a guest of honour in Syria. Class schedules were moved to accommodate fasting Muslims, and most of the cafes and restaurants around the university campus closed during the day or for the whole month. Non-Muslims were expected to respect the majority fasting for a month. In the old days, there used to be a fine or jail time until the end of the month for anyone caught eating or drinking in public.

'The good old days, when Islam was respected,' my father would say. Back then, it made my blood boil to see someone eating on the streets, as if disrespecting Islam.

Classes seemed longer during Ramadan, but knowing I would be rewarded in the afterlife helped me bear the thirst and hunger. The streets of Damascus flooded with traffic just before sunset, when everyone rushed home to break the fast with their families. That was when the *adhan* burst out loudly from the mosques' speakers, allowing Muslims to end a day of fasting, only to start again with the dawn of the next day.

It was recommended to break the fast with an odd number of dates before eating anything else: one or three, usually, but not two. Many theories tried to explain the scientific reasons behind this, but no one really knew why. We just knew it was a *sunnah*, a ritual that the Prophet Muhammad used to do, and Muslims were encouraged to follow in his footsteps in everything.

Following the main meal, there were usually many delicious types of sweets to enjoy, like baklava and *katayef*: golden pastries stuffed with nuts and cream and dunked in thick sugar-syrup. After eating what felt like a heavy feast, the nights of Ramadan were my favourite part, when I got to pray in the mosque. During the rest of the year, it was uncommon to see women in mosques, so this was a rare chance to feel closer to God. Although during the Prophet's times women would pray along with men – or, more precisely, *behind* men – the new Islamic laws had replaced this with two separate rooms inside the mosque, and two entrances, one for each gender, with the female entrance usually at the back of the mosque. The imam who led the prayer was a man, never a woman. He would stand in the front row of the men's space with a microphone next to him. That microphone carried the prayer to the multiple speakers in the women's space.

Al-Maliki Mosque was a hotspot in Ramadan. People came from all around Damascus to listen to the mellow voice of the imam reading the Quran. Even the president attended the Eid prayer with a special entourage after Ramadan was over.

Each day after breaking fast, or *iftar*, I would go with my brother to pray, splitting up at our separate entrances. The mosque's floor was covered with neat rows of long carpets. I usually sat in a spot near the open window, the ceiling fans or the A/C if it was a hot summer day. If Nadia hadn't arrived yet, I would grab a Quran from the many on the shelves and read some pages. If she was there, we would end up chatting like the rest of the women until the place became a loud beehive. The women in the first row, usually seniors and more conservative, would raise their voices to shush us, but we only stopped talking when the imam called '*Allahu Akbar*' through the speakers, announcing the start of the prayer.

The first-row ladies had another task, too. I only noticed when one of them approached, asking for my personal details and writing my answers in a notebook. When I glanced at it, I saw other records of girls split into columns of name, age, address, phone number. It was a matchmaking book. Before then, I didn't realize that the mosque was a centre for matchmaking. Every woman in that place was eyeing the younger ones, looking for a potential bride for her brother, son, or even grandson. The other girls knew it and wore their best clothes and attitudes to the mosque in the hope of getting married, ideally into a rich family from Al-Maliki.

The nights in Ramadan were long and filled with food and new TV series that lasted till dawn. Ramadan was a hot season for TV production. Many devout Muslim voices could be heard warning people against getting distracted by those sinful shows and wasting those blessed days. I tried to find a balance between the two, picking a show or two while maintaining my religious rituals of praying and reading the Quran. Like many Muslims, it was the only month in the year when I would open the Quran at home. For some, Ramadan was the only time they prayed. We all competed with each other in that month: who read more pages, who prayed for longer and who suffered more during fasting. Although God was watching us all the time, we made sure we watched each other, too.

Before the sun rose again, announcing the start of the next fasting day, we would be up to eat and drink till the last allowed minute of *suhoor*, the pre-dawn meal. I didn't like waking up for that meal; I valued my sleep over food. On normal days I wouldn't eat anything straight after waking up, but during Ramadan I had to eat before the dawn to store some energy for the fasting day. Because I was the female in the house, it was naturally my duty to prepare food and wake up my brother.

Damascus looked like it never slept during Ramadan. Restaurants were open late, until an hour or two before dawn, for those who wanted to enjoy *suhoor* outside their homes. The shops were also open for anyone who wanted to go out after fasting and praying. The last ten days of Ramadan are considered the most precious, and the city seemed at its busiest then. During those ten days is one famous night, Lailat al-Kadr, which is believed to be the best night of the year, when God sends down his angels to answer all the prayers. The specific night is left vague in the ancient books as an odd-numbered one in the last third of Ramadan, so it could be the twenty-first, twenty-third or twenty-fifth night, but many believe it is the twenty-seventh. That day is sacred in Damascus, with mosques packed and praying time extended from nightfall till dawn. The lines of carpets would pour out of the mosques and on to the streets and pavements to accommodate more Muslims who didn't want to miss that holy event. Sometimes I spotted colleagues of mine who didn't usually pray or fast. A few girls also made the decision to commit to hijab, carried by the emotions of Lailat al-Kadr. While some kept wearing it for ever, others took it off after waking up from the religious hangover.

I cried a lot during Lailat al-Kadr. I would ask God for forgiveness for all the sins that I did or didn't commit. The prophet said: 'The eyes that cried out of the fear of God are not to be touched by the flames of hell.' The imam's beautiful recitation of the Quran was like a good therapy session for hundreds of praying Muslims. The mosque was the only place where men were allowed to cry. Lailat al-Kadr would leave me feeling good, like a new soul.

When the holy night was over, Ramadan had only two or three nights left. People got busy with the preparations for Eid by shopping for new clothes, cleaning their houses and making *ma'amoul*, the famous Eid sweet. Eid al-Fitr, which means 'breaking-the-fast festival', comes after Ramadan – twenty-nine or thirty days of fasting, depending on the solar month – and lasts for three days. It's all about visiting the extended family and spreading joy, especially among kids, who spend the days at funfairs.

A typical Eid for me started with the mosque speakers repeatedly chanting '*Allahu Akbar*,' with a short prayer. Our house was less than ten metres from the neighbourhood mosque, which made me feel like the loudspeaker was inside my bedroom. Men would go to the mosques to perform the Eid prayer and later visit the graves of deceased family members. My first visit would usually be to my mother's family in Al-Midan. *Tete* Jihan, my grandmother, would have her apartment spotless for the day – as she did every day, just like my mother. That seemed to be the most important rule in their world. The sweets would be spread on trays and ready to serve to the waves of visitors in the guest room – the tidiest and most perfect room in every Syrian house, which no family member was allowed to enter when there were no visitors. Even if that meant the family had to squeeze into the rest of the apartment. The guest room showed how much we valued outsiders' opinions and comfort over our own. Something I wished I understood back then.

It was hard to tell if Tete enjoyed the crowds of visitors or was annoyed by them. It was common to have people ringing the doorbell unannounced. That meant being prepared twenty-four hours a day for three days and sometimes longer. She always welcomed the guests with a smile, even if she was not in the mood. Her smiles seemed to be reserved for the guest room and were rarely seen in the living room. Tete Jihan had raised seven kids who left their mark on her knees, back and blood sugar. Her diabetes was triggered after watching the shocking news of a plane crash, thinking my uncle Khaled was on it. He was on the next plane to Abu Dhabi, where he worked in the oil industry, but it was too late for my grandmother's blood sugar levels. Every time she invited me over to dinner, I watched her lift her shirt or dress, inject herself with insulin and carry on as if nothing was wrong. She was tough, like every Syrian woman who was raised at that time. Being weak was not an option.

Although I enjoyed Ramadan, for me Eid was a series of endless disruptions and invasion of my personal space: the loudspeakers, the unscheduled visits, accepting endless sweets out of politeness, the ongoing judgement by my religious aunts or my grandmother's strange visitors who wanted to know when I would get married.

After Eid, things went back to normal. Ramadan was the guest room of the year, where everyone was on their best behaviour. Their true faces appeared as soon as they left it.

~

By the time my parents came for their annual summer break, I was already a new person – more comfortable in my new environment, and dangerously independent. But for them, they were still the parents; they expected everything to be the way it was back in Saudi Arabia.

After a year of temporary freedom, my father was again questioning my every move, while my mother focused on teaching me better manners and new dishes. My movement outside the house was restricted. It was strange for my parents to see me going out for a walk or to meet with Salma or Nadia, and it was also strange for me to change my routine to accompany their previous image of me. It caused many fights and made summers unbearable.

These arguments didn't happen between my father and Walid. He was allowed to go out and come back, no questions asked, as long as he was home before midnight. Men rarely had any restrictions on the time they spent outside on the streets; they could laugh out loud and wear whatever they wanted. This lifestyle made them more relaxed and fun, while we women were tense and cautious in our every word and action.

When I finally passed the first year, I exhaled. I had managed to prove to myself, and the rest of my family, that I could be the first woman in the family to walk the engineering path.

Chapter 7

New and Old Relationships

MY WRITING PEAKED IN Damascus. I wrote about the city's wild beauty, the smell of the first raindrops and the cosiness of watching the snow fall. Everything around me inspired my most passionate words. Damascus turned me into a romantic without a lover.

'Have you considered submitting your writings to a newspaper?' Omar texted. I had met Omar online; he admired my writing and had followed it while he was working in the US after graduating as an engineer from Damascus University. We kept in touch online until he returned to settle in Syria and asked to meet in person. I hesitated, but agreed as long it was in a public place. I dragged Nadia with me just in case he turned out to be a psychopath.

It was the first time I had met up with a guy. I was trying to live my life, finding a middle ground between religion and normal life. As his messages implied, Omar turned out to be a nice guy with a bright smile. He'd got me a book as a gift, and I kept feeling the urge to return home to open my laptop and send him an email instead of talking to him in person. Omar and I became close friends shortly after he helped me publish my first essay in *As-Safir* newspaper under my pen name. The only people in Syria who knew who was behind those words were me, Omar and Nadia. He was an avid reader and always talked about the poems of Mahmoud Darwish, the Palestinian poet. He often shared pieces with me until I too was hooked on them.

Omar and I met either in his favourite coffee shop or in mine. We talked about books and movies and music and technology. I knew I would be in trouble if anyone from my family saw us, but I kept reminding myself that I wasn't doing anything wrong.

'So, what, now you are just friends?' Nadia asked one day, pressing on the phrase 'just friends'. She didn't like this relationship and always had a suspicious look on her face every time I mentioned Omar.

'Yes, Nadia,' I sighed. 'For the millionth time, we are just friends!'

The conversation halted as we reached Exlibris, the fancy bookshop in Al-Maliki. It was owned by Rima, an elegant Syrian lady who used to live in the UK. She looked modern and confident with her blonde-dyed hair and the makeup she wore with a bright smile. A look that I never saw on the women in my family. The bookshop was packed with English books for all ages and categories. It was probably the only place to find books of such quality and variety.

I scanned the titles with hunger before picking one called *Where Rainbows End* by Cecelia Ahern. I flipped through the first pages and saw it was written in messages, online chats, emails and postcards, something similar to the online life I lived back in Saudi Arabia. Cecelia's book was my first experience of Ireland, a place that was somewhere in the mysterious West, which I knew little about but was curious to explore.

When I was in my second year, Sami joined Walid and me at university and enrolled in the Computer Institute. The three of us had many good times while trying to integrate in our place of origin. My second year was overloaded with ten modules, but I was determined to pass, and I did. I also managed to get a temporary job at Exlibris, helping out at the summer book festival – my favourite event of the year.

During the summer, my father's restrictions kept getting tighter. I tried to avoid getting into any arguments with him and stayed reading in my room, as I wasn't allowed to go outside alone when my parents were in Syria. One day, after he snapped at me out of nowhere, I stormed to my room and buried my tears in my pillow. Minutes later, my mother joined me, trying to calm me down. My tears froze on my cheeks when she told me he had overheard Nadia and me speaking on the phone about a guy.

The fear of my father knowing about a guy in my life was worse than the shame of having him invade my privacy. I stopped crying and tried to remember how much I'd blurted out over the phone.

'He is worried you'll grow up to be like her.' My mother stopped talking, not sure how to explain.

'Like who?'

My mother sighed, got up and went to her room. Minutes later, she returned with a photo.

Years before, I'd found a photo album in my parents' wardrobe. There were pictures of my parents' trip to Palmyra along with my father's family: my deceased grandmother, my two uncles, two aunts, and a woman who I was told was a friend of my aunt. I'd never doubted my mother when I asked her about the photo many years ago, but now she was telling a new story.

'That woman is your third aunt, Sanaa.'

*

My father's relationship with his family was always shaky. Every time he hung up the loud weekly international phone call from Syria, he would look distressed. My father's family blamed him for leaving, just like he blamed his father for dying. He was in charge of the family, and he didn't like it. My father's way of protecting was by overprotecting. He rejected any suitors who proposed to his sisters, while he sent money to support them. My youngest uncle travelled to Russia to study Engineering, but years later he came back home with a Russian wife and a baby girl. I saw the picture of the baby girl in my father's family house, but no one answered when I asked who she was. My father cut ties with my uncle and no one would dare speak of him again.

'Sanaa was the most beautiful among your aunts,' my mother explained while I was still looking at her in disbelief, trying to comprehend. 'One day, she fell in love with a man from a different faith, an Alawite man. She ran away with him after your father rejected him remotely and without meeting him.'

I couldn't believe it. *How could she break my father's heart like that? And the shame that she brought to the family must have been unbearable for him.* The anger towards my father that had piled up inside me was replaced by sympathy. I started understanding his overprotective love.

I would never break his heart like that. Never.

~

By the time I started my third year at university, I had become more comfortable in my field. I met Lara and Nisreen, my new project partners. Lara was Christian, and Nisreen was Druze, two religious groups I knew nothing about. Despite our many differences, we clicked straight away.

When I visited Lara's house for the first time, I felt the love of her parents. I envied how understanding they were, how they hosted her group of friends of mixed genders and even accepted her having a boyfriend. I guess I was also Lara's first Muslim friend. So far, she had only gone to Christian schools and lived in the Christian part of Damascus. Most of us were exposed to a new, diverse world at university and had to meet and partner with people outside our regular circles. Lara told me one day that her father had read the Quran. I was surprised that he'd chosen to stay a Christian even after reading it. I didn't comment, but hoped that one day Lara and her family would find the right path.

Nadia got engaged quicker than I'd thought she would. It was an arranged marriage that she didn't see coming. She was ready to reject the offer, but found herself falling for him. I didn't know how serious it was until I was making fun of the idea on one of our endless phone calls and she got upset. A few days later, she told me she wanted to give this relationship a chance. Soon after, both families held an elegant party at the Palace of Nobles to celebrate the engagement. Nadia looked stunning in a chic green dress. But after her new relationship status was confirmed, our friendship was never the same again.

From then on, our phone calls would always include her fiancé, who also happened to join some of our outings, turning me instantly into a third wheel. The heart-warming beginnings of love were nauseating to the eye of an outsider. Their jokes, their laughter, the way they teased each other all made me want to stay away. *Am I jealous?* I was against arranged marriage, but

I wanted to feel that silly unexplainable feeling that seemed to make Nadia smile more. My father seemed restless whenever a family called asking to pay a visit with a view to an arranged marriage. I felt restless, too, and didn't mind when he refused those visits, just as he had done for his sisters. I knew love outside an arranged marriage was a dangerous thing to pursue. My brain knew – if only my heart did.

~

The sun was still shy when I left Damascus behind and headed on a bus trip towards the ancient city of Palmyra. I'd never gone on a trip before. My father had only allowed me to go on this one if Sami accompanied me. Although thousands of kilometres away in Riyadh, he still managed to control my choices. I sat next to the window with my brother next to me. Nadia and her new fiancé sat in the seats in front of us and around twenty of our friends from the Syrian online forum took their places around us.

I didn't like mornings, but I made an exception that day so I could explore a mysterious part of my country. My friends were already awake and energized. The loud singing started as soon as the bus engine roared and a *derbakkeh*, the famously musical drum, appeared out of nowhere to accompany the chaotic, happy voices.

I turned my head to the back of the bus where all the noise was coming from and saw a new face. The man was holding the drum and singing with the rest.

'Who's that?' I asked Rana, who was sitting behind me.

'That's Housam, Salman's friend.' Salman was her husband.

'I thought we were going to keep the group small?' I sighed.

'He is a nice guy. Salman invited him.'

I sat back in my seat, annoyed by the loud music and the new faces. The imaginary walls I put between myself and other people made it hard for me to get along with strangers easily. I pulled out my MP3 player and tried to block out the noise. After the city started disappearing and the road became less crowded, the party inside the bus got louder. Now there was dancing, mostly by the guys. They could shout, swear and shake their bodies as freely as they wished with no eyes judging them.

Housam passed his *derbakkeh* to another guy in the group and stood in the aisle as he declared it was his dance session. The loud cheers made me pause my music and watch. To the rhythms of the drum, Housam started bending his body to imitate a belly dancer. The bursts of laughter were contagious. The more he tried to act like a sexy dancer, the louder everyone cheered. The guys started throwing some banknotes at Housam, who arched his back while rubbing his belly. I took off my headphones and joined the others in their laughter. It had been a long time since I'd laughed like that. Housam took joy in pushing his act to the extreme until laughter turned into tears of mirth.

Palmyra, the ancient Semitic city, had been waiting for us for many thousands of years. The magnificent ruins of the old city stood tall to tell us stories about old times, when emperors and queens lived lives we knew little about. Our big group split into smaller ones, spreading out to explore every corner. I was winding my headphones up when someone approached.

'I have a similar one in black!'

I turned around to see the new guy taking a similar model of MP3 player out of his pocket with a big smile.

'Oh, yes, it is the same!' I smiled back, not sure what to add.

'I work for that company.' Housam pointed to the silver logo on the player.

'Ah, cool.'

'If you ever face any technical issues with it, just let me know.' Housam smiled and walked past me and Sami to catch up with the group gathered at the Temple of Bel. We all walked inside, and after taking more pictures than we needed, we rested on the stairs. Rami took out his oud and turned our chatter to a peaceful melody. Housam took a place next to him and started singing along with a soft and deep voice that echoed inside the temple.

At a restaurant nearby, a dinner was set up for us in a large Bedouin tent that shielded us from a sandy storm. It was an authentic local meal of rice and lamb. After that, we formed a circle around the fire and sang and laughed until it was time to head back.

The night was magical, and the ghosts of the past were surrounding us. Everything seemed perfect, and I was blissfully unaware of all the disasters that would hit in the years after that moment. How could I know that ISIS would invade this enchanting spot years later and destroy the temples to erase the already dead gods? How could I foresee that this beautiful group of friends would split up into supporters and opposers, some ending up in prison while others took boats across the deep blue sea? As I caught Housam's eye across the dancing flames, I had no idea that love was closer than I thought it would be.

The next time I saw him, it was a month later with the same group of friends, celebrating my birthday in a restaurant in the Old City. He handed me a wrapped gift and whispered, 'There is a story behind this gift. I will tell you later. Hope you like it.'

Later that night, I sat on my bed with the unwrapped presents around me. A teddy bear, a book, a mug, but the best of all was a mirror in a handcrafted walnut frame, beautifully inlaid with mother-of-pearl. When I held the mirror in my hands, my phone beeped with a message. It was him. 'I was looking for a fine piece of art that reflected you.' The mirror reflected my smile as I blushed reading the message.

Serendipity brought Housam and me together again a few weeks later, this time at the annual Syrian Technical Expo. I was sent by the IT university to be part of the exhibition's registration team, while Housam had to represent his company at one of the kiosks. Although he was an English Literature graduate, he'd taught himself graphic design, web programming and market-ing. Housam passed me every morning to wish me a good day. I only smiled back in return. By the end of the exhibition, I'd got up the courage to go to his stand. He was packing up when I entered. When he raised his head, our eyes locked, and we knew something was happening.

The expo took place on spacious grounds on the city outskirts, where it was quiet and beautiful. Housam and I went for a walk in the open space as it began to empty. The night surrounded us, and the scattered yellow lights of the expo were shining in place of stars.

We sat on a bench, Housam making nervous jokes about the stand next to him that had kept playing annoying music for the past three days while I laughed. When an awkward silence crawled between us, I asked him, 'Where are you originally from?'

'I think you know.'

'No, I don't.' I needed him to say it, and I needed to put it out in the open.

I learnt then that Housam was half Palestinian. His grand-father Saeed Zayyad was forced to leave Nazareth in 1945 during the Israeli occupation of Palestine. He walked with his wife and kids to Lebanon and then to Syria, where he lived for over fifty years, waiting for this temporary situation to resolve itself so he could return home. Saeed had a son in Damascus, who grew up and fell in love with a Damascene woman from Al-Midan. They got married and had Housam. Housam and his father were two of many Palestinians who never saw Palestine – who were never allowed to – but were never granted a Syrian passport. They were labelled as 'Palestinian Syrians' with a Syrian travel document for refugees. They belonged to neither country.

By the time Housam had finished explaining, I couldn't stop my heart from pounding. All I could think of was my father's face if I told him I was in love with a refugee. It would be over six years until I saw the irony of this.

Being in a relationship back then was not as easy as the Western movies showed. Love was frowned upon, and relationships were only for married people. The prying society of Damascus made it harder for us to be together, so we only saw each other at the university or in casual meetings with other friends. We were never alone. We kept platonic conversations for the day and the romantic ones for the nights' texts and calls. My heart was ach-ing from love and guilt.

When my family came over that summer, I told my mother about Housam while I was helping her in the kitchen. She looked like I'd told her I was pregnant.

'Your father will never approve!' My mother rarely gave her opinion on things. After marrying my father, her opinion didn't seem to exist, and sometimes it backfired when it turned out to be a wrong one. She learnt to keep her thoughts to herself or frame them as my father's.

That summer witnessed the escalated military conflict between Hezbollah in Lebanon and Israel. Rockets were fired by both parties for thirty-four days. As Lebanese people poured across Syria's borders, Syrians were on the alert in case the country was dragged into this war. My father was nervous all the time, and my mother kept postponing the conversation.

'Now is not the right time for such a thing,' she would say. 'We have to wait for a suitable day when your father is in a good mood.'

There was never a day good enough in that summer. It was challenging to do anything, as every normal thing seemed controversial in my father's eyes. Nadia, like many others, was busy volunteering with the Syrian Red Crescent to help displaced Lebanese people settle. I wasn't allowed to join her.

I went one day to the annual book festival and returned with a pile of books. My father went mad over one choice: *Season of Migration to the North*. He called for my mother and brothers and asked them to read some lines. I couldn't see the words in question, but I could see the uncomfortable faces of my family as they read them.

My attempts to explain that I'd never read the novel before were useless. My father didn't want to listen. I stood in the living room while he passed the book between my brothers and flipped the pages to show them what apparently was inappropriate content for me but OK for them. The novel, which my father seemed to know by heart, was considered one of the *Guardian*'s hundred best books of all time, but it was one of the worst ones to pick up on that day.

I went back to my room with what was left of my dignity. I called Housam from under the covers and cried and whispered how much I hated my father, but I didn't explain why.

'Did he hit you?' Housam asked in concern, and I cried more as I remembered my father's words of wisdom: 'Never get your hands dirty by hitting a woman.'

Housam took all my anger and heartbreak and turned it into calmness. I stayed in my room, broken, wishing to escape that bad day. I could still hear my father's angry yells as he blamed my mother, and I wished I had enough courage to go out and take her away for ever. The door opened suddenly, and Walid's face appeared behind it, looking upset. 'Are you happy now?' I stared at him blankly. 'This mess is all because of you!' Walid had never yelled at me before. Like me, he grew up helplessly watching my parents argue. Blaming it on me was perhaps easier to process. He slammed the door and left me in the darkness of my room, hoping I might vanish into the void.

The stressful summer was over, and the cold breezes of autumn came back, carrying my temporary freedom. Autumn became associated with a sense of relief as my parents returned to Saudi Arabia. Walid left with them after that summer to start a new job in Riyadh and stay by their side. Autumn's fresh breeze and the smell of my new textbooks and stationery were enough of a distraction to make me forget whatever arguments I'd had with my father. The fourth year of university focused on my specialism in Software Engineering. It had taken three years until I started learning what inspired me to choose IT in the first place: websites. My days had never seemed busier as I tried to learn everything related to building web pages. The excitement every time I saw my lines of code turned into display in the browser was inexplicable.

Housam and I kept meeting occasionally with friends. I didn't dare to go out alone with him because I wanted to be able to look my father in the eye and tell him I was waiting for his approval, even if I wasn't sure when that day would arrive. Meanwhile, the guilt mounted. Every time I talked to Housam, a fire lit inside me. I was doing what Khalil Gibran advised me not to do.

> *Do not live half a life*
> *and do not die a half death*
> *[. . .]*
> *Half a life is a life you didn't live,*
> *A word you have not said*
> *A smile you postponed*
> *A love you have not had*
> *A friendship you did not know*

I resented my half-life and my half-love. I wanted to break free of all the constraints and be with Housam, but to do so, I had to be patient and play by the unreasonable rules.

When Ramadan came around again, I prayed a lot during Lailat al-Kadr, asking God to forgive me for falling in love, to make my father approve, and to guide me and choose the best for me because He knew better.

Housam was more practical. He took on additional freelancing jobs to save more money, applied for a mortgage and bought an apartment to be our future nest in a new housing project in Jisreen, a village to the east of Damascus. In some sweet moments, I managed to let myself dream with Housam about a future in that place: a boy and a girl. Maybe a cat. Lots of books and pot plants. We would wait a year before having kids and enjoy being together, in love, holding hands in our favourite streets of Damascus. That image was so vivid and real I could see the faces of my kids and hear their laughter while chasing the cat.

I managed to set aside my doubts and throw myself into university and eventually passed my fourth year with high grades. The summer came, but my father didn't visit due to work commitments. I was disappointed to postpone the moment of confrontation again, anticipating the inevitable battle with my prejudiced father.

The fifth and final year of university was exhausting, and I couldn't wait to graduate and start my career. I met up with Lara and Nisreen regularly to finish our graduation project. We worked for as long as we could at university and met up at weekends or talked on the phone late at night to discuss urgent technical updates. We became inseparable, like conjoined triplets. We wrote lines of code together, we stressed out, we argued, we laughed, and we shared our best and worst days. I never knew what it was like to have a sister before knowing them. They kept me sane and encouraged me never to give up on love. Housam joined us sometimes at the end of our sessions. I realized then why Nadia's fiancé, who was now her husband, had been joining us all that time.

The summer of 2008 was supposed to be bright; I graduated as a software engineer, and I was in love. I was ready to move on to the next chapter in my life, but my father was not. Everything changed with one single word when I told my father about Housam. That ugly word of two letters: No.

Chapter 8

War Against Love

THE RESIDENTS OF AL-MAZZEH neighbourhood could probably hear my father's yelling from the streets as he declared his definite rejection. The word 'refugee' was repeated, sometimes with disgust, and other times with fear. It sounded like a crime, like an infectious disease that could be transmitted through marriage. Attempting any means of reasoning was only pushing the Hulk to grow more furious.

Shaking, I withdrew to my room and wondered if I was indeed a bad and stubborn girl after all. My father had acted exactly like I'd thought he would, but nothing like I'd hoped. The door to my bedroom burst open and my mother stood there looking pale.

'Come right now and tell your father that this was a mistake. Tell him you'll never think of it again. NOW!'

I knew from my father's level of anger and my mother's fear that there was no room to argue. I followed her like a zombie, numb. I said all the things that my mother asked me to. I apologized, he yelled, and I wished I didn't exist. I hadn't made a mistake. I was the mistake.

The next day, life went back to normal in our house while I remained in shock at what had happened. I texted Nadia, broke the news to her in a short message and asked her to update

Housam, terrified I would be caught contacting him. Mostly, I was terrified of breaking his heart. *It's over. Isn't it?*

When my parents went out later that day, Nadia came over to check on me.

'Your father has officially gone crazy!' She was angry and sad and disappointed, but I wasn't any of those. I was lost. She kept suggesting solutions while I looked distant, hypnotized by the flashing red 'breaking news' bar on the screen. The poet Mahmoud Darwish had been declared dead after failed heart surgery. I thought about how Omar must be devastated. I thought about how convenient it would've been if my name had been written on that red bar instead of Darwish's. That lucky fugitive.

A few days after the Big Bang in our house, I called Housam. When he answered, I realized I couldn't say, '*Marhaba habibi* – my love', like I used to, and he couldn't say, 'Hi, *hayati* – my life.' I'd missed our breakup when I'd asked Nadia to do it, and now I had to face a formal heartbroken version of him. We talked in short sentences interspersed with long pauses of unspoken words.

'I don't want this to end.' I teared up.

'I don't want that either.'

We ran out of allowed words and solutions, so we hung up.

Over the next weeks, first my colon rejected what had happened in the shape of constant abdominal pain, then a double root-canal surgery pushed my body to its limit. Nothing seemed to function in my body any more and I was crumbling away. As I started losing the will to live in a world that didn't make sense, it didn't take my father long before he took the final decision: I was going back to Saudi Arabia. Full stop.

~

The white room was half full when my mother and I entered and took a seat. A giant TV screen was hanging on the wall showing a muted live scene of prayer from the Kaaba. Three of the four women in the room were covered in black, wearing *abayas* and burqas. I couldn't stare into their faces, but they stared at mine.

'Madame Huda.'

A nurse in white came through the door and called in Filipino-accented English, looking around the room. One of the women stood up and followed her to an examination room. When she opened the door, I caught a glimpse of my father sitting in the men's waiting area. It was easy to spot my father in the crowd with his tall frame and white head of hair. He had always had white hair, ever since I could remember. He was forty years old when I was born, had already lived his life. A life he rarely spoke about. I didn't know my father as a child or as a teenager. I didn't know about his first love or first heartbreak. But he knew about mine. He caused mine, and I could never look at him again. I turned my face away when I saw him looking at me.

'Saud . . . Mr Saud.' I heard the nurse calling in the men's waiting room. 'Mr Saud Aldarra.' I rolled my eyes and stood up. My name was always misread in English as Saud, the male version of my name and one of the most common male names in Saudi.

My father joined us as we followed the nurse to the doctor's room. This was not my first doctor's appointment. In the first month of my return, my parents sat and listened to the doctors saying again and again that the main reason behind my symptoms was psychological. My nervous colon, my low blood pressure, my teeth grinding when I slept. My father casually paid for the prescription like I had a cold. Meanwhile, my symptoms didn't go away with medicine. *Is there a pill for heartbreak?* I sat silently in the back seat, staring out of the window while he drove us back home through the streets.

Riyadh hadn't changed. I had.

I'd left this city as a young girl full of curiosity to explore the outside world, and now I was back, broken. My mother cooked all my favourite dishes, and Walid bought my favourite snacks and offered to drive me around now that he had his own car. Despite everyone's welcoming behaviour, I couldn't shake that one fact that they seemed to ignore: I was here against my will. Nothing in the world could make me feel better here. The silence of our house was suffocating. I avoided my father and he didn't try to change that. No one talked about what had happened. Everyone avoided mentioning Housam and I didn't mention that I was still in touch with him. The only solution that made sense to me was to wait for a miracle. If it was meant to be, then God would find a way to reunite us.

Meanwhile, Housam had decided to try a different path and accepted a job offer in Dubai; maybe a refugee with a better salary in a Gulf country would be harder for my father to reject. Housam and I talked daily. The pain of the separation was hard to grasp. We were miserable apart, failing to fit in. Everything becomes harder when you are far from home. Housam's new life in Dubai was harsh and lonely. He shared an apartment with eight Syrians and was lost in a city that only looked after wealthy people. During his time away from his family, his paternal grandmother passed away in Syria, and his mother underwent heart bypass surgery.

Slowly, I recovered while isolating myself in the abandoned guest room. We rarely had any visitors, so my mother turned it into a space for me. There was nothing for me to do. No studying, no job. Just passing time. My laptop was my only companion. Online, I saw my friends back in Syria celebrating their graduation with family and friends. A few got engaged and married. Many started new jobs, while the rest travelled abroad and started a Master's in Europe or the US. What update could I post about myself? That I was eating all kinds of junk food and had already gained back the weight I'd lost while sick – and more? That I had watched all the shows there were to watch? The fictional characters were my friends. I wished I were Rory from *Gilmore Girls*, Yale-educated and best friends with her mother. I wished I were on *The Amazing Race*, travelling the world with Housam. I wished I were anyone, any character, but this overweight, heartbroken, unemployed failure version of myself.

Day or night didn't seem to make any difference. I slept whenever the heartache felt unbearable. Having nothing to wake up for was daunting. *Now what?*

Through my mother's connections, I was set up with a job interview at a telecommunications company. I worried that accepting a job meant accepting this new life my father had chosen for me, but I was also worried that I would lose my technical muscles if I remained in this limbo, that I would lose my mind.

The job gave me a reason to wake up in the morning, dress up and talk to other people who knew nothing about my broken heart. It also introduced me to a new friend, Sherien, who took me under her wing and shared lunchtimes and gossip about the company with me. My tasks were barely meaningful and my manager seemed out of reach in the men's section in the gender-segregated company. Lots of days passed as I stared at my screen, waiting for a task and not allowed to join my tech team, who were all in the other division.

Frustrated, I decided one day to confess to my mother that I was still in touch with Housam. It was hard for me to have a conversation with her about this forbidden relationship. She would feel sorry for me one day but attack me on another, as she believed that if there were any good in marrying Housam then God would've made things easier for it to happen; God would choose the best for me.

In an attempt to bring me back to the real world, my mother told me she'd convinced my father to meet Housam in the summer. This update turned my gloomy mood upside-down. Seeds of hope got me out of my isolation, and I started joining my family and being friendlier to my father, who had finally agreed to meet me halfway, or so I thought.

After eight months away from the life I longed for in Syria, I couldn't wait to get it back on track. Housam and I discussed plans to reunite in Syria. Within a few weeks, he'd quit his job and booked his ticket back home, but I knew my return would be harder.

My father picked me up every day from work and saw how unhappy I was. He tried to ignore it, along with my hints about going back to Syria. Eventually, on one of those rides, I burst.

'I don't want to live here any more.'

'You should be more appreciative,' my father said, keeping his eyes on the road. 'This country provided me with opportunities that I wouldn't have dreamt of back in Syria.'

'Fine, then you stay! Why do I have to stay?! Why can't I decide where I want to live my life?'

We argued for the whole forty-minute trip back home. We yelled our opposite opinions; I cried while his voice trembled. Then we arrived home and went silently to our separate rooms. I felt lighter yet nervous, not sure about the consequences of my freedom of speech. The next day my mother told me he'd agreed to let me go. Something I'd said must have worked. As my face lit up with joy, hers didn't. She wasn't happy with the decision. I was slipping out of her hands for the second time. She wanted me to be happy, but only next to her, stuck in the same place that she couldn't escape.

On my departure day, before heading to the airport with my family, my father called me to his room. He was dressed up and sitting on the edge of his bed with my mother next to him. He looked at me and then looked away before saying calmly, 'Listen.'

My heart sank, as I could feel a disaster was about to happen.

'I agreed to you going back to Syria on one condition: you may never contact *that guy* in any way. Is that clear?'

I froze. I looked at my mother, but she didn't share my surprise. My father left the room without waiting for my answer.

'But ... you said ... you promised he would meet him!' I stared at my mother in shock.

'I never promised you anything,' my mother said in defence. 'I said I would *try* to convince him to meet him at least. What else can I do?! You know your father when he says no.'

I knew what she'd said, and she knew what she'd said. But she'd had no other option but to lie to me, and probably lie to my father, saying I'd moved on, in the hope that time would solve the matter. But time was only making it more complicated. My freedom that I'd thought had come in easily overnight was a conditional one after all.

~

A few weeks after returning to Damascus, I managed to find a job in a small programming office where Nisreen worked. My parents decided to renovate the family house, pushing me and Sami to move in with my grandmother in Al-Midan. I don't know if that decision was to tighten security or because they'd given up on finding an affordable house in Damascus, but that move was the chance to get closer to my grandmother's world.

From first thing in the morning, after coffee, Tete spent most of her hours in her small kitchen preparing food. She would sometimes ask me to climb the stairs in the kitchen to her pantry, and bring her green or black olives from the big jars, or whatever else was missing, like *za'atar* or jam. She also stocked bags of flatbread in the freezer, as bread was present in all Syrian meals.

Like many Syrians who witnessed the war in the seventies, Tete stored tons of food at a time. She also never threw anything away. The empty medicine bottles carried minced garlic; the yoghurt bucket was used for storing leftover vegetables. In Tete's kitchen, I learnt the mystery of Syrian cuisine; dishes my mother wouldn't make back in Riyadh due to lack of time or fresh ingredients, or my father's dietary requests.

There was a season for each vegetable, during which Syrian women bought and stored them for consumption during the rest of the year. When it was the pea season, I learnt how to dive with Tete into the massive box of peas, shell them one by one and fill a huge bucket with the green balls. I learnt how to boil them, add a bit of sugar, drain, store them in plastic bags and freeze them. Whenever Tete ran out of dinner ideas, she would grab a bag of peas from the fridge and cook them with rice and minced meat. The whole city looked like it was doing the same thing. If you walked down the streets of Damascus, you would see in the waste bins, depending on the season, empty cardboard boxes of peas in the summer or aubergine during the autumn. Small aubergines were boiled, stuffed with walnuts, red pepper and garlic, then stacked in jars of olive oil, resulting in the delicious *makdous*.

Despite my admiration for Syrian cuisine, I thought of all the work behind it as a waste of time and energy. Women clearly had lots of spare time on their hands and few things to do if they could come up with such innovative dishes. Over the years, some semi-ready options were made available in a dedicated corner of Al-Shaa'lan Street called 'The Lazy People Market'. Upper-class women – and, later, working mothers – could find empty, ready-to-be-stuffed courgettes, peeled garlic and shelled peas.

In the evening, the TV was allowed to be on and Tete would flick through the channels before stopping at her favourite Turkish show, which didn't go off even if there were visitors over.

'What a liar! *Wli aleki sho kazzabeh!*' Tete talked to the screen. I smiled and pretended to follow as she explained the last few episodes that I had missed. Tete was strict with her sons and daughters, but she was softer with me. My grandmother knew about Housam, and felt sorry for the way my father had handled it. I have to thank those romantic shows that had become popular among Syrian society. Because of them, Tete understood how vital love was for me, and she took my side against my father's, while my mother disliked those shows and said they were all a bunch of lies.

At night, I slept in the same room as Tete. After Jiddo, my grandfather, passed away, Tete had separated their twin beds, and I slept in his bed while Sami slept on a mattress in the living room. I envied him, as I missed my bedtime phone calls with Housam, and also because Tete snored.

Since I had graduated and was already working, it was hard for the relatives who often came to visit Tete to understand why I wasn't married yet, or why I refused to meet any suitors or their mothers when they called to set a date. Living with my grandmother meant I was more exposed to those calls since she was very social and well connected, unlike my mother, who'd lost many ties by living abroad with a snobbish husband.

The marriage proposals were often from very weird suitors. The last one was a doctor who lived in the US and was coming for a short visit back home, hoping his mother had prepared a list of suitable girls. He was looking for a pharmacist, but was willing to make an exception for a software engineer. My grandmother's home had become a strange shop, and I was the merchandise. Customers enquired about my age, height and weight, degree, family's name and origins, hair and eye colour; and some might even ask about breast size. 'You know, these days guys are watching all kinds of girls on that damn satellite TV, so I'd better find him a good-looking wife before he ends up dragged into haram,' a caller said once to my friend's mother, who politely hung up the phone. My degree in Computer Engineering didn't serve me well. I was overqualified for the position of housewife.

'No, Tete,' I said to my grandmother after she told me about another caller, feeling overwhelmed.

'But what should I tell her?' she said.

'To wait until my mother is back in the summer?' I replied, embarrassed to look her in the eyes. She sighed and ended the conversation, asking God to choose the best for me: '*Allah ykhtarlek elkher.*'

*

97

Finding a job gave me a good excuse to leave the house for nine hours a day, five days a week, but to meet Housam after work I had to be creative.

The French Cultural Centre (CCF) was a tall building in the Al-Bahsa neighbourhood, just beside the pirated software valley. The lobby was usually occupied by an art exhibit, giving it a different, interesting new look every week or two. I took the stairs to the third floor, where my class was located, and sat in my usual spot. We all had different reasons to study French – some to get a scholarship, some just for the thrill of learning a new language – but I doubt anyone had the same reason as I did. I glanced beside me at Housam, scribbled a note on a piece of paper like a teenager, and we both hid a laugh.

L'amour.

For two hours, three times a week, I got to spend time with Housam, guilt-free. I'd always wanted to learn French and had fantasized about spending my honeymoon in Paris, the Capital of Love. At the same time, Housam believed having good French would be an asset if he ever migrated to Canada.

The class was the best part of my week: Housam's warm company, the walks with hands intertwined before and after the class, the nearby bakery's deliciously seductive aroma that reached the third floor, and the minibus that allowed us to sit closer together while pretending we were strangers in front of prying eyes.

Although I thought I had my life back, knowing my father was against my love ruined most of my days. I was depressed and lonely when I was far from Housam. I would wake up in the middle of the night spooked out by nightmares of my father shouting. I was drowning or falling from a cliff or getting strangled. Those nightmares followed me during the day like my shadow.

My father and I didn't talk, but he occasionally sent me offensive emails about ungrateful daughters or Quran verses warning against disobeying parents. His emails and the way he considered himself the victim sparked my rage whenever they arrived. We were miles from reaching a midpoint. I deleted his emails without opening them. I didn't have the courage to run away and I couldn't bear living with a forbidden relationship. I thought of taking a year to travel and study for a Master's in the UK or US, but that plan was rejected. 'Since when do girls travel on their own?' my mother stated. 'When you get married, go wherever you want.' That was my mother's – and most mothers' – answer to anything asked by a girl. When Nisreen got married shortly after and travelled to do a Master's in Ireland along with her husband, my mother kept referring to her as a perfect example.

'When I get married?' I felt a pinch in my heart. My mother spoke about it like nothing had happened. 'As if that's an option, Mama!'

'You CAN get married. Suitors are calling your grandmother all the time! You are just being stubborn.'

Desperate, frustrated and helpless, I decided to seek help from my estranged aunt, Sanaa.

~

'What's the occasion?' the florist asked inside the tiny shop. I froze for a second. *How do I explain this to him?*

'No occasion.'

As if there would be a special flower arrangement for this event. I hadn't told anyone besides Housam about my meeting my aunt. I didn't want anyone to change my mind. There was always a chance that it would backfire, but this was my only hope. If I could understand what had happened back then, I might find a way of being with Housam. My father had left me no other option; he was too stubborn to change his mind, and I was too determined to break free without breaking his heart. So, I asked my second aunt, Falak, my father's other younger sister, to arrange a meeting with Aunt Sanaa. She was the only one who was in touch with her and whom I could trust to keep this a secret. Both aunts were thrilled to learn of my wish.

I held the no-occasion flower bouquet in my hand as I walked towards my aunt's house. I imagined all the possible scenarios on the way there, but the reality was even better. Aunt Sanaa's place was as warm as her smile. She hugged me like I had just come back from a trip, even though we'd never met. My aunt had five kids. Five cousins I could've had in my life: twin girls around my age; one boy who studied the same subject as me; and two younger ones, a boy and a girl. I instantly bonded with them as a conversation started about how we all had the same body structure and chubby faces. I shared my genes with them.

'I went through a hard time as a fatherless and attractive young girl; everyone wanted to take advantage of me,' my aunt said while pouring me a cup of tea. 'I just wanted to get married and have someone to protect me, but your father never agreed. Every time women knocked on our door, asking to see me and your aunts for marriage, he would kick them out. No one was good enough.'

No one is ever good enough for my father, I thought.

'When I fell in love, your father was in Saudi Arabia. Your late grandmother told him over the phone, and he rejected the proposal instantly, knowing my husband's Alawite origins. I had no option but to run away.' My aunt was telling her story without my asking. She was defending herself like she probably had done for many years. I listened to her and watched her facial expressions harden and soften as she relived the story. However, she always smiled and her eyes glowed with love whenever she mentioned her five beautiful children.

I told her about Housam and my father, the same man who had cut her out.

'Do you know that your father was a romantic?' Aunt Sanaa said. 'He fell in love with a Kurdish girl and proposed to her, but her father rejected him. He wanted a Kurdish man for his daughter.'

My heart raced. *This. This is the missing puzzle piece that I needed to know about my father.*

My father's heart had been broken!

'And then he married another woman who also broke his heart. He spoilt her, but she always refused to follow his wishes. His marriage didn't last a year.'

I knew my father had a failed first marriage, but that part was rarely spoken of. My father was a broken romantic monster. This explained his soft heart and explosive rage. This explained why he kept his sisters, and now me, from love.

I left my aunt's house that evening content that I'd taken the risk, yet overwhelmed by my father's complicated past. Maybe there was a way to convince my father after all and make everyone happy. Maybe is a dangerous word.

Chapter 9

Love Against War

I WAS NEVER A fan of watching the news, but since a man had burnt himself in Tunis in December 2010 to protest against police corruption, I had been glued to the live news reports, flagged with the red flashing 'breaking news', showing waves of angry shouts from fed-up civilians rising up against years of unjust and brutal regimes. I followed the revolution train, labelled as the Arab Spring, as it moved within months from Tunis to Egypt to Libya, never expecting it to hit Syria. Life wasn't perfect in Syria, but it was much better than the dystopian one I pictured in my mind when listening to stories from relatives, close friends and Housam. Stories, horror stories, that people only dared to whisper from one generation to the other, because 'walls had ears'. The security was well known to be tight. I wanted Syria to be the best country in the world but had my doubts about whether an Arab Spring would stand a chance.

Still, I kept an eye on the increasing number of subscribers to the Syrian Revolution event page on Facebook that called people to march against the regime. Facebook was blocked by the government, but once again VPNs and proxies opened all the doors. And in mid-March, Friday prayers turned into protests calling for freedom, dignity, social equality and, most importantly, an overthrow of the illegal regime. The mosques flooded with protestors, mostly young men and, later, women. The president spoke on TV, promising reforms. He deactivated the State of Emergency that had been in place since the sixties – which gave the government extra power to take actions that wouldn't normally be permitted – replaced the government ministers with new ones, and tried to reassure everyone that things would change. His speech could be heard in Damascus's streets, which held their breath to listen. However, the changes weren't enough to calm the growing waves of protestors who had been waiting for decades for such a moment. They weren't enough for me.

On the other hand, some people in Damascus seemed annoyed that the Friday protests were ruining their only day off. Some didn't believe this would lead to any good, while others were simply tired of working six days a week, in more than one job and for minimum wage. They longed to have some peace on Friday before going back to the harsh life of providing for their families, and couldn't afford to care about politics.

During that time when Syria was about to split, I was trying to get my life together. The renovation of my parents' house was now over. Moving back to the family house with Sami gave me more freedom to spend my time as I wished.

My relationship with Sami was very strained at the time. He wanted to return to Riyadh like Walid had, but couldn't leave me alone in Syria. It was like I was still a seven-year-old girl going to a party at my friend's house and having to be accompanied by my brother. It was like we'd never grown up. We both wanted the exact opposite things, and we were only left with resentment – lots of it.

*

By the third presidential speech in late June, the tone had changed: the government condemned the protestors as terrorists invading the country whom the army needed to wipe out. Soon enough, the supporters' clapping was louder than the protestors' shouts, and blood flooded the streets. The violence escalated quickly in other Syrian cities like Homs and Hama, while Damascus became quiet, too quiet, as protests were suppressed.

My city turned into the most 'secure' place in the country with the introduction of checkpoints. I learnt how to avoid these, when possible, by taking shortcuts or at least not talking back to the armed soldiers standing in front of my car. They checked IDs, mostly the men's. They sometimes asked to see our phones and scrolled through photos, messages and emails. Most importantly, they asked for Facebook accounts. They checked posts, photos, liked groups and friends, looking for any indication as to whether one was loyal or a traitor. Sometimes, they didn't know what a Facebook was and thought it might be a threatening device, a weapon. And it was indeed, only not as physical as they imagined.

'Do you have a Facebook on you?' a soldier would ask, not sure what he was expecting. Protestors learnt how to overcome the Facebook trap and started creating dummy accounts filled with pro-regime content to fool them.

The war between the regime supporters and opposers wasn't only on Facebook. Pro-regime marches and celebrations were spread across the city as a reply to the smaller, and abruptly ended, protests. Meanwhile, patriotic anthems were broadcast from shops, cars and checkpoints all around Damascus, remind-ing people how much they loved their country and, more importantly, their leader.

I don't remember being afraid back then – not yet. There was something empowering about watching revolutionary acts. Something that was close to my nature. I also hoped that my father's increased worry while following the situation on the news would help sway his heart and change his attitude in return for my safety.

By August, the international community had declared that the Syrian regime had lost control and that al-Assad had to step down.

It's only a matter of time.

That's what everyone had in mind as we watched the clashes continue. We all saw how the Arab Spring was over in other countries in a matter of weeks and months. The people had their say, and they got what they asked for. Only that was not the story for Syria, as al-Assad refused to step down.

Meanwhile, the tension between Sami and me began to thaw. When he fell in love with a girl from a town a few kilometres outside the ancient walls of Damascus, he started understanding my dismal world under our father's rules. He announced it when my mother came to visit us alone during her mid-term break in November. And while she felt the pressure of having to help yet another romantic relationship, I felt less lonely. Sami had changed his attitude towards Housam and me, and became more accepting. That meant the world to me.

That winter, my mother realized she needed to do something, besides praying, in order for a change to happen. Encouraged by her own mother, she finally agreed to meet Housam, the man who was still in love with her daughter despite the obstacles and rejections. She was probably looking for a flaw to convince me to quit this suffering relationship, but I trusted Housam would be able to make a good impression.

At the cafe, I sat awkwardly between the two of them, but before I knew it, they were making jokes about my stubbornness and impulsive attitude. Despite being under attack, I took a sip of my hot chocolate and smiled, feeling my heart warm up. My mother was finally on my side.

For a while, in the winter of 2011, I was optimistic. I was in good shape after losing all the weight I'd gained back in Riyadh. I adopted Beso, a fluffy black-and-white cat, who made the house less gloomy; I was learning French, piano and how to drive, despite everyone's discouragement. I had a satisfying new job in a promising company and fun friends; I was deeply in love and feeling positive about both Syria and me getting our happy revolutionary endings.

Little did I know that I was about to witness what the UN would go on to describe six years later as the worst humanitarian crisis since World War Two.

~

I flipped the light switch as I entered the house after work, but it remained dark. I sighed. This was becoming a regular occurrence. I lit the candles already placed in each room, then went to the kitchen to prepare a quick meal. *Good thing the stove is gas*, I thought, before realizing this too wasn't working. The gas tank was empty.

It will take ages to get a replacement!

I made a cheese sandwich by candlelight and left the dish in the dark sink. The house felt like a cave. I grabbed my thick wool jacket and put it on while moving around the house, trying to warm up. Time went slowly without electricity. I caught up on my literature reading with the aid of my mobile's torch, but three hours in the dark was still a long time.

2012 was not a happy new year. We'd sensed this was coming as 2011 ended with random explosions in the city. The regime opposers were now an army of rebels that had managed to break through the tight security and reach the suburbs, a few kilometres from the heart of Damascus. And as much as we anticipated that moment, it was still stressful, being unable to imagine the aftermath of the zero hour.

Despite the cold weather, I went out on to the balcony to check for lights outside. The street drowned in darkness. A loud song burst from a speaker somewhere in the night around me, praising the regime fighters. I cringed and went back inside.

Every neighbourhood had a different schedule for the government-controlled power cuts. Al-Mazzeh, where I lived, alternated between darkness and light every two to three hours. Nadia's neighbourhood, Al-Maliki, was off that schedule and the lights there were always on, as they were in other places where government officials lived. On the other hand, places known to be full of opposers, like the Damascus suburbs, were cut off for longer hours, sometimes days, punished like a naughty child.

It was easier to deal with the power outages during the week when I spent my time at work. Most companies and shops had a power generator used as a backup during the power cuts. This made us stretch our hours in the office as long as possible to benefit from electricity, heat and the illusion of a safe space and the company of friends. It was hard to focus on work, glued to the news websites like addicts. We soon realized that social media was best for unfiltered and real-time news. Websites like Twitter, Facebook and Google Plus covered hundreds of events that the official news was too biased to mention. It was hard to know which accounts to trust. Fear had already invaded the country, and anything was possible.

The CEO sent us an email warning that he would be monitoring our website activities after noticing our minds were too occupied with our reality. The same reality that he was denying, living in a posh, quiet and secure neighbourhood. He didn't tolerate any conflict-related excuses from people who couldn't show up to work because their area was declared closed or besieged. Affected employees had to apply for day leave or an unpaid absence.

It was impossible not to follow the news. It was no longer only happening in other cities or countries. It was happening here, to our families and friends. To us. We were the news.

While some employees would come to the office saying life was normal outside, others would come shouting, 'War! There is war outside! How are you guys still working?!'

The political debates in the office were hard to avoid. It was risky to speak your mind, as many people were being detained at work after someone had reported them as traitors. No one in my workplace had been detained yet, but trust was as rare as electricity and gas. There were eyes and ears everywhere.

'So what if Rami Makhlouf was stealing money from the country?' a girl in the office exclaimed, defending the president's cousin who had shares in almost every company in Syria. 'Every country has its mafia, but that doesn't mean we go and destroy everything. Look at Italy, they are fine!'

By the spring of 2012, weapons were being heavily smuggled into Syria through several countries backing their own agenda. Violence was now faced with more violence. During that time, the company offered us a first-aid course with a paramedic named Taha from the Syrian Red Crescent (SRC). Besides *Grey's Anatomy*, I wasn't interested in learning anything medical, but with everything going on, we all felt the need to enrol.

Taha was young, tall and kind. He had been volunteering with the Red Crescent for years, but in the last few months he had found himself rescuing civilians injured during the conflict. When Taha told us how he'd helped evacuate the besieged residents of Al-Zabadani in the Damascus suburbs, his red medical vest suddenly looked like a superhero's cape. I realized then that this was what I wanted to do. I wanted to save lives. I never wanted to leave Syria. I needed to protect my home and my people. As soon as I was done with the course, I called the SRC to volunteer and waited for the call to make a change. The need to throw myself into danger was fuelled by the love of my homeland, which was falling apart. It was also a statement to my parents: I am never leaving love behind, even if it costs my life.

By summer, things seemed to have calmed down in Damascus momentarily, and I managed to convince my parents to visit for their annual holiday. I wanted closure to my on-hold relationship, even if it meant picking one side for ever.

Even though Lara got married in a beautiful ceremony in Al-Zeitoun Church and my cousin got engaged, June turned out to be a terrible month. Happy moments were overshadowed by the war that was crawling towards us. The ongoing battles had reached Damascus despite increased security measures. A civilian call for strikes was announced to pressure the regime to resign, asking people to close their shops. Many responded but were forced to open the next day.

News of arrests and deaths was spreading online. Our friend

Rami was detained while secretly taking videos of the protests, like many did to share online with the world. Housam's cousin, along with a colleague from my previous job, was also detained. A resentful statement on Facebook, or taking part in a political conversation, was enough to get you behind bars without a clear charge. The list got bigger than we thought possible. It was when a guy from my university went to Homs with his camera to document the war and was shot dead that we felt that death was closer than ever.

I fell sick with a nasty throat infection that kept getting worse, as if my body sensed what was about to happen. My parents were very nervous all the time, and my father was checking the news and the flights back to Riyadh as rumours circulated that the airport would shut down soon. The sounds of war woke us up at night. And during the day, we managed to find some time to argue over and over about my relationship with Housam. It was no longer something I wanted to hide. It was clear that my father was not going to change his mind and that my mother was unable to help.

The next day, my fed-up father came up with new orders: everyone would have to travel back with him to Saudi Arabia or otherwise be denounced. The house would be locked for ever. I'd got dressed and was about to leave the house for work, even though I was coughing badly.

'Look at me.' My father's voice echoed, holding me back as I reached the front door. My father looked tall and angry. He didn't look like my father, not like any father.

'Don't bother coming back home.'

I walked aimlessly in the streets of Damascus, making sure I was far enough away before stopping to catch my breath. My phone was ringing with my mother's name on the display.

'Come back home. We'll talk,' my mother said firmly.

'I am not coming back, Mama. Not to the house, not to Saudi. I can't do this any more,' I said, realizing this was turning into a goodbye.

'Come. Back. Home. I won't let him touch you.' My mother sounded stronger than usual. But there was nothing she could do now.

I told her not to worry about me, and I hung up and cried in the middle of the street like a lost girl. With trembling hands I called Housam, and I told him everything. He took the day off and came to the rescue. I was losing my balance as we walked. My face was pale, and my cough was getting more violent.

'You have to see a doctor.'

Housam took me to A&E. My throat infection was getting worse. Two injections, an IV bag and a prescription for an antibiotic. We walked to a cafe to eat a bite and rest.

'Don't worry. We'll get our happily-ever-after. We did our best, and now we have to move on and get officially married. I can't let you go back to him, not any more.'

Housam was calm and confident. For a second, when I'd called him earlier, I'd thought he would feel the need to run away from this mad family, but here he was telling me how he would fix it all. His eyes were the only safe spot in my crumbling world.

'Drink some of the juice. You need to get better now.'

My mother was calling restlessly, worried I would run away. I returned home, planning to see her and pack my things. I was so tired from the dramatic day and the medication was kicking in. I went into my room and slept for many hours. I woke up to more yelling. *Am I still in that nightmare?*

I recognized Sami's voice. He was in a heated argument with my father. I'd never seen Sami so angry and loud, and, for the first time, he was standing up for me and for himself. Everyone was fed up.

I was allowed to stay a few more days either to pack my things or change my mind and go back with them to Saudi Arabia. A girl was not supposed to be kicked out of her family's house. She was never supposed to leave her family home unless she was going to get married. *From her family's house to her husband's house to the grave.* That's what the older people used to say about a girl's life cycle. Those were the three places she was allowed to live or die in. If she misbehaved, then she would be locked in, not kicked out.

During the whole time, I could hear my father's insults and my mother's prayers. While missiles were hitting somewhere else in Damascus, our house was falling apart in a different way. A dictator lived in it, and no matter how loud we yelled or how hard we fought back, we could only lose. Freedom was impossible. Years wasted trying to reason with my father to accept Housam, praying to God to help me change the things that I could not control, asking others to intervene and waiting impatiently for a miracle to happen. It was finally clear to me that nothing would change. If I stayed, my life would be forever trapped with him in Saudi Arabia, waiting for the perfect suitor who would never meet my father's standards.

The last couple of days I spent in the house were enough to eliminate any doubts I had about leaving. The ultimatum that he gave me as a means of pressure helped me see things clearly. The game was about to end, there were only two options left, and I made my choice very clear. I chose love over hatred. I chose unknown freedom over apparent injustice. I chose me.

I took out my passport from my desk drawer and turned to

where the Saudi re-entry visa was printed on a piece of A4, folded and attached with a clip. I considered my whole life in Saudi Arabia. There was no returning from this. I pulled the paper from the passport and slowly tore it into two halves. My heart was racing, but as soon as I shredded the paper, it slowed. *Now, I am free.*

I went to my parents' bedroom, where my father was having his afternoon nap, quietly placed the shredded paper on his nightstand and left.

I am not going back. Not any more.

~

I stood in the street in front of my family's house, holding my bag and whatever was left of my dignity. The sun was about to set, and cars were rushing to get back to their safe houses instead of wandering in the unknown night. I was hoping to reach Tete's. She was the only one who would be willing to hide this *shame*. The only problem was that the Al-Midan neighbourhood had recently turned into a conflict zone and taxi drivers looked at me like I was crazy when I mentioned my destination.

A taxi finally stopped, and I told him the scary word. He paused and looked confused.

'Do you know what is happening over there right now?' His voice was concerned.

'Yes, I know.' I held tight to my bag and tried to sound strong again, but my voice sounded like pleading. 'But I need to be there urgently.'

The driver seemed to be thinking about it for a second and must have felt sorry for me because he agreed to take me with him.

'Fine, get in, but I will only drop you at the entrance of the neighbourhood. I am not going inside, OK?'

'That's more than enough!' I lightened with hope. 'I can walk the rest. *Shokran* – thanks!'

By the time I reached my grandmother's warm house, I could hear a few gunshots in the distance. There was no smell of cooking and no sounds of kids playing around. There was fear in the air and the scent of a disaster that was about to happen.

My grandmother greeted me, tired and distressed. The security situation, the summer heat and the power cuts were taking their toll. My cousin was staying with her, as he couldn't return to his house in Darayya due to the conflict and roadblocks. No one was in the mood to talk. We spoke in short sentences before the night crawled in, and the few distant gunshots became closer and louder. We pretended not to hear them, like we pretended I hadn't just been kicked out of the house, causing scandal for my family.

When the morning came, I got dressed and snuck out of the house before my grandmother woke up. I wanted to leave behind that feeling of shame. I walked away from Al-Midan towards my work in Al-Baramkeh. The buses had disappeared, so I kept walking, exhausted and stressed out. When I arrived, I realized it was naive to think I could distract myself with work. Everyone was following the news on social media. Things were getting more dangerous in Al-Midan.

I called my mother and acted tough while she worried. The whole situation was confusing and unreal for her. Standing up to my father was something she made sure my brothers and I avoided at all costs.

'Mama, listen to me.' I interrupted her countless questions, afraid that her worries would sneak into my mind.

'I am OK. But you have to get Tete out of Al-Midan. The area is going to be in danger very soon, and she might get stuck in there.'

The harsh reality of my words made my mother freeze.

'*Wo ente?* What about you?'

'I have a plan,' I lied. 'Just get her out, please, do something!'

I hung up the phone and went to the toilets to pull myself together. My whole body was shaking.

I tried to concentrate at work, but after a couple of hours I noticed my colleagues were packing to leave. I opened Facebook and found out that an explosion had taken place at the National Security Headquarters, resulting in the death of the Syrian defence minister, the deputy defence minister, and other top military and security officials. Most of my company's employees lived in the suburbs and were worried about road closures in and out of Damascus. In no time the office was empty, and I had to leave, but where to?

Sami called and picked me up later. After some discussion, we agreed it was best to stay in his room for the time being. Tete and my cousin were already at home with my mother, who sighed in relief when she saw me. She told me my father was worried when he didn't see me earlier with Tete. When he heard I was there he was quiet but also relieved. That was a non-verbal agreement allowing me to stay for the moment, and I had to swallow my pride and be pragmatic. It took every cell of my body to force myself to come back to the dragon's nest again and hope not to get burnt.

The next days were tense as events in Damascus escalated very quickly. I avoided being in the same room as my father as much as possible. My aunt Razan and her three children were forced to flee their home in Al-Midan and come to live with us. Every room in the house was occupied. Although all I wanted was to be alone with my thoughts and sob, I had to make small talk and smile along with my family like a good host, welcoming guests in a house that no longer welcomed me.

In the kitchen, the food supplies started draining quickly as our numbers increased, and I wondered if anyone would be able to go out to find more. My mother tried to cook basic meals that would keep us full for hours, like *mujadara*, which contained bulgur and lentils. However, her Syrian hospitality skills made her always go the extra mile with side dishes and appetizers. Even in the darkest days, my mother was the perfect hostess.

The living-room couches were full as we sat together listening to the bombshells exploding around Damascus and aircraft breaking the sky above us. When the internet was available, we would all be on our phones searching for updates. The living room turned into a news report room as everyone raced to announce a scoop every minute. Whether it was true or false, it only made us feel worse.

Later that day, a piece of information circulated on social media pages warning all residents of our neighbourhood to remain indoors and take all measures of protection. The Alawites of Mazzeh 86 were invading the streets with knives and planning to kill all Sunnis. That line of news spread like fire. We scattered around the house, making sure every window and door was locked. The wooden blinds, metal barriers and cloth curtains were all down, standing between us and the madness outside. We sat in the darkness of our fear and sweat while my aunt started reciting the Quran and prayers, asking God to protect us all.

Every time a missile exploded somewhere, she would raise her voice to cover it, to stop it like a magical spell. The mix of both sounds was making me more anxious, and closing all the windows in the hot Syrian summer made it hard to take a breath.

'Enough!'

I lost my temper and stood up to crack a small opening in the window, allowing a breeze to enter my lungs. I wondered, what if the Alawites were sitting locked down in their houses, imagining Sunnis attacking them as well? I thought of the Alawite classmates I knew at university. Would they really attack me?

A deafening roar from an aircraft made me close the window and go back, choosing to suffocate with the others rather than listening to the war roaring outside. We were stuck inside, like a scene in a horror movie where a group of friends hides from the zombies outside. *Are 'they' going to break in and kill us all? Is the house going to explode? Or are we just going to run out of supplies and starve to death?*

Between the sounds of Damascus under fire and my constant cough, I couldn't get any sleep. My mother told me I was hallucinating one night and gasping for a breath with a high fever. She saw me fading away in my sorrows and sickness as she stood there, helpless.

The date for my father to return to his work in Saudi Arabia arrived soon and the airlines confirmed his return flight. He wanted to leave this madness after the war had prevented his plan to force everyone back to Saudi. He was obliged to host relatives who had fled their dangerous neighbourhoods and keep the house open. My mother's return flight was already scheduled for a later date and, due to the ongoing conflict, changing it to an earlier date was impossible. With my father gone, we were relieved from one battle but still left with another.

I managed to get out of the house during a reprieve in the shooting. Al-Mazzeh had turned into a ghost town. The area that used to buzz with shops and restaurants now had barely anything left on the shelves. I tried to find some basic food supplies, but all I managed to buy was breadsticks and a bag of pasta.

Bins overflowed with rubbish bags as the refuse collectors didn't come for them. I wondered if they couldn't make it or weren't allowed. After a few days, the residents were sick of the smell. A lit matchstick gave birth to a fire that did the job. Only then did a fire engine show up and clear the vast smoke cloud.

Life, or what was left of it, returned gradually to Al-Mazzeh after a few days when the rebels lost their battle with the army and withdrew from the area. This wasn't the case in Al-Yarmouk, where Housam was living the worst days of his life. The whole neighbourhood and the area surrounding it were under heavy military attack. Tanks blocked all exits and Housam and his family were stuck. We could only call or text for a few minutes, enough to update each other and make sure we were still alive. Minutes of hope and desperation, happiness and deep sadness, good and bad news. Those minutes were our oxygen masks. I can't remember which was harder: to call Housam and not get through, or to hear his soothing voice mixed with explosions in the background. This was not how it was all supposed to happen.

My mother was booked to leave two weeks after my father, in the middle of Ramadan. She first had to clean up the mess he'd left behind. After consulting her brother and her religious uncle, they supported her decision to get Housam and me at least engaged for now. After Ramadan, we could finish the paperwork and get officially married. My mother took a huge risk in being part of this after my father had made it clear he would cut ties with any-one who helped me out, but she had to put an end to the situation. She knew this was the last thing she could offer me before going back to her life with him, without me.

The preparations for my engagement ceremony were made quickly and in tears, like a funeral. My mother was blue and wor-ried all the time about my father finding out. I was still coughing and sick. The whole country was at war, and here we were, trying to celebrate.

People usually don't get engaged or married during Ramadan as it is dedicated to worship, but we had to move quickly. Since Housam and his family were stuck in Al-Yarmouk and my mother had to leave soon, we decided to drop some of the pro-tocols of an engagement. The traditional visits between both families to agree on dates, dowry and other details were done over the phone. We had to wait a few days until roads opened temporarily in Al-Yarmouk so Housam could get out during the day and meet me to pick our engagement rings.

As we walked through Al-Salhiyah, most of the shops looked deserted. Shop owners were afraid of riots, so took down their displays and kept only a few options in the shops, while others decided to clear their shops entirely and close until things settled or they simply left the country for good.

There was nothing much on offer. After searching for an hour, I decided I would choose the first ring I saw in the next shop so we could all go home and have some rest. Luckily, I found a ring that I fell in love with.

'Good for you, getting together in such circumstances! Con-gratulations!' the jeweller said as he placed our rings in a red velvet box. I didn't think I could smile in those days. The ring made me feel like a real bride for a minute, about to marry the man I loved. If everything had been black and white so far, that moment was full of colour.

The engagement date was set. My mother ordered a cassata ice-cream cake from a well-known bakery in Al-Mazzeh that had managed to stay open for business. I got a neat lilac-and-beige dress, while Housam bought a new black suit. He called me to ask about the colour of my dress so he could buy a matching tie, as advised by the seller. I laughed, my cheeks hurting from moving an unused muscle. So far, the jeweller and the tailor seemed to be the only two people who were happy about this engagement. Everyone else seemed to want it to be over, with the exception of Nadia, who insisted on joining the celebration. I was glad she did. I needed a friend, someone to lighten up the air in our house and joke about the ridiculous situation. Someone who didn't care about how this looked to society or how my father would react if he knew. Someone who knew Housam and me and was genuinely happy about us being together. That was Nadia.

At 10 p.m., after *iftar* and the *taraweeh* prayer, Housam and his family took a complicated trip through the unpredictable roads from Al-Yarmouk to Al-Mazzeh. I was putting the last touches on my makeup with Nadia when the doorbell rang, announcing their arrival.

When Housam and I saw each other, we smiled like the day our eyes locked at the exhibition.

'Is that what you call purple?' Housam whispered, referring to my dress.

'Well, your tie is definitely not,' I said, noticing that we'd got our shades mismatched.

I couldn't have cared less about the purple. I would've been fine wearing pyjamas for this just to move on. It was a good feeling, calm, to know I was finally able to sit next to my love without the need to hide any more, without the fear of being seen or being in sin.

The men talked, and the women nodded. Housam's father proposed on behalf of Housam, asking the men in my family, my mother's brother and uncle, for permission to allow this union. It was a cultural act in which Housam and I had no say. We just had to sit there and let them talk on our behalf and agree to everything that the women had already discussed over the phone. This was just a symbolic announcement to tell the world we were in a relationship. Official marriage paperwork was to follow after my mother's departure.

When the talk was over, Housam's mother handed him the box of rings. As Sami prepared his camera to capture this long-awaited moment, Nadia rushed to grab her handbag.

'Wait, wait, don't start yet!'

We all stopped and looked at her in confusion before a melody started playing from her mobile phone. It was the famous celebration song 'Mabrouk' – 'Congratulations'. I had always listened to it while dreaming of this day. The song drew a spontaneous smile to everyone's faces; even my mother, through her anxiety and stress, was smiling.

> *Congratulations, congratulations,*
> *O my heart's life, congratulations.*
> *This happiness is our happiness.*

And happiness has gathered us.
How sweet is our world,
Congratulations.

Nadia accompanied the song with an excited *zaghrouta* – a wavering, high-pitched sound – encouraging the women to participate in her joyful cheers. Those sounds were for me, for my stolen moment of happiness.

Sami took lots of photos of Housam and me, standing next to each other politely. We couldn't kiss or hug despite the formal announcement, not until we were officially married. Still, my romantic grandmother poked Housam to put his arm around me when we took the picture. We all laughed, and Sami's camera clicked. He told me he'd never seen me smiling as much as I did then, even though I was still coughing. I did not want the night to end, but Housam had to get his family back home before midnight.

'Call me as soon as you arrive, don't let me worry.'

Housam gave me a warm smile before he left with his family. When he finally called me later that night, I could hear the gunshots in the background. He told me how the taxi they'd booked never came to pick them up, and he'd had to find another driver in the middle of the night and hope he was not another kidnapper taking advantage of the chaos in the country. He was stressed the whole way, feeling guilty about putting his family through a dangerous trip.

'I love you, my fiancé,' I said, holding the phone tight in my hands. Hoping if I said it loud enough, the war would stop for a second and let us be two lovers.

Chapter 10

Love and War

Suad Aldarra is engaged to Housam Zayyad

I STARED IN DISBELIEF at my relationship status on Facebook. The red notification alert kept popping up in the corner of my screen as our friends created an instant digital celebration through their flood of comments and happy emojis.

My mother and Sami left the day after the engagement. I drove them to the airport and tried to stay strong as I hugged them, knowing the chances of reuniting again were slim. 'We'll meet soon, *inshallah*,' we lied to each other before they disappeared into the departure lounge. When I got back to the house that had once been so overcrowded, it hit me how quiet it was. Even my grandmother had returned home after things had relatively calmed down in her neighbourhood. I sighed deeply, the scent of Housam's bouquet reminding me that I was not alone. I was one step closer to being with him, yet separated by many more.

The first step was to make our relationship official at the court-house as soon as possible. Housam worried that the place might be closed or destroyed, and we'd end up with an unnecessary obstacle if we decided to travel. In Syria and generally in the Middle East, this process was called *katb kitab*. It would usually occur along with the engagement to make it halal for a man and a woman to go out in public or spend some private time together. In stricter households, it would happen just before the wedding, for the exact opposite reason: to prevent a man and a woman being alone before the wedding night.

An official piece of paper with my and Housam's full names was all it took for us to be allowed to be together, for me to take off my hijab and literally let my hair down. That piece of paper meant that I didn't need to worry if we touched, kissed or let sparks fly.

As the war battled on, we had our own truce. An embrace was enough to shield us from the missiles and a candle seemed more than enough to light our way when the electricity went out. As long as we didn't discuss when or how we could live together, we were like two lovebirds.

The following steps were still not clear, and all we could do was plan each day as it came. *Are we staying, or are we travelling? Where do we stay now that our future house is besieged, and where do we go if we leave?*

Housam was torn between his family's safety and mine. We couldn't travel while they remained in danger, and we couldn't stay in Syria while I remained alone in my family's house. I couldn't move in with his family, and we couldn't rent, as the market was going crazy with more and more displaced people choosing to move to Damascus, where security seemed to be tightest.

Explosions were still happening. One took place in the Radio and Television Building near my work. Another day it happened at a checkpoint near my home. Every time a thunderous bang made me jump, I'd go first to check Facebook and assess whether I needed to leave where I was or stay inside, depending on the location. I'd call Housam, or he'd call me, if there was phone coverage, to check that we were still alive. Once, he couldn't reach me on the phone after a car explosion took place in Al-Mazzeh, so he came over and knocked desperately on my door until I showed up still in one piece.

In August, two weeks after my engagement, Nadia left. The situation in her neighbourhood was tense, her husband was let go from his job, and her family were already waiting for her in Istanbul, pressuring her to leave. We went for a walk the night before her flight. The Al-Shaa'lan shopping area was open and busy despite the random gunshots and ambulance sirens. When the electricity went off, the streets sank into darkness for several seconds before the buzzing of the electricity generators roared and brought the city back to life. People were adapting to the conflict and resuming what was left of their lives, hoping things would be over soon. Nadia assured me she'd be back, that she'd taken a leave of absence from her job instead of quitting because she'd be back. I couldn't argue. She had a two-year-old daughter now, and children should never have to adapt to this madness.

Back in Saudi, my father gave Sami a hard time. He was still upset about what had happened, and took his passport away. He asked my mother about me but she told him to forget me. That I was living with Tete and would never come back. We'd broken each other's hearts and there was no return from there.

Despite the war, I was free of everyone's hold over me. My mother's worries transferred to me over our stolen phone calls whenever she could slip away. She hated not knowing what my plans were, while I hid how nervous I was about an unknown future. She hated knowing that I was living in the house on my own. I'd slept for one night at Tete's, but it was chaos at her place.

My aunt – her daughter – and her big family were staying there temporarily after they'd had to leave their house in Darayya, so I decided to stay on my own at my family's house. I preferred loneliness and solitude in my own house to feeling like an intruder in a crowded house. *This is temporary*, I kept reminding myself. But temporary looked like an endless dark ocean.

In September, the conflict calmed around Jisreen, the small town where Housam had bought our future house. His father went first to check the area and said the roads were open again, and that most of the checkpoints were cleared except for one. After a few days, I went there with Housam and his father. The apartment was brand new, well designed and empty, waiting to be filled with our stories and memories. However, the surrounding area was completely deserted and eerie. A big construction site in front of the building was supposed to be a park and a school, but when the war started construction had been halted, leaving a massive dump in its place. Jisreen looked like a ghost town with only a few families left who had no other options. Housam's father was trying to be optimistic about us living there. Theoretically, we only needed some furniture, but I felt nervous, and Housam could read my face. I tried to discuss it with him when his father gave us some privacy, but he was quiet and said we should get back before it got dark.

In the evening, my mother-in-law called and said Housam had been quiet since he'd come back. She passed the phone to him, but he barely spoke. The house was everything Housam had saved up for, and now he had to let it go and spend more money on renting somewhere else. He knew it wasn't a suitable option and that the area could burst into flames all over again.

Yet it was not easy to digest, and I couldn't find the courage to say, 'Let's go and live or die there.'

The next day, Housam was on his way to work when a soldier stopped him at a checkpoint in Damascus and asked to see his ID. Realizing Housam was Palestinian, he refused to let him pass. 'Go back to Palestine!' He smirked and threw back Housam's ID. It was that day that Housam truly felt the urge to leave, that this country was not home any more.

He talked to his friend in Dubai, who was a partner in a tech company. He offered Housam a job as a web developer, but both work and tourist visas were almost impossible for someone with a Syrian-Palestinian passport to obtain at that point, even though he had held one when he worked previously in Dubai. All Arab countries made sure their doors remained locked to his cursed passport. As panicked people migrated towards the neighbouring countries that had their doors open for Syrians at the time, Housam and many Palestinians in his shoes had to stand still in a death zone, waiting slowly for their unknown fate.

We decided to postpone the wedding until we figured out our options. However, I still went to a gynaecologist to have a pre-marital exam and be ready when the time came. It was my first time at this type of clinic and I wasn't feeling very comfortable. My blood tests and an ultrasound of my uterus showed that I had what the doctor explained was Polycystic Ovary Syndrome (PCOS). She told me it was common, and that I shouldn't worry about it unless I wanted to get pregnant. She prescribed birth control pills that were supposed to take care of the issue.

I felt lonely as I left the clinic. I didn't know how serious PCOS was or if I even wanted to get pregnant. I had always felt lucky compared to Nadia or anyone trying to go through this war with kids. What would I tell them when they heard the roaring of a missile? How would I explain why soldiers were holding guns at checkpoints? And all the videos online about death – how would I hide all that? Yet I wished I had my mother or Nadia to accompany me and share the weight of that bleak moment, or talk it through.

I wrote an email to Nadia about it and she told me to get used to the nausea that came with birth control pills. Nadia didn't stop worrying about me all the way from Istanbul. She kept checking on the situation in Damascus and my future plans. She sent me an email whenever she read about an explosion, but at some point they became so frequent I could no longer tell which explosion she was referring to. They became the daily sound-track of our lives, mixed with the sounds of the cars beeping, the birds humming and the desperate prayers of mothers.

Work didn't make sense amid war. The CEO reminded us in the monthly meeting how lucky we were to be still employed and getting paid at the end of the month despite the financial crisis. Most companies in Damascus had gone bust and laid off their employees. Our company was making a fortune as it dealt in dollars and other currencies, while we got paid in Syrian pounds, which were falling apart day after day. He urged us to take work seriously and warned us about slacking and 'wasting' time reading the news.

My manager, Ahmad, came into the office one day saying he had accepted a job offer in Egypt and would be leaving soon. He seemed cheerful and relieved, despite having to abandon his brand-new home. He was grateful enough to be leaving at all. Every week, someone else came into the office to inform us that they were leaving work and the country. The chairs around me emptied one after the other, and I wished I would be the next to resign and go.

I told Housam about Egypt as an option. He didn't think it would be possible for Palestinians, as he already had an aunt who had got married to an Egyptian and was now living there, and who could never see her family in Syria again. But after another rejection from Dubai came through, he decided to give it a try and check the new regulations for an Egyptian visa. To his surprise, Housam found out that the rules had changed since the newly elected President Morsi had opened the door wide for Syrians and Palestinians. Housam immediately started an application for both of us, and we began counting down. How many days left, how many more explosions to endure, and how much money we were losing due to the currency collapse. In November, a door of hope opened as we got approval for an Egyptian tourist visa.

The countdown to escape death had now begun.

The first of December was set to be our wedding day and our flight was booked for the third. No plans for the wedding yet. The calendar dates looked like a countdown on a ticking bomb. I met Lara one day after work and told her about Egypt. After Lara had got married in June and come back from her honeymoon, she went to start her new life in a town close to Jisreen. She was forced to leave her new place a few days later as war crawled to that area, and she moved in with her in-laws in Damascus. I walked with Lara as she told me her story, laughing about the awkwardness of her unfortunate new life. We had to joke; we had to take our unbelievable life lightly to remain sane. But when Lara asked if I was planning to have a wedding, I couldn't tell if she was being serious.

'How can I get married and wear a white dress in these circumstances?' My voice choked. 'And without my family?'

'Stop this nonsense!' Lara stopped walking and turned to me. 'Look at me,' she said firmly. 'You've waited years for this, and you'll only do it once. You'll wear a white dress, and you'll have a wedding, and we'll dance and have fun!'

I let my tears fall as she hugged me. The guilt of having a wedding my father was against and my mother couldn't attend was hard to bear. Lara reminded me that I was a bride-to-be despite the ongoing war and my family's absence. Although it wasn't traditional to have a bridesmaid in Islamic weddings, I always called Lara my bridesmaid. I don't think I'd have had a wedding if it hadn't been for her.

Things started falling into place once we received our Egyptian visas and decided to leave. With the help of Lara, I found the most beautiful wedding dress in the Christian part of Damascus. The electricity was off when I went with her into the shop, and I could only see the classy off-white dress by the light of the LED chargers and candles, but I knew it was the one. I'd never imagined renting my wedding dress, but given the circumstances, it was the reasonable thing to do. I couldn't carry a wedding dress with me all the way to Egypt. Luckily, the dress was new so I would be the first to wear it. It fitted me perfectly.

For the wedding, Housam and I agreed to hold a dinner in a restaurant instead of a party in a hall. Syrian weddings usually took place in halls with two separate rooms: one for women and one for men. Since we had already done the official marriage during *katb kitab* in the presence of a sheikh, a court official, there were no special rituals during the actual wedding party. It looked mostly like a Western wedding: walking down the aisle to put on rings, having a giant cake to cut and dancing all night. At conservative weddings the parties were separated, and the bride walked down the aisle alone, only in the presence of the women. Then, after a couple of hours, the women would cover up, so the groom and some of the men from the bride's side could come over to the women's hall accompanied by *a'arada*, a group of men chanting traditional songs for the newlyweds with drums and pipes. The couple would walk the aisle again and resume the party. If the families were from a very conservative background, the two groups never mixed. Housam and I never liked the separation idea, so we took advantage of the chaotic circumstances and managed to get away with having one party.

We skipped the step of printing cards and invited our close relatives on the phone. I called Tete and told her the plan, and she took charge of calling my uncles and aunts, only from my mother's side. For friends, we created a Facebook event. When people asked about my family's attendance, I'd use the war as an excuse. In the back of my mind, I imagined meeting them again soon and holding another celebration, but I knew it would never happen. I also decided to broadcast the party for my family and Nadia on a friend's laptop. That helped ease the burden of their absence.

Packing for an unknown life in Egypt was the hardest part of all. I couldn't leave anything behind, as I wasn't sure what would happen to my family's house. I started putting ads on Facebook groups where people bought and sold things second hand. Those groups became very popular during the war as many people needed to sell their belongings quickly before leaving, while others needed temporary things quickly after relocating to Damascus. Every time someone replied to an ad I felt a pull in my stomach. With every item I cleared out of the house, my heart cracked a little bit: my schoolbooks, my romantic novels and my silent piano. At least my used things didn't know what was hitting them when they were put in boxes and given to strangers. But Beso, my cat, knew when he saw his carrier. He ran around the house, hiding behind the couches. It took all my energy combined with Housam's to grab hold of him during a power cut, using torchlight to finally put him in his portable home. His frightened and pleading mews still haunt me to this day. They didn't rest for a second as I drove him to the friendly family who had agreed to look after him.

He'll be fine. He'll be fine. He'll be fine.

I kept repeating it to myself as I went back to the silent car that now reeked of his urine. He knew.

A day before the wedding, the internet was cut off. The government announced they were fixing the issue, but this meant that my plans to have my family watch my wedding online were ruined. I had to go through this on my own.

After I packed the lucky things I'd decided to keep and filled two bags for charity, I cleaned the house thoroughly and covered the furniture with old sheets, as my mother used to do every summer when we all travelled back to Riyadh. I was so tired I couldn't feel my body any more. I was exhausted mentally and physically by everything that had happened since the beginning of 2012. Trying to plan a wedding and an escape at the same time was more stressful than I could ever have imagined. I pushed myself through each situation, hoping it was the last one, but there was always a new struggle.

I turned off the lights for the last time, packed my bags in the car and went to spend the night at Tete's. She welcomed me with her warm smile and later gave me half of a relaxant pill. I went to dream.

On the morning of the wedding, Lara drove me to the hair salon and then to the hotel. My mother's sisters joined me as I put on my dress and prepared. Housam arrived in a charming new suit and fresh haircut. His best friend drove us to the party, where our loved ones were waiting for us. We weren't allowed to use the horn in the car to celebrate, as is customary, nor were we allowed to decorate it. It moved silently and slowly in the streets of stressed-out Damascus.

The party was a stolen moment of happiness amid the darkest days in the city. We all pretended everything was fine, danced to the songs that Housam and I had picked, and had a lovely dinner and slices of a nicely decorated cake. It all looked unreal. Me in a white dress, Housam in a black suit. A moment that we'd imagined and fought for for many years was now happening, and it was nothing like any dream we'd had. My heart was full yet aching for not having my mother, brothers and Nadia there. My mother's family were in tears every time I glanced at them. We didn't say it, but we were all thinking about my mother missing her only daughter's wedding. That moment was now something we would never share.

The internet lines came back to life in the middle of the party, and our friend, who was ready with his laptop, managed to connect me with my mother for a few seconds. The fragile line carried her voice as she faked courage, told me I looked beautiful and wished me all the best. I closed the laptop and handed it back, ignoring the confused looks on people's faces. They'd probably never seen a bride with a laptop. But again, amid everything else happening around us, that was the least weird thing.

Later came hugs that were both congratulations and goodbyes. We were about to leave everyone behind and start our journey together, far from the war but also far from friends and family love. As the guests left one after the other, I turned my back to the room and looked at my reflection in a mirror. *Is this a dream or a nightmare? Should I wake up or keep dreaming?* I couldn't tell.

Housam's steps echoed in the empty space as he walked his family to the main door and returned to stand with me after everyone had left us to our long-awaited happy ending.

Chapter 11

Dreams and Deaths

MY BODY FLOATED IN the warm water of the pool under the sun's rays. I wasn't worried about getting sunburnt because I had a full swimsuit on. Nothing showed of my body except my face, hands and feet. The sky was bluer than I could remember – no helicopters, no missiles, nothing but chirping birds. I didn't realize how much I'd missed the water until I went back to it. My muscles remembered all the moves straight away and took me back to our summers at the beach. Housam swam up from behind and held my head gently, blocking the sun behind him.

'Hello, sleeping beauty.' He leant forward and kissed me. 'Did you come to the pool to sleep?' I adjusted my position in the water and stood up next to him, trying to touch the pool floor with my toes while holding on to his wet shoulders. Being with him, being here in this beautiful place, felt more like heaven.

Are we finally safe? Is this what normal life looks like?

We swam for a while and then headed back to our honeymoon room in the sprawling resort. I struggled to take off my wet swimsuit that stuck to my body like skin. I got in the shower and turned on the water, still adjusting to the fact that water was there all the time.

Housam joined me in the luxurious bathroom. I felt the urge to hide my exposed body before remembering that we were husband and wife now. Lying next to him at night and opening my eyes to see him first thing in the morning was the safest feeling I had experienced in my life.

The flight from Cairo to Sharm El Sheikh was the last leg of our long journey out of Syria. When we first arrived at Cairo Airport after finally boarding a plane from Beirut, the flight agency notified us that because we'd rebooked our trip from Damascus to Lebanon, the part of the ticket that covered Cairo to Sharm was lost. We had to rebook and pay additional fees for our baggage, considered overweight for a domestic flight. Although every single step of the way seemed complicated, we paid and were relieved that we had reached the end of our arduous journey.

For seven days, Sharm El Sheikh welcomed us with open arms after an exhausting trip. Despite parts of it looking artificial, the city was fascinating. The salty sea breeze that hit us as soon as we stepped off the plane was a good change from the freezing weather back in Syria and Lebanon – *this must be what a happy life smells like!*

The resort was even more astonishing than the pictures on the website. The staff greeted us with cold *sharbat* – a famous crimson drink made from hibiscus. They also left us a delicious chocolate cake in our room with a note that said, 'Congratulations on your wedding!' It was surprisingly easy to forget about the traumatic events that happened outside the walls of our resort. We spent the time swimming in the pool, doing water sports, going for dinner cruises or just walking on the beach, holding hands. That was all that we had wanted for the last six years and hadn't been allowed to have – that peace in sharing a simple moment, without the fear of being caught in a conflict.

We were still not sure what would happen when we headed to Cairo to settle after our honeymoon, but Housam's friend Ismail had assured us life was good and renting was easy. Immersed in our joyful moments, we trusted him. The worst was behind us now.

Our back-to-reality moment came on our last day in Sharm El Sheikh when Housam's family called at night and told us about the Al-Yarmouk invasion. They had had to flee the house, carrying only their valuables, before the whole area was besieged and turned into a conflict zone. Housam was devastated, but his father assured him that they were fine and renting in a safe neighbourhood with his brother and his family. Guilt for having left crawled into Housam's mind, but there was nothing he could do.

After a week in heaven, we headed to Cairo. It was almost evening when Ismail picked us up from Cairo Airport. His excitement to see Housam, a familiar face from back home, was clear. I stood beside them, smiling as they hugged. Ismail was an old colleague of Housam's and had fled to Egypt with his family a few months before us. He'd offered to help us find a place and settle in. However, by the time we reached Egypt, many Syrians had already taken the same journey, affecting the rental market. Rent was much higher due to the increased demand and our options were limited.

'A Nigerian company relocated to Egypt just a few days ago,' Ismail said. 'They rented most of the apartments here for their employees. Your luck is just terrible! There were many available when we last spoke but now they are all gone.' Despite his attempts to arrange a couple of meetings for us with landlords, the idea of not knowing where to spend the night was enough to make my stomach cramp.

'Don't worry; there is still one place we can see tonight. If it's not suitable, you will stay with us.'

Although Ismail lived in a small one-bedroom apartment with his wife and little daughter, he insisted on hosting us.

The sun was setting in Cairo as we drove through its streets. Ismail was talking non-stop, but when we passed Tahrir Square, he became quiet. I recognized the place from all the news reports that I'd inhaled during the Egyptian revolution.

Here is where it all happened.

This was the iconic space that had held thousands of protestors shouting for freedom. Although it was deserted, the graffiti was still there. For a second, I could hear the protestors' chants of '*Alshaab yoreed isqat alnezam!* – The people want to overthrow the regime!' sending chills over my body. *Here is where freedom was born. Here is where people died for it.* In a few months, the Egyptians had managed to overthrow their corrupt regime and pick a new leader democratically. The country was relatively calm now.

After more than an hour, we arrived at a massive gate that opened for us. Ismail lived in a compound secured by a guard. All new compounds were built this way to provide a degree of urbanity and safety from the real world outside that we'd be lost in as newcomers. The grass inside the compound was greener than the dry roads outside it. It was easy to spot the difference between the two worlds at first glance. The neat buildings were almost identical, with swimming pools scattered between them. I remembered watching promotional ads for this place on Egyptian TV channels. I wasn't sure if we could afford it, but Ismail insisted that it was safer for us to look for a rental here and stay close to him so he could look after us.

Ismail pulled his car over in front of a building. A retired Egyptian man welcomed us to his apartment with a smile. The furniture looked older than him. The living room was packed with ornaments and plastic flowers. While the guys talked about renting that apartment, I remained silent, staring at my flat shoes that didn't suit Cairo's cold weather.

'I heard a couple were coming from Syria, and I felt the need to do something for you. I am sorry about what is going on in your country.' Haj Ibrahim put on a sympathetic face. 'It is getting late, and I am sure you had a long trip, so I am going to save you some time. Let's talk about the details.'

When Haj Ibrahim mentioned the price for renting his place, I lifted my head and looked at him in shock, and then at Housam's face. He knew the price was unreasonable, but he also knew we were out of options, like the rest of the Syrians who'd left. Ismail tried to negotiate, while Housam looked like he was doing maths in his head. The guys finally reached a deal to rent the apartment for five days, starting tomorrow, while looking for a longer-term option.

As they shook hands, I glanced at the bedroom with the old brown blanket on top of the double bed. This was not what I'd had in mind when I pictured my future house with Housam.

Ismail took us back us to his apartment, which was a few minutes away.

'*Ya ahla wsahla, tfaddalo* – welcome!' Ismail introduced us to his wife and unfolded the only couch in the empty living room, turning it into a bed, while his wife insisted on preparing a light dinner. I was embarrassed for invading his small space. He was generous despite having little to offer.

Housam brought a change of clothes from our packed bags that were still in Ismail's car boot. After we'd had a few bites, Ismail and his wife left for their room and Housam and I lay on the sofa bed meant to fit one person. As Ismail and his family had only recently moved in, they didn't have any extra sheets or blankets. Unlike Haj Ibrahim's, their house had only the basics. In our houses back in Syria, we'd had extra of everything and expected visitors at all times. Now we were the unexpected visitors. Housam wrapped his arms around me, and I buried my head in his chest where dark thoughts didn't reach, hoping the next days in Egypt would be better than this one.

As soon as the sun came up the next day, we moved our luggage to our temporary residence at Haj Ibrahim's apartment. It was not the best place, but it was ours for a few days. Several menus for food delivery were laid around the kitchen table. Housam and Ismail left to hunt for more apartments and buy SIM cards, while I stayed in, unpacking the necessary stuff for the following days. I cleaned the house, but I still didn't feel comfortable touching anything. When Housam was back, we ordered two meals from McDonald's that arrived late, cold and tasteless, and, by the next day, had made us both sick.

Before the end of the fifth day, Housam managed to find us a place. He signed a year's contract without giving me a chance to check it first.

'That's the only good option we have. If I hadn't sealed the deal, it would have gone in two minutes,' Housam explained as he put his clothes back in our luggage. The apartment was in the same compound but, due to increased demand, it was double the price range that Ismail had told us about on the phone, with an extra-big deposit and one month upfront. Housam ended up paying what he had thought would last us for three months just for the first month.

The new place was more modern than Haj Ibrahim's apartment, but a much smaller space. The kitchen and the living room were combined. The kitchen was not meant for cooking and the living room was not meant for living. They comprised a fridge, a microwave, two stove burners with no oven, and two couches. It took ten steps to walk from one end of the apartment to the other.

The first room in the apartment, which had previously been a proper kitchen, had been turned into a bedroom that fit only two bunk beds with no windows or space for anything else. The main bedroom had two single beds.

'We'll push them together, see . . .' Housam noticed my expression and went to rearrange the beds. Given the overall situation we were in, I didn't think this would disappoint me, but it did. I remembered the two linen sheets I'd carried from Syria, like any other new bride. What a waste of luggage allowance.

'You'll never notice the difference, believe me,' Housam assured me.

'Did you have to spend all that money on our honeymoon?' I said, leaving the bedroom. 'Now we barely have any savings left!'

'How could I predict rents would go up in seven days?' Housam looked at me in disbelief. 'And we have money left. I have a job, and I will get some freelance projects.'

I pretended to be busy moving bags around to avoid looking at him, to avoid being seen. That house was not mine. It would never be home. Housam came closer and looked me in the eyes. 'We deserved every night of that honeymoon. And I don't regret spending money on it. We'll be fine. Never worry when you are with me.'

I cried as he hugged me. I trusted his words, but I didn't trust our luck.

On our first trip to the city, we decided to visit the Canadian Embassy to enquire about immigration. Canada seemed like a decent option to start a new life and migration had been eased for Iraqi refugees by the embassy in Damascus. The two guards at the embassy door were busy eating fried chicken, so we waited on the side of the road. When they were done, one of them pointed to a bulletin board next to the gate.

'This document here has all the details you want.' The document didn't have many details but provided a website that we checked later at home and found useless. There was no mention of a special process for accepting Syrian migrants or refugees, so we had to look into the general immigration process.

Housam managed to contact an immigration lawyer who was offering advice online for Syrians. He advised us to start with getting an English qualification certificate (IELTS), which was normally a requirement, and to check again in a couple of months for new regulations for Syrians. We registered online for the nearest exam and started preparing.

Egypt hosted millions of Syrians, though none that we knew besides Ismail and his family. The few Syrian families in the compound were mostly wealthy people and businessmen. Most Syrians in Egypt chose to live in 6th of October, a satellite town of Cairo named after the war in October 1973 fought by Syria and Egypt against Israel. The town had a famous street called Al-Husari where we managed to find our bread, cheese, falafel and other familiar products made by Syrian hands. Holding those items always made me feel like I was not too far from home. We considered moving to be closer to that area, which was about fifteen minutes from where we lived, but house hunting was a daunting laborious task with more Syrians coming over daily.

In other parts of the town there were malls, hypermarkets, cinemas and restaurants much larger than those in Syria, and bookshops with a wider collection than I'd ever seen, with relatively fewer sanctions on literature.

At weekends we would buy groceries, watch a movie or have a meal outside the house. I couldn't find a job as easily as I'd thought. The salaries were low, and commuting from the far-flung outskirts of Cairo was challenging for a foreign woman like me. While Housam worked two jobs, I was doing household chores. I shared some of the freelancing projects with him to keep busy and contribute a bit, but it wasn't enough. At night, we would go out for walks inside the dreary compound. Having nothing to do in a new, temporary world was making me feel useless and pushing me to doubt the move. This was supposed to be the exciting new start that I'd longed for. Why did it feel like a trap?

~

It had been almost a month since we'd moved. I was still in bed, while Housam was working in the living room. I heard a shout, followed by a wail. I jumped out of bed to see Housam in tears, struggling to catch his breath.

'He is dead. Baba *mat.*'

I felt dizzy, like there was an earthquake happening.

'He was shot by a sniper in Al-Yarmouk while checking on the house.' I couldn't believe what Housam was saying; neither could he. His mother had received a call from his father's mobile phone and assumed it was him. The caller said the phone was found on a dead man and that was the last number he'd called.

My brain was shutting down. *This can't be happening.*

'What if someone had stolen his phone and that person died? His phone was stolen before!' My brain was hallucinating, but it was enough to make Housam stop sobbing and think. He tried to call his mother again to pursue the truth, but couldn't get through. Not sure what to say or what to do, Housam opened his laptop to check the current situation on Facebook.

One search was enough to confirm the news.

A photo of my father-in-law, lying on a floor, his face covered in blood and his eyes shut, while his body was wrapped in a blanket.

The photo was on a page titled 'Unidentified Dead Bodies'.

'Be grateful that he was buried.'

Abu Kasim, a friend of Housam's father, told him this over the phone. Dead bodies were left all over the streets in Al-Yarmouk, as people feared being shot by a sniper if they dared to carry them away. Housam's father was considered 'lucky' that his body reached the civil hospital and that his best friend, who was still in Al-Yarmouk, got to bury him at the Martyrs' Graveyard. No funeral, no goodbyes, and despite Abu Kasim's assurance that he'd marked the grave, Housam knew that he would never find it.

My mother-in-law, Sabah, was not crying when I talked to her over the phone. The tragedy was bigger than her. In the space of a month she'd said goodbye to Housam, was forced to leave her house under gunfire, and then this. Her world, the only world she knew, had changed for ever. She asked over the phone if I was pregnant already or feeling any nausea, and asked God to bless me with a child. I didn't know how to respond. She asked me to read a few chapters of the Quran for the soul of the dead.

Housam's eyes were blurry. I glanced at him while he hid his face and emotions behind the laptop, working days and nights. He was distant. The worst thing I did was try to reason his father's death by saying he was a martyr now, alive with God – the highest honour for a Muslim. Hearing this made Housam angry. 'What's the point! I want him to be alive with us.'

Watching Housam lose his faith was scary. I felt it was my responsibility to keep him strong and stable. But how could I? Questioning God's will was a dangerous path that we avoided by praying and reading the Quran. Still, I couldn't help wondering why God chose my kind father-in-law instead of my father.

For weeks, I tried to protect Housam from his dark thoughts. I tried to comfort him but ended up saying the wrong things. I made sure he took breaks from work and had a bite to eat while watching TV to change the mood. I avoided the news as it always brought up the war in Syria.

I became alert when we watched any show, trying to predict if a character's father would die or someone would mention the war. I kept looking at Housam from the corner of my eye and made an excuse to change the channel if any scene was too dramatic.

I tried to push Housam to sleep so he could rest, but he would lie beside me, staring at the ceiling with his eyes wide open. One night he broke down in tears, asking about his father.

'Where is he? Is he cold down there? I want my father,' Housam repeated over and over. And there was no word that I could say that could possibly help. I wrapped my arms around him and cried with him, wishing I could take his pain into me.

A month later, our friend Rami joined us in our solitude in Cairo. We were relieved to see him in person following news of his detention when he had been caught recording the protests in Damascus. He was one of the lucky ones, released after only ninety days. Having him around helped Housam slowly come out of his grief, although he never let go of his anger and urge for revenge. With Rami, we explored Cairo together, the old city and Al-Azhar Mosque and Park. We spent a lovely evening in Alfishawi, one of the most ancient folk cafes, joking around like old times and imagining for once that we were all OK and that our scars were healed.

My mother-in-law called us two months after the incident to tell Housam to expect his sister, Amani, to come over. 'Girls are being kidnapped, and I am worried about her.'

Despite our pleas for my mother-in-law to come too, she refused. It was tradition for a widow to stay indoors and not be seen by any men for three months.

Our flat was small; it was filled with sorrow and disappointments. Amani stayed in the extra room and didn't leave it much. Although she was grieving, she and Housam didn't talk a lot. He faced his laptop most of the time, so it was my duty to comfort her. But I didn't know how. I didn't know how to be a sister for Amani.

In April, an unknown number flashed up on Housam's mobile screen. He was being summoned by the Security Directorate to speak about his visa for Egypt. Housam was used to the special treatment of a Palestinian Syrian who was always considered an alien. Even his tourist visa was limited to three months, compared to mine that stretched to six. I was worried, but Housam assured me it was a routine visit.

The next day Housam went to the address in the middle of a deserted area, but found himself in a military zone. An irritated soldier showed him the correct way and pointed far down the road, but the address turned out to be even further than that. When Housam noticed he was late he began to run down the deserted road, but this caused one of his asthma attacks. As he leant over one of the rocks to catch his breath, a few eagles floated over him, covering the sun.

When he reached the correct place, a soldier registered his name and took his passport and phone. Then he led him to a filthy room with a stinking toilet buzzing with insects. The only light in the room was a small ray escaping from a broken window.

'Wait here until we call your name.'

A door was slammed shut and he was left for over an hour. People around him were handcuffed and it hit him that he was in a jail cell. Later, a soldier called his name and asked someone to take him to the *pasha* – the lieutenant.

Housam was met with a stream of racist insults from the lieutenant before finally being asked some basic questions about his residency, the answers to which were all written in his visa renewal application. The lieutenant then told Housam to check back in fifteen days to pick up a three-month tourist visa from the residency department. This humiliating process would be repeated every time he wanted to renew his tourist visa as a

Palestinian Syrian. On the way back, Housam sat on a rock in the sandy road to rest and watched a stray dog staring at him. Housam smiled, thinking how much easier his life would be if he were a dog.

My mother-in-law finished her mourning period and booked a flight to Cairo. We picked her up from the airport and carried her heavy bags, wondering what she had inside them. She'd lost some weight and was dressed entirely in black.

When we arrived, she took one look at the extra room and said, 'I am not sleeping in there.' She left the room for Amani and chose the couch in the living room to be her bed. 'Why couldn't you find a better place?!'

She didn't like anything about our apartment: the isolated location, limited space, the lack of a Turkish coffee set despite the fact that neither Housam nor I drank it. She was happy, though, with dinner. Housam had told me her favourite dish was *horrak esba'ao*, a lentil dish with square-shaped dough, soaked in tamarind sauce and topped with pieces of fried onion and bread, and garnished with pomegranate seeds and parsley. For dessert, since we didn't have an oven, I'd looked up a recipe for a micro-wave chocolate cake that turned out very well. I wanted her to feel at home, though this place didn't feel like home to me.

As I cleared the dishes with Amani, Housam listened to his mother's stories about everything that had happened since he'd left, who'd died and who'd survived. All the things that she couldn't share over their monitored phone calls. She gave him a copy of a Quran printed especially for his father's death, as is the tradition in Syria, in the hope of sending blessings to his soul every time someone used it. She cried, and Housam fought his tears, while I went to the bedroom to give them some space and cried on my own.

~

'That's not how we do this dish.'

My mother-in-law murmured from her place on the couch while a Turkish actor was shouting on the TV screen with a Syrian voiceover. I stood at the kitchen counter and continued cooking, pretending not to hear her comment. I didn't realize that the open kitchen space I enjoyed preparing dishes in would be an easy way for my mother-in-law to watch my every move while she followed her favourite TV series.

Housam was busy working and I was taking online courses to refresh my technical knowledge, so there wasn't much for her to do besides watching TV, reading the Quran and calling her siblings back in Syria. Having retired a few months ago and recently lost her duties as a mother and a housewife, she was left with a huge space that was hard to fill. Sabah was used to waking up early before going to work and preparing the family dinner, but she found it hard to change that habit. We got used to waking up to the smell of fried food or the washing machine's loud sound.

Talking to Housam became limited to the bedroom. Any conversation in the living room would welcome everyone's opinion, no matter how small or personal the matter was. On some days, it felt like there was a curse on our relationship. It was to remain a forbidden love for ever.

I stayed in the bedroom most of the day and kept myself busy studying for a programming certification by Oracle that I had wanted to take for a long while. I didn't know how to interact with my family-in-law. I barely knew how to talk to my own family. My naive solution was to keep quiet and avoid pointless arguments, but I felt like I was walking on eggshells. My mother-in-law, despite her uncalled-for comments, was very sensitive and always apologized for being a burden on us. She wasn't happy either; she didn't like living in Egypt and longed to go back home. I heard her weeping at night when we went to our room. Despite our efforts to make her happy, it was not an easy task to cheer someone who'd been through what she had.

The next day I tried to come up with a way to make Sabah enjoy her time. As she'd loved mosques back in Syria, I suggested she check out the mosque in the heart of the compound. I had visited the mosque several times, and it was soothing and well looked after. I often saw elderly Syrian women chatting, but I wasn't very interested in starting a conversation. I just wanted to talk to God and cry it all out. My mother-in-law liked the idea and went to explore the mosque, but after an hour she came back with a broken look on her face. She told us how she'd tried to talk to the women over there, but when they asked her where she was from and she said Al-Yarmouk, they looked down at her and turned their backs, assuming she was a Palestinian refugee. I felt the urge to go and yell at the snobby women, but I knew better. The war had taught us nothing.

One evening, we were all drinking tea after dinner when Housam got a work call and went into the bedroom to take it.

'Are you taking any pills?' Sabah asked. I looked at her in confusion. I knew what pills she was referring to. Amani sensed the awkwardness and left for her room.

'Yes,' I replied and looked away.

'*Ya Allah* – oh God! Why would you do that? Those things are harmful! You should not be taking those!'

'My doctor prescribed them to me.' I avoided mentioning my PCOS to prevent more private questions.

'Your doctor doesn't know a thing. *Allah yehdeke* – may God guide you!'

I swallowed every word I thought of saying as if they were razors. My stomach was bleeding sharp words.

'Don't tell Housam I asked. *Amaneh* – please!'

I nodded as I felt the room run out of air. I went to the bathroom to take a shower. The loud noise of the water covered my tears as I sobbed under it. How could I possibly conceive in such a situation? How unfair it would be to bring a baby into this mess! The crisp future image I'd always had for our happy kids was now blurry, like a hallucination. Housam and I were grateful we could control not having kids, grateful our children were unborn.

Still, my mother-in-law's comments managed to poison my mind with doubts. *Are birth control pills really harmful?*

I heard knocks on the door. Housam appeared. It was easy to hide the tears under the shower this time.

'Amani heard you crying.' Housam's face was covered with sorrow. 'Please don't cry, *habibi*. She told me what my mother asked you. I am sorry about that. I will talk to her. Don't worry.'

The stress of our unpredicted new life took its toll on us. My sensitive colon felt like a rock, while Housam felt chest pains and had difficulty breathing. The ramifications of his father's loss, his responsibility towards his family and me, his job and the uncertainty of Egypt's situation found their way to his heart. Despite the doctors saying he was fine, I knew he wasn't. None of us were.

One night, in a bid to cheer us up, I lay in bed and asked Housam for the things he was grateful for. I was thinking how things would've been much harder if we were separated. Sleepy and grumpy, he said: 'I am grateful for the extra-salty fried-chicken meal we had today.' I laughed and poked him to be serious. To think about us being together, or having a decent place to live.

'I am grateful for the cold Coke that I had with the chicken,' Housam added.

'How about the chocolate cake we had afterwards?' I went along.

'Oh, that was delicious – now I am just hungry! What is this game again?'

We chuckled and hugged and sighed. Over the coming nights, we managed to have that moment to thank God for the good things we had in our life. Whether it was food or something deeper.

The Oracle exam was the perfect distraction for several months from everything that was going on. I was nervous but eager to pass it and feel accomplished again.

The tall Egyptian man behind the reception desk at the exam centre greeted me and asked for my ID. I handed him my passport, feeling ready to take the test, but I was not ready to learn that I wasn't allowed to.

'I am really, really sorry, but ... unfortunately, you are not allowed to take the exam with this ID. Due to US sanctions—'

'I know about the sanctions,' I defended myself, 'and all Syrians take those tests outside Syria.'

'Yes, but you have to show another non-Syrian ID or have

residency in the country. You have only a tourist visa, and that doesn't work, I am afraid.'

'But nothing on the website mentioned anything about eligibility. Why would Oracle let me register, pay money and spend all those months studying?!'

'I am not sure why. I am truly sorry.'

My stomach tightened. I wanted to shout, but nothing came out.

'I wish there was something I could do. This is completely out of my hands.' The man gave me back my passport, and I took it in defeat.

Housam was surprised to see me back in the lobby so soon.

I explained what had happened. As the words came out of my mouth, I thought the whole thing was ridiculous. Housam told me everything would be OK, but it was not true.

'I spent my entire life being told I was not allowed to do stuff because I'm Palestinian,' Housam said as we walked down Cairo's busy roads. 'I got angry and frustrated a lot, but it didn't hurt anyone but me. The sooner you get used to this situation, the better for your sanity.'

But I couldn't let go. Oracle eventually reimbursed me for the exam fees after a few weeks of chasing, but they couldn't compensate me for the disappointment. No one knew why the website didn't mention the banned countries or why it allowed those citizens to register. I couldn't move on, and my sanity was the price.

By the end of June 2013, the Egyptian people had had enough of the Muslim Brotherhood and their elected president, Morsi. Again, they went on to the streets to protest with the blessing of the Egyptian army, who protected their demonstrations and gave the president forty-eight hours to resign.

In our packed living room, we held our breath as we watched Morsi give a live, heated speech detailing his plan to fix the situation. We gasped when he announced cutting ties with the Syrian regime and closing the Syrian Embassy in Cairo. A decision that would only complicate the lives of thousands of Syrians in Egypt and make it impossible to issue any important official documents.

After the forty-eight hours had passed, the military spokesman announced the end of Morsi's era; they shut down all media channels that supported the Muslim Brotherhood and arrested many essential figures in the Egyptian regime, including the president. A temporary president was assigned to lead the country while the supporters and opposers of Morsi clashed in protests, spilling more blood on the streets and sacrificing the country's youth.

More bad news came soon after. Due to some Syrian involvement in the now-ousted Muslim Brotherhood, a ban was announced on Syrians, effective immediately. Syrians were not allowed entry to the country or to have their tourist visas renewed. As Housam and I digested the heavy news, we realized that, in a few months, if we didn't leave the country, we would be illegals.

Chapter 12

Illegals

WHEN THE NIGHT CURFEW was enforced in Egypt, it came as no surprise to us. We were well used to curfews in Syria. However, as news circulated on the Syrian Facebook pages that checkpoints were arresting Syrians with expired visas and deporting them, we found ourselves facing another unofficial curfew exclusively for Syrians. Other news reported police officers raiding apartments in Al-Housari, searching for Syrians. Looters took advantage of the situation and robbed houses by impersonating Egyptian officers. They knew Syrians had cash and jewellery in their houses since they'd sold everything back home and carried it with them. Banks didn't authorize accounts with a tourist visa, but Syrians didn't trust banks anyway.

A couple of weeks after the coup, curfew was lifted but the situation didn't change much. When we went to Al-Housari to get some groceries from the Syrian shops, I could see military tanks from the bus's window. I hadn't expected that I'd see tanks so soon after leaving Syria.

Later that week, Housam went to pick up his salary from Western Union. Seconds after he left the place, a guy pointed a knife at him. He didn't want Housam's money; he wanted his Syrian passport. Luckily, Housam managed to run away with his life and passport.

'What would they possibly do with a Syrian passport? It's use-less!' I said in shock.

'Many things,' Housam said. 'They could use it to seek asylum in Europe. They could use it to plant evidence at a crime scene and blame a Syrian. And, of course, they could use it just to blackmail its owner for money since they know how compli-cated it is to get a new one.'

After six months in Egypt, it was clear that our time there was over. We had to find an alternative. My mother-in-law wanted to go back to Syria, and Amani had an Egyptian suitor proposing to her and wanted to stay in Egypt. Countries that allowed entry for Syrians without a visa didn't admit Palestinian Syrians like Housam. Our best chance was to secure a work visa. Our days turned into job hunting and reading about visa regulations all over the world. Housam's previous manager in Dubai contacted him after hearing about the situation in Egypt and offered him his job back, but UAE rules regarding Syrians were changing overnight. At first, he was allowed to get a work visa, but I could not get a dependant visa. After a few weeks, I was allowed to get a tourist visa, but then Housam was not allowed any type of visa, even with a job contract.

A visa agent promised us that, with money and connections, we could get a visa anyway, so we sent our documents and started focusing on leaving for Dubai. We told the landlord of our inten-tions to leave as soon as we received a visa so that we wouldn't lose our deposit. Every month for several months we told him that this would be our last month in the apartment, but the end of the month would come, and our visa would still be processing. The agent would keep promising us that the rules were about to loosen up, but they never did.

The situation in Syria was only getting worse. My friends started leaving one after the other, changing their Facebook location to a new country. In August 2013, a chemical attack wiped out a whole village in Syria, killing its residents in their sleep. That tragic event left us speechless, scrolling through pictures of dead bodies on social media. Obama said something about chemical weapons being a red line and how crossing it would entail 'enormous consequences', so we kept the TV on news channels all day just in case of an American announcement of war. Nothing happened but an agreement between Syria and America to dispose of the chemical weapons through Russia. 'You can continue killing each other as long as you only use non-chemical weapons,' I imagined Obama saying.

The suffocation of many Syrians, both from the chemical attack and the harsh life they were living, pushed more to leave the country. They had lost their last drop of hope that the situation would get better. The huge flocks of Syrians alarmed Arab countries and made them rush to put up paper borders. Egypt and UAE now weren't the only two countries that made it hard for us to seek a safe life. Soon after, all Arabian Gulf countries followed the same pattern of tightening the rules for Syrians. A member of the Kuwaiti parliament explained on TV how the expensive Kuwaiti lifestyle didn't suit traumatized and stressed-out Syrians. That they should aim for Lebanon or Turkey, which had a similar lifestyle to what they were used to back in Syria. Rich and spacious Gulf countries didn't mind donating large sums of money to aid the Syrian cause, but when it came to hosting them and allowing them to work, that was a big 'no'.

'Believe me, if you were an Indian worker, your visa would've been issued in a few minutes,' the UAE visa agent told Housam over the phone. Racism was universal.

Lebanon, Jordan and Turkey kept their doors open for some time. Still, Syrians were reportedly subject to abuse, unfair wages and trafficking, and deprived of education, all in return for having a safe place to stay after losing everything in the war.

All of this pushed Syrians to follow another route that seemed at the time to have more mercy than the Arab governments – the deep dark sea.

A new trend started showing up between the images of dead bodies on Facebook pages. Pictures of boats started to appear, promising Syrians a better future in a magical land far away for a mere $3,500 per person. Of course, no one mentioned that this package included the risk of drowning or human trafficking or rape or robbery: only bright sun and a bright future.

Images of my friends in Europe looked magical. Some were in Germany, others in Ireland or Sweden. Some had been there since before the war and some had just arrived across the sea. They seemed happy and worry-free. *And the grass, how green it is! Could this be the only way out?*

'Why aren't you considering it yet?' My former manager Ahmad's question showed up on a Facebook chat as we discussed our current situations.

I stopped typing. *Why am I not considering it? Is that my only option now?*

'You don't have a kid, so you have nothing to worry about. I have two!' he continued. 'Just put yourselves on a boat and get out of here!'

'Well, we definitely don't have that kind of money,' I replied and wondered, *Would I do it if I did?*

I tried to keep in touch with my friends, but our chats were mostly about visas and regulations.

'How did you reach this place? How did you get this visa? Did your partner get a dependant visa?'

Most of my friends were in Turkey, besides Lara, who had found a job in Dubai while her husband waited in Syria for a way to join her. Nisreen had already finished her Master's in Ireland and was starting a new job there.

I told Nisreen in one of our conversations about the situation in Egypt, about the boats. '*Oa'ek* – don't dare! Either go legally or don't!' she replied, but what did she know about the situation we were trapped in? I was willing to take my chances with the sea rather than stay there as a trapped and unwelcome guest for one more day.

A few days later, Nisreen sent me an email titled: 'Apply ASAP'. I opened it while I was half asleep in bed. It was a web developer job ad from Fujitsu, her current workplace. Although it was a temporary contract, it sounded perfect. I applied immediately, making sure I kept my hopes as low as possible.

To my surprise, a few days later my dull inbox announced a new message: an email from Fujitsu's HR department inviting me to a video interview. I read the email multiple times to make sure I understood.

Nisreen answered my questions and coached me through my worries.

'But this is in a research lab! I know nothing about research!'

'We did something similar during college. Remember?' Nisreen was sure I would be fine, but I wasn't. Something else worried me: how would I interview in our tiny apartment? The bedroom would look very unprofessional, and the TV was always on in the background of our conversations.

I didn't want to mention the interview or the thought of travelling abroad in front of my mother-in-law, to avoid unnecessary stress, so Housam suggested taking her along with his sister to the shopping mall for the day, which would give me the place to myself.

After days of preparing and trying hard not to consider that this job interview was literally a life-or-death opportunity, the day arrived. I put on a formal white blouse over my pyjama trousers and placed my laptop on the plastic dining table. I wore a white-and-blue-striped hijab and sat alone in the warm apartment, sweating as I waited for the call that would determine my future.

A few technical issues later, I found myself looking at two blond guys smiling all the way from Ireland. Their smiles were relaxed and polite, while mine was forced and desperate. They introduced themselves, but my heartbeats were louder than their voices.

The interview started quickly, and the ice between us stayed there the whole time, unbroken. I spoke about my expertise and answered their technical questions – most of them, at least. The interview ended, and I couldn't tell how it had gone. I hadn't had similar interviews before to compare it to. Those two guys were the first Europeans I'd met. *They probably found my hijab too weird*, I thought before I took it off and stood under the A/C. *Now all I can do is wait.*

Another email from Fujitsu arrived in my inbox after a few anxious days, asking for a second interview with a member of HR. I was much more comfortable and confident when meeting Roisin because I knew I had passed the technical part. After she finished her questions, she asked if I had any. I had one: 'If I was successful, would my husband be able to get a visa too?' I didn't ask about the company, the benefits or the salary. I was ready to say yes to anything. Roisin assured me that it shouldn't be a problem and that she would ask further.

My email notification sound became as stressful as the wailing of a fire alarm. Every time that envelope popped up on my phone, my heart stopped beating. Everything was hanging on that interview's outcome. Days became a week, and a week became two. I emailed asking for updates, but I got a disappointing automated out-of-the-office reply.

Housam decided to take me out for lunch and away from my anxiety. I dressed up and put all my effort into relaxing and forgetting about the job interview, but it was all I could talk about in the restaurant.

'What if they hire me? What if they don't? Could you imagine us living abroad? I don't want to stay here for ever!'

Housam looked calm on the surface, but I knew deep down he was even more stressed out. This job was the light at the end of that long, dark, hopeless tunnel. It was the only thing that kept us waking up in the morning.

I was about to take a bite of my beef burger when my mobile screen flashed with an international number.

'It's them!' I grabbed my phone and rushed outside the restaurant for some quiet. This was it – the moment of truth.

On the other end, Roisin's voice was not very clear, so I kept walking in the hope of getting better coverage. I didn't notice how far I'd walked until I finished the call. I turned around to see Housam staring at me through the window, trying to read my face.

'YES! I got the job!' I yelled and put my fists up in the air. Housam tried to control his reaction as he was still in the restaurant, but his face was lighter than the sun. I ran my way back to him and stormed into the restaurant as everyone stared at me.

'I am accepted! They want me to start ASAP!'

I was too happy to finish my burger. I kept talking non-stop, telling Housam about the phone call and the next steps. Part of me kept nagging that this was too good to be true. That after all the misfortune in our lives, we shouldn't be too excited until we had in hand two visas and two plane tickets. As Syrians, life had taught us to be careful when receiving happiness. It might be just an illusion created by our exhausted brains.

Two problems came afterwards.

First, the visa required a passport that was valid for at least another year, and second – which was even worse – for Housam to get a dependant visa, my salary had to be over thirty thousand euros per year. It was not.

'I am not leaving without you,' I cried in disbelief. How could we be that close, just to lose again?

'Maybe I can apply for a tourist visa and then see how it goes,' Housam said softly as he held me in the tightness of our bedroom's four walls. 'Let's figure out the passport validity first. One problem at a time.'

ILLEGALS

My passport was eight months away from its expiry date. Due to high demand on issuing passports, the Syrian Embassy in Egypt was prioritizing only passports with less than six months of validity left.

'What do you mean you are not allowed to renew your passport?' the nice lady at the Irish Embassy declared when I tried to explain my situation to her. 'That's nonsense! Your embassy should make an exception to support your trip!' She was Egyptian-Irish, yet she spoke as if she had never met someone from the Arab world. She was genuinely confused. I thought maybe that's how Ireland would manage it if the situation were reversed.

My enthusiasm at getting the job offer was fading quickly. This shouldn't have been that complicated. Luckily, Roisin and the team were understanding when I asked for more time.

A few weeks later, the rules changed. The Syrian government announced that all its embassies were now to renew all passports. It was unclear whether the motivation behind that decision was to help their citizens or the urgent need for cash flow to the Syrian government. However, that was enough to solve my passport's shortage of validity.

The next day, I joined the crowds of Syrians of all ages that gathered in front of the yet-to-open embassy doors. Peddlers moved around holding trays of snacks. It was like a carnival – the carnival of the Syrian passports.

An exception allowed women to enter first, which saved me from an endless wait. After a few hours, my passport was officially extended for another two years. Now all I needed was to apply for my Irish work visa. I learnt from Nisreen that because the job was in a research lab, my work visa would be categorized as a research visa; these were fast-tracked and relatively easy to obtain compared to work permits.

For Housam's tourist visa, he needed to show a bank statement to prove he had the money to support himself for the duration of his stay. However, because our stay in Egypt was also on a tourist visa, we weren't allowed to open a bank account. We prepared our documents without the bank statement and submitted our applications, hoping for the best, three months after my interview. The whole time, I was worried that Roisin would send me an email saying that they couldn't wait for me any longer.

Fortunately, the team waited. Two weeks later, I checked the embassy's website for updates on my visa application status. Approved. Housam's was rejected.

I sobbed while I told Housam I was not leaving without him, and he smiled. We both knew that there was no other choice.

It was December, over two months after receiving my job offer, when I finally held my renewed passport with the Irish visa. Roisin suggested pushing my start date until the new year, as the team might have already left for the holidays by the time I arrived.

I agreed, relieved to have more time with Housam. I booked my flight to be on the last night of December 2013; it was cheaper, and I wanted to have a fresh start with the new year. The flight had an eight-hour stopover in Istanbul. Perhaps I could meet with Nadia?

As my excitement grew, Nisreen tried to manage my expectations. She talked about taxes and rentals and the wet weather. 'I don't mind the rain, I love it, remember!' I naively told her, not knowing what rain meant in Ireland. I googled Ireland, then Galway, where the job was based. I walked virtually in the wet streets using Google Street View, holding my breath, admiring the enchanting world I was about to enter.

Nisreen had invited me to stay with her until I found a place of my own. Two other classmates from university were married and in Ireland as well. They were both undertaking a Master's in the same research institute where Fujitsu's labs were located. They texted me once they heard the news of my visa and offered their apartment during their New Year's holiday. I hadn't been in touch with them for a long time, but their kind gesture warmed my heart. Knowing there were familiar faces in Ireland helped ease my stress at leaving for the unknown. It also helped my mother accept the idea after I broke the news to her over the phone. I wasn't sure which was the worst part for her: the fact that I was travelling to Europe, a place she knew nothing about, or the fact that I was travelling there alone, without a man.

Housam decided to leave the apartment after my departure and move with his mother to Suez, where Amani was moving to after accepting a marriage proposal.

'Too many bad memories in this apartment,' Housam said as he taped up a box of his things. 'And the good ones will make me miss you.'

A few days before my departure, Housam, his mother and I travelled to Suez for Amani's wedding day. She rented a white dress, but there was no party out of respect for her late father. We joined the bride and groom driving around Suez's streets in three beeping cars to spread some joy before reaching the married couple's house. I hugged Amani goodbye. I thought my wedding was sad until I attended Amani's. She was far from home, without her friends and missing her father. Still, I was happy she had found a soulmate to heal her wounds and start her life with. That was the last time I saw Amani, the broken bride with a smile and a tear.

Cairo was cold that year – colder than usual, as the airport taxi driver was saying. I held on to my wool jacket, the same one I was wearing when I left Syria, the one that smelled like home.

I'd promised Housam the night before that I wouldn't cry. I didn't want the last image he had of me to be gloomy. I forced a wide smile as I walked with him inside the airport until we reached security. Housam slipped his warm fingers out of my trembling ones and kissed me goodbye. I swallowed the ball of tears that accumulated in my throat and told him to take care of himself. I had to walk the rest of the road alone.

When the airplane took off violently against gravity, I felt like someone had yanked me out of Housam's arms, forcing me, again, to leave him behind.

Chapter 13

A Stranger in Ireland

I SPENT THE FIRST night of the new 2014 in Istanbul at Nadia's place. I hadn't seen her for over a year, but we talked like we'd been parted only yesterday. We jumped from one topic to another and never finished a story. Her four-year old daughter, Layal, was too excited to sleep knowing there was a guest in the house, and kept running back and forth to her room and showing me her toys. She looked bigger than the last time I'd seen her, especially with a new baby in the house. Nadia led me quietly to her bedroom to show me her new baby boy dreaming in his crib.

Spending the night's late hours at Nadia's warm house was exactly what I needed before taking my next step towards the unknown. We hugged tightly and promised to keep in touch before I left with her husband, who generously insisted on accompanying me to the airport to catch my early flight.

With two hours to go until my flight's departure, I decided to spend the time waiting in front of my gate, worried that if I moved I'd miss it. My body ached in the metal airport chair. The adrenaline had prevented me from sleeping. I scanned the passengers around me, trying to guess their stories. Some looked relaxed, as if they were going on holiday. Perhaps those ones over there were about to meet with family and friends. Some men in suits passed by – a business trip? A couple couldn't stop kissing and cuddling – a honeymoon? I laid my head back and wondered if anyone here was travelling for the same reason as me: survival.

My flight number was announced through the speakers for boarding. I moved my achy bones towards the gate. Four long hours later, I arrived safe and sound at Dublin Airport, in the country of luck. My knowledge about Ireland was all taken from Cecelia Ahern's sweet novels. I didn't know much else about this country, and never in my wildest imagination had I thought I would end up here one day.

The stream of passengers carried me towards the passport control counters. I double-checked that all my documents were in my handbag, whispering a little prayer to myself. I glanced at the officer at the front of the queue. I'd learnt during my travels with my parents not to argue with a government officer. No matter his seniority, he still had the power to complicate my journey in every possible way.

It was my turn. I stepped forward and smiled at the officer with silver hair. He looked calm and unamused until he glanced at my passport. A flash of déjà vu dragged me back to the Lebanese border and I wasn't sure what to expect.

'Syria? Wow!' he exclaimed, flipping my blue ID in his hands.

I gathered what was left of my courage and said in a shaking voice, 'I am here because I have a job contract.' I handed the officer the file of my documents, my story.

'How are things goin' on back there?' the officer asked in a concerned voice.

I stared at him in confusion. *Does he really want to know? Or is he just being polite and making conversation?*

'It's bad,' I summarized.

'Is it getting any better?'

'No,' I sighed. 'It's getting worse,' I murmured, avoiding any direct eye contact. I felt ashamed of all the horrible things happening in my country, like it was my fault.

'Do you have any relatives there?' The officer wanted to know more. Maybe he did care. But what if he did not? What if he was just asking all these questions to know how long I would be staying there or how many other miserable Syrians I would bring over to his country?

I decided to keep my answers foggy until I knew his real intention.

'Well, some were lucky to be able to leave, but not everyone wants to leave. Not everyone can afford to, either.'

The officer flipped through my documents and then started typing my data into the system. *Was that it? Did I pass? Is he really smiling?*

That officer was the first Irish person I had ever met, the first of many friendly Irish people I would meet. He returned my documents and passport, wishing me luck. I admired the Irish stamp on my passport for a second before moving to pick up my luggage. I took a step on to the escalator and let it lift me to the new world. As I took my first steps on Irish soil, I closed my eyes and inhaled the soft rain and the freezing breeze of freedom. As I opened them again, I caught a glimpse of a policeman marching towards the airport entrance. My heart sank inside my chest, ready for him to arrest me. It took me some months before I got used to the police's friendliness in Ireland. *Gardaí* – Guards, those who protect; a concept that was unfamiliar to me.

'Everything is bright green.' I texted Housam from the airport bus as soon as I got an internet connection. 'And there are so many sheep! It is like *Shaun the Sheep* here!' I smiled as I remembered how much he enjoyed watching that show. It was still early in the morning and there was one hour of difference between our time zones, but Housam was already up. He'd spent the night following my long flights' updates online and couldn't sleep for a minute.

I took a picture of the bright green scenery around me and another one of a water bottle with the word 'Galway' written on the label. The driver who handed me the bottle looked too friendly compared to the drivers I'd seen before in my life. Housam texted, saying he would sleep a bit now that I was safe, and I promised to check in again in three hours.

At Galway bus station, I thought of Al-Baramkeh and the loud buses that roamed around Damascus. It was quiet here. I waited for a few minutes before Nisreen showed up with her husband, Basel. I hadn't seen her in over five years and rushed to hug her. We split the bags between us and dragged them through the rain to their apartment, which was only a few metres from the station.

The place was small and cosy with a modern design. The ceiling-to-floor glass window at the end of the living area over-looked the station that I had just left, blurred with raindrops.

'I will go grab some pizzas,' Basel announced. 'Suad, vegetar-ian pizza?'

'Don't bother, please,' I replied shyly.

'No bother at all!'

When the door was shut after Basel, I took off my headscarf and passed my fingers through my dull hair to give it some life after being covered for over twenty-four hours. I opened my bags and grabbed a small canvas painted in Arabic calligraphy with a proverb, 'Al Sadeek Wakt Al Deek', which translates to 'A friend in need is a friend indeed'. Nisreen smiled and hung it on one of the walls, using a piece of Blu Tack.

'It's beautiful. You didn't have to,' she said while stretching her body to reach a better place for the painting.

'It's nothing. I really appreciate what you did for me.'

Nisreen opened the door to the only other room in the apartment and pulled my luggage inside.

'You'll be sleeping here,' she said, standing in front of her bed.

'What? But what about you two?'

'Basel will sleep on the couch, and you and I can share the bed. It is a big one!'

'No way! I can't possibly do that to you guys!'

Nisreen and I argued until Basel entered with two large pizzas. I covered my hair as soon as I heard the door opening. Basel placed the boxes on the dining table and took Nisreen's side in insisting he would sleep on the couch.

'I work late on my PhD thesis, so believe me, it's for the best!'

I didn't have the strength to argue and my stomach started speaking for itself when the smell of pizza wafted from the boxes. Having a good meal and talking to old friends helped me overcome the fear of being in a strange land. After lunch, Basel cleared the table, and I whispered to Nisreen, 'That's nice that Basel helps around the house, no?'

'Of course he helps! All men here chip in. It is not like back home where women are expected to do it all.'

The night arrived early at 4 p.m. Nisreen suggested we go for a walk to show me the city. I put on my jacket and a woollen hat and scarf instead of my hijab. I hadn't seen any women in hijabs since arriving, nor over the preceding year in the pictures Nisreen had posted from this city. I didn't want to stand out, and the weather was perfect for making that change.

Eyre Square was a few steps away. The leftover Christmas lights hung over our heads as we walked on the stone-paved road towards the High Street. The shops were closed, but a small cafe was open. Nisreen ordered two waffles and two coffees, and we sat outside under an electric heater that hung on the wall. I wrapped my fingers around the paper cup to get some of its warmth. A few steps away, a man played a beautiful melody on his guitar. I took a sip of my coffee and thought I had ended up in a romantic Western movie.

'So, how did you get your father to approve of your marriage?' Nisreen asked.

'He didn't.' I looked away. 'It is a long story.' Longer than I wanted it to be.

After we had finished our coffees and sufficiently warmed up, we strolled down the rest of the street.

'There is a beautiful pub here that plays Irish music every night.' Nisreen was excited to show me her world. We shared a similar taste in music and books. The sign on the wooden door said the music wouldn't start for another hour. I took a look at the inside.

'So, this is like a bar?' I thought of the *hadith* about how God cursed anyone who looked at alcoholic drinks.

'It's more like a restaurant, really. You can have tea or coffee. The atmosphere is cosy,' Nisreen said casually. The only bars I'd seen before were in Syrian shows as places only the bad characters visited.

'Maybe another day?' I told Nisreen and continued walking.

*

The rain didn't seem to have stopped since I'd arrived. It was still raining when I went to work with Nisreen and Basel five days later. The air in Galway was always humid, and I felt I didn't have the right gear; my socks were always getting wet, and my jacket never managed to protect my clothes, so I was lucky to have the option of Nisreen's car. However, her tiny car, like her apartment, reminded me that there was not enough space for the three of us.

'*Wasalna* – we are here.' Nisreen showed me the office, filled with six desks and lots of plants. The extra-wide window over-looked the business park that housed the research building. Green scenery stretched around us, making it look like it was built in the middle of a forest. We were the first to arrive, so Nisreen took me for a quick tour of the building. She greeted people as we passed by and introduced me quickly to them. The people I met were from a mix of different cultures, and the brief words we shared were delivered in a huge range of accents.

When we came back, my manager, Raphael, the tall blond guy I had had my interview with, was waiting in the office. He greeted me with a polite smile and showed me where I would be sitting. My desk mates were men from Egypt, Italy, Chile and Japan. I was fascinated by the diverse nationalities in the office, some-thing I wasn't used to, as I rarely knew any foreigners in Syria or Saudi Arabia. Later, I met people from other countries I knew almost nothing about. Every person opened a window for me to a whole nation and culture. I learnt about their traditions and tasted ethnic dishes without leaving my office.

Fujitsu's red logo on the corner of my screen, the mouse pad, the notebook and the pen shone all day, reminding me that this was not a dream, like the totem in *Inception*.

At lunchtime, we went to the canteen. A place that didn't exist in most Syrian companies, as we used to eat at our desks to avoid wasting working hours. I followed Nisreen as she explained how the system worked, and I copied her moves: I grabbed a tray when she did, a plate and cutlery, and stood in line behind her while trying to read the menu on the blackboard.

Tuna was the only thing that I could eat without doubt. Fish was the only meat that was halal no matter how it was cut. The other types of meat were less certain and I didn't want to ask what it was or how it was prepared.

I took my tray back to the table and joined my team. I was shy and uncomfortable, so I kept busy eating while listening attentively to their stories.

'So.' Raphael looked at me, and I smiled in advance. 'You managed to ditch your husband back in Egypt and come alone. Good job!'

The joke was meant to be an icebreaker, but somehow, it broke my heart.

'Yeah . . .' My smile trembled as I started picking at my food with the fork.

'No, I am joking. I hope he can manage to join you soon,' Raphael said politely, and I wondered what Housam was doing right now.

Work was intense for the next two weeks. I learnt from Raphael that the Japanese senior managers were coming to Ireland for an annual meeting and expecting to see a demo of the research project they were funding. That demo was supposed to have been ready months ago, and would have been if my paperwork had been faster. The academic research behind the demo was all done, but it was missing an interactive web user interface to make it more visual and easier for the managers to understand. That was my task.

Fuelled by pressure, I dived into work day and night. Being unable to work much in Egypt made me excited to handle any kind of job, and this one reminded me how much I enjoyed solving web development problems. I also felt that I had already let my team down. I could have saved everyone this stressful time if I had been here earlier. I needed to prove that I was worth all the trouble they'd had to go through to hire me.

What if I fail to deliver this? Will I have to go back to Syria? I blocked my brain from asking those questions and tried to focus on the task. This job was my raft across the dark ocean.

On top of my bursting workload, I was still trying to set up my life in Ireland. I had visa-related paperwork to complete and was looking for an apartment. A mandatory pre-employment health check took me to a hospital far from the city centre. For the entire bus journey, I kept looking at the map on my phone, worried I might have taken the wrong bus, or that I might be late to the appointment. The doctor was friendly and spoke to me slowly and carefully, emphasizing each word, like you'd talk to an older person with a hearing problem. Although I understood everything she said, when it was my turn to speak I lost all the words. I realized at that moment that I didn't know medical terms in English. *How do I say colon? Constipation? Anxiety?* Like a lost tourist, I tried to explain using the words I knew, and the doctor tried to make sense of what I said. Blood rushed to my cheeks as I saw the blank look in her eyes. She told me to check in with my GP if the problem persisted.

My immigration appointment to register as a resident in Ireland went much more smoothly. An officer took a photo of me and explained he would need to scan my fingerprints. I put my hands where he pointed and felt my wedding ring preventing them from lying flat.

'Should I take off my ring?' I asked nervously, afraid of ruining the process.

'Is this your wedding ring?' the officer asked.

'Yes?'

He looked at me with a smile on the corner of his lips and said, 'Then don't ever take it off.'

The mountain my shoulders were carrying crumbled, and I smiled, grateful he understood my husband's abstract presence in that ring. I needed that.

I also needed to set up an Irish bank account so I could get paid. The bank visit was arranged by Mary, a project manager at Fujitsu. Mary was an Irish woman with a lovely heart. So far, I hadn't met anyone Irish at work yet. We had been emailing back and forth until she came over to Galway from where she was based in Dublin to meet me. I was standing at the corner of Mainguard Street on a rainy morning when she arrived with a handbag and a smile so big that it made her eyes look smaller. Mary hugged me; until then, I hadn't realized how much I needed to be embraced.

'Oh, you poor thing! What a journey you had!' Mary's face looked concerned while she patted my shoulder and looked deep into my eyes. I smiled foolishly and said I was OK. I never let myself admit how challenging my journey was, but she was the first to say it aloud.

We walked side by side to the bank, set up my account and lodged my humble cash savings that I'd carried all the way from Syria in a currency I'd never dealt with before.

Afterwards, Mary invited me to lunch in a nearby pub. I was embarrassed to object, so I followed her inside, and it was not like the wild places portrayed in Arab dramas. It looked more like a restaurant – just like Nisreen had described it, only darker. The place was empty except for us. We ordered some soup and two sandwiches while Mary fussed over me.

'How are you finding Galway? Where are you staying? Have you found a place? Did you find where you can buy your food?'

Galway was cold in January, but Mary's presence and concern warmed my heart. I couldn't understand why my food would be special enough to be sold in a specific shop. I realized then that to her I was a foreigner.

'Everything is fine.' I smiled politely. 'I am just concerned about my husband's visa situation.'

'Send me his CV, and I will share it with my network,' Mary said without hesitation.

The hope that she gave me was like a candle lit inside my dark heart. I relaxed my back against the black leather seat and enjoyed Mary's confidence. I would have Housam back soon.

Nisreen introduced me to a small network of Arab friends in Galway. Ashraf, a hilarious Egyptian guy who worked with us in the same team. A lovely Tunisian couple, and Hadeel, a Palestinian girl with long dark hair and the most welcoming smile. Hadeel invited us for dinner at her place in Salthill. Her one-bedroom apartment was cosy and decorated with Arabic souvenirs from Palestine. Printed on her coasters were short poems by Mahmoud Darwish, and her wall was covered with photos of her family and friends. I admired Hadeel's lifestyle. She was confident and independent and passionate about her

PhD in humanitarian law. This was what my life would probably look like if my parents had let me travel to study abroad.

Dinner was the special *makluba*, common in Syria but prepared differently in Palestine. I hesitated when I saw the chicken cubes in the rice. When Hadeel was in the kitchen bringing the glasses, I asked Nisreen if the meat was halal, but she didn't know.

'Are you vegetarian?' Hadeel asked, noticing me picking at my chicken and pushing it with my fork to the side of the plate.

'Yeah . . . kind of.' I smiled nervously. She apologized for not asking ahead and I sensed the awkwardness that I'd triggered in the room. *I must have embarrassed Nisreen*. I didn't speak much until the end of the visit.

This awkwardness stretched over to my stay at Nisreen's. The chain of constraints I carried with me to Ireland affected my choices for eating, drinking and having a good time. I had to keep wearing my hijab in the presence of Basel, which was not very comfortable after a long day of wearing it at the office. Whenever I tried to help, I made trouble instead – putting dishes in the wrong cupboards or buying the wrong brands of groceries. I thought that once I got my first salary, I could take Nisreen and Basel to dinner at the Moroccan restaurant that we all loved, but my first salary didn't amount to much. With an emergency tax deduction, I was left with around a thousand euros. How would I afford a deposit and a month's rent if I did ever manage to find a place?

The apartment situation in Galway was trickier than I'd thought. There were only a few apartment blocks, and they were always occupied and overpriced. Nisreen suggested sharing a house with others, but I wasn't comfortable enough to take that step.

Although I couldn't wait for the weekend to come, to go and

explore the city on my own, when it did arrive I couldn't leave Nisreen's place. The worry that I would get lost started crippling me. I felt the need to stay by her side, despite picking up on her hints encouraging me to go for a walk.

Soon the air between Nisreen and me felt tight. She was looking for a familiar friend from back home to share good times and have some fun with, but all she got was a tired and worried shadow of her friend. The differences that we had back in Damascus seemed amplified outside it.

I tried. I wanted to be that outgoing girl in a new world. Still, I couldn't not worry about the unknown future of my partner; I couldn't not worry about the job, about the paperwork, about finding a place to stay, about the halal meat, about how I looked in my hijab, and all the big and small things. When you don't have a home, everything seems more challenging. My mother's daily calls, reminding me to find a place of my own and stop bothering my friend, didn't help. After a week or two, I insisted on sleeping on the couch but I still felt like an inconvenience despite my hosts' welcoming gestures.

The meeting with the Japanese team finally came, and I managed to finish developing the requested interface after long nights in the office. Filled with pride and an overwhelming sense of achievement, I joined my team to welcome five Japanese men in suits in the meeting room. The meeting was a success, and I finally exhaled after holding my breath for the past few weeks.

After weeks of searching, I had an appointment to view an apartment. It was Sunday night, and a storm was hitting Galway, but I insisted on going over when I called the landlady. I'd learnt by now that I had to be competitive to find a place. The lady described the location, but I couldn't understand anything but the street name. The English in this country was not the English I was used to. I tried to look up what she'd said on Google Maps, but I couldn't find it. *Where is this 'rondabot'?* I tried different spellings, but the map didn't show me anything that made sense.

Nisreen offered to drive, and I was relieved that I wouldn't get lost alone in the middle of a storm. I called the lady after reaching the street, but her voice was cutting out like she was underwater. She suggested coming out to the main door, and we finally saw her waving.

Patricia greeted us in the rain and showed us where to park. She pointed to the traffic circle at the end of the road and said, 'That's the roundabout I was talking about.'

Roundabout. A word I will never forget!

The house was old, but well looked after. The bedroom was wide with big wardrobes. There was a small bathroom with a shower, a storage room, and an open-plan living room and kitchen/dining room with a red couch, a square dinner table and two wooden chairs. A locked door linked the small house to Patricia's basement.

'I will take it!' I told Patricia after less than five minutes.

'Oh, shall we wait for tomorrow to discuss?'

'No need. I can pay you a deposit right now.'

I was desperate for a place of my own and the stormy weather had prevented any other renters from coming to a viewing. Patricia agreed to lease the apartment to me but she needed some time to get it ready.

'A week from now. Is that OK?'

I wanted the place now, I wanted it yesterday, but I didn't have a better option, so I agreed and thanked her before leaving with Nisreen. We were both happy.

After a week, I finally moved in. In the living room, a small note lay on the dining table:

> Saud,
> Patricia Here
> You are very
> <u>Welcome</u>
> I will chat to you later,
> Bye

I smiled at the spelling mistake in my name and teared up at the three-times-underlined 'welcome'. I threw myself on the couch and let myself have a good cry for the first time since I'd arrived in Ireland. For all the trips and travel, for all the luggage and burdens I carried with me, and for not being able to have Housam beside me at that moment. Now I had a home – a cold and empty one, but it was mine. I could sleep on the bed and eat whatever I desired. I could take off my hijab, and I could cry.

I picked up a dessert from the shelf and flipped it in my hand. 'INGREDIENTS: Wheat, sugar, eggs, rum.' *Shit*. I sighed and put it back on the shelf. I placed my groceries on the conveyor while a middle-aged woman in front of me moved her items forward. I played a quick game of 'spot the haram products': a bottle of wine, a pack of sliced ham and a bag of Haribo. I looked back at my carefully picked halal items, and a feeling of pride passed through me.

When I returned home from my first Irish supermarket shop, I saw Patricia in the garden and asked her about the heating system. My first night in the house was spent shivering. Patricia introduced me to the concept of a storage heater. They stored heat in the evening, when electricity is cheaper, to be used during the day. She said she'd turned it on so I would be warm on my first morning, but apparently I'd switched it off, assuming I was turning it on.

'So, what do I do if I get cold in the evening?' I asked, still trying to comprehend.

'I will bring you an electric heater,' Patricia said and went off to her house to find one. This place was nothing like Nisreen's, which was centrally heated and well insulated. The water also came from two separate taps, either burning hot or freezing cold.

At weekends, I went for walks around the city. Galway was peaceful and suited this post-traumatic phase of my life. It felt like I'd passed into a parallel universe. The streets were quieter and less busy. The air was fresh. People were relaxed and never seemed to rush. 'Thank you' and 'sorry' were common in any conversation. It felt miles away from the bustling Damascene streets.

The buses were clean, and the bus driver always nodded when I got on. When my eyes accidentally met someone else's, they smiled back while I looked away or changed my direction. Years of learning not to smile or look at strangers, to avoid giving them the wrong impression, were becoming a problem. Looking people in the eye and smiling felt like a huge effort that I tried to teach myself, but I made sure to start with smiling at women only. After a while, I began to realize men were not staring at me – not at any woman who walked alone in the streets – like some men used to back in the Middle East.

After a month, I felt more confident with both the streets and people of Galway. I knew how to move around and where to find everything I needed.

The Irish accent was still a struggle – even when I understood the words, the meaning seemed to be new. Like the first time I went shopping, feeling lonely and overwhelmed, and the shop assistant asked me, 'Are you OK?' I stared at him in surprise for a second. *Is it that obvious that I am not OK?* He probably read my confusion so he said, 'Are you looking for something specific?'

Oh. That's what he meant!

I found a cosy French cafe that stayed open until late and served delicious crêpes and hot drinks, so I often went there at weekends with a book to read and a notebook to write down my new daily life. I couldn't get used to the fact that everything closed early in that city. I was used to restaurants and cafes open-ing late back home. Families stayed until the late hours, having food comas and drinking tea or shisha. That was our guilty pleasure and the way we spent the weekends. The only places open late in Galway were pubs. The places that I couldn't seem to enjoy.

On 17 March, I left the house early to meet Nisreen and join the crowds at Eyre Square to celebrate my first St Patrick's Day. I didn't have anything green with me, so Nisreen lent me a wig coloured green, white and orange, while she wore a long green leprechaun hat. I put the wig over my woollen hat and stood among the crowds, watching the joyful parade passing me. I wondered what my religion teacher would think if she could see me celebrating this non-Muslim holiday.

*

Housam's attempts to apply for jobs in Ireland were all failures. Not all companies were willing to invest time and money to provide a work visa for someone outside the country. We found ourselves back in time, when our relationship was limited to phone calls and texts. Every time I had a nice moment in Galway, it was weighted with guilt that Housam was not there to share it.

After a month of living with his mother in Suez, he learnt that the Lebanese government was allowing access for Palestinian Syrians, so he decided to move there with his mother, who desperately missed home. Lebanon's short distance from Syria allowed brief visits back and forth, which sounded more appealing than being trapped in Egypt.

They packed their few belongings, travelled to Lebanon and rented an apartment in a small town near the Syrian border so my mother-in-law could go back and forth between the two countries while Housam stayed behind, as it was less risky for women to move between checkpoints. After they'd spent a few days settling in in Lebanon, she went for a day to visit her family in Syria and finish some paperwork, but that day turned into a week and the week turned into a month as she found it hard to leave home and go back to Lebanon. In the meantime, Housam's work as a freelancer kept him busy, and mostly he appreciated his solitude, until one day he got sick and wondered who would find him if he died. I stayed on the phone with him and tried to act strong while worry invaded every inch of my body.

Mary kept her promises and introduced me to Magda from Euraxess, an organization that provided support for researchers in Ireland. She was responsible for my visa. I told her about my husband's situation, and she promised to look into it. After many emails, proof documents, signed letters and a bank statement showing payslips and the money I'd borrowed from my mother, I managed to prove that I had sufficient funds to support Housam; that he wouldn't be a liability to the country.

By the end of the month Housam's visa had been issued, and on the first day of April he arrived in Ireland. I couldn't help but think that this was an April Fool's prank until I saw him at Dublin Airport and held him after what felt like the longest three months of my life.

Shakriyeh was Housam's favourite meal.

It's a rich stew made of lamb and slowly cooked yoghurt. I missed cooking for him and I made sure to have a big bowl of it on the dining table under a banner that said 'Welcome back!' I couldn't find any that said 'Welcome home'.

I was excited to show him my world, to unfold Galway for him, but his eyelids were getting heavy, and his head was starting to sway while I talked non-stop.

'*Habibi*, you should rest a bit,' I said softly.

'What? No, I am awake.' Housam adjusted his body, trying to sit correctly, and forced his eyes open. 'Tell me what happened next.'

'We have all the time in the world.' I kissed him on his forehead and covered him with the white throw on the couch. It was hard to let him go to sleep. I had missed his presence so much that I couldn't bear to lose it again. But he hadn't slept for the last day out of excitement and anxiety that something would go wrong. And something always did.

When Housam and I were reunited, my mother exhaled. Her phone calls became less stressful now that I had a man beside me. Many relatives and friends began to contact us, asking questions about the situation for Syrians in Ireland. They had assumed Housam had joined me through a reunification programme for refugees, and that I had applied for asylum, and were hoping to do the same.

Things in Ireland weren't easy for Housam. His dependant visa didn't allow him to work, or open a bank account. It frustrated him to sit at home all day while I was at work. We managed to create a limited life with my low salary, and he kept applying for jobs, hoping they might sponsor a working visa for him, but with no luck. Companies preferred someone who already had a work visa or, even better, a European passport.

I decided to cheer him up by buying him a bike. It kept him busy and excited while he explored Galway during the day and occasionally came over to my workplace for lunch. Watching him ride made me realize that I wanted to ride a bike, too. I was never allowed to back in Syria. When my friend told me she was selling her bike, I didn't hesitate to buy it and start practising. Soon enough, after a few falls on the streets of Galway, I knew the joyful feeling of flying along on a bike.

While Housam's frustration with being unemployed was growing, I secretly wished I could switch places with him, that he would go to work instead of me while I could spend the day on my bike and in the public library, browsing books and writing.

I was struggling with *being* employed. Working in research was something new and an unfamiliar path for someone coming from industry. When my team members took turns sharing updates about their work in every Monday meeting, I would sit there quiet and distracted. I didn't know the jargon, conferences or papers, or big players in the field. As a developer, I was used to having precise requirements and designs for the system that I needed to build to solve a problem. In research, I had to come up with the problem and the solution, and if it didn't work I could write a paper about my failed attempt and publish an article about it. It was a different mindset that required a certain amount of passion and curiosity in the domain. For me, it was a survival job.

After my first project, which didn't require getting into the research side of things, I was tasked to program a system described in an academic research paper.

The words, although written in English, seemed to be in a language I hadn't learnt. *What the — is 'et al.'?!*

Deep breath.

I took the stack of papers outside, and sat by a tree behind the building to get some fresh air and focus. As Ashraf came out for his smoke break, he noticed the piles of papers in front of me and asked what I was working on. In less than twenty minutes, we managed to decrypt the paper and work out the requirements. Ashraf's friendly gesture gave me the first push towards my work, but I was still sinking in a pond of self-doubt, and I was only going deeper.

Everyone around seemed to already have a PhD or be doing one, while I had an undergraduate degree from the University of Nowhere. Even Nisreen had already achieved a Master's in Ireland and gained experience and confidence in the research domain. I went from being the expert in the team back in Syria to the slowest team member in Ireland. It was enough to keep me up at night.

I didn't know that I was experiencing imposter syndrome

until I stumbled upon a book called *The Secret Thoughts of Successful Women* by Dr Valerie Young. The cover was made up of quotes that were the exact thoughts I didn't allow myself to speak out loud: 'They felt sorry for me'; 'I have no idea what I am doing'. It helped a lot to understand my feelings, but the struggle was still there. I tried working around it by concentrating on other achievements besides my work.

I looked for online courses and started teaching myself the topics I needed for my job. I read any technical book I found lying around in the office. I also started looking into the tech community in Ireland and went to Dublin to attend events and listen to motivational speakers, especially women who had managed to break barriers. I finally registered to take that technical Oracle certificate exam, now that I had Irish residency. I double-checked this time that I was eligible to take the exam before I began to study. Earning that certificate was probably not essential for my job, but it was more for me. To prove I could overcome anything and that no one could deprive me of a learning opportunity.

Besides tech, I started writing. I created a blog where I recorded stories about my life in that unique city. I found myself scribbling on the back page of my Fujitsu notebook to escape the anxiety I felt at work. I started reading novels again after I found a stash of second-hand books at Charlie Byrne's Bookshop. The bulletin board at the entrance of the bookshop led me to a creative writing class. Two hours a week in the evening after work when I escaped to be a writer. The weekly writing assignments helped wake up my pen after a long hibernation.

Chapter 14

Uncovered

THE HOLY MONTH OF Ramadan came in June amid the summer heat, the long, warm days that we had heard of but not yet experienced. Ramadan, the lunar month, moved slowly between seasons over the year. Back in the Middle East, when it fell in the summer it was hot yet bearable, as each day's fasting lasted for around fifteen hours, some of them spent asleep. Back home, the world seemed to change to accommodate Ramadan. Ireland, however, didn't. The working hours were still the same. The restaurants and cafes were open during their regular hours. The supermarkets displayed the same products and the TV broadcast the same daily shows.

Days before Ramadan arrived, I was out for lunch with my team. I can't remember how the conversation turned into discussing Ramadan, but suddenly all eyes were on me.

'Are you really going to fast for twenty hours?' someone asked.

'Yes,' I replied to the absurd question that sounded like, 'Are you really going to breathe?'

'With no food at all? Wow! You can still drink water, right?'

'Nope. Not even water.'

'What! That's crazy!'

'But that's not really fasting, right?' A new colleague joined the conversation from the end of the table. 'I mean, that's cheating. You get to eat after sunset. That's not proper fasting.'

It took me a second to realize he was comparing Muslims' fasting to Christians' fasting for Lent. I remembered when Lara had fasted for forty days before Easter back in Syria, and how she'd checked the packaging of any snack to make sure it didn't contain any animal products. I thought THAT was cheating!

I had never had open discussions about religion. I had never had to answer for my religion before. I was sure my way of fasting was the true one but, deep down, his comment never left me.

Once Ramadan started, I skipped lunch at work and stayed in the office while my team went to the canteen as usual. I tried to stay focused on work, but it was hard with the enticing smells of food and coffee. I left work an hour earlier to make up for the missed lunch hour and stopped cycling for the duration of Ramadan to save my energy. I would arrive home around 5 p.m., but knowing there were still five more hours to kill was enough to give me a headache that prevented me from sleeping.

When sunset finally came late in the day, we put on a video of the *adhan* from Umayyad Mosque on YouTube and pictured ourselves back in Damascus with family and friends. It was hard to arrange breaking the fast with friends in Galway, as the hour was late and we were all drained. By the time we finished eating, it was dark and we just wanted to sleep, but we had only a few hours to eat and drink until first light came at 2 a.m.

Housam's body didn't cope well with the long hours. The headaches he had were intense to the point that he vomited the moment he began eating. After a few days of this torture, he stopped fasting for a day, as Islam allowed it for the sick. I searched online to see how people tolerated this in other countries with long daylight hours, or if there was a *fatwa* – a ruling on a point of Islamic law by a sheikh or an Islamic authority – which would make it easier for people in our situation. The answers were contradictory.

Some people fasted only for the length of fasting hours in Mecca. So, if sunrise in Mecca was at 6 a.m. and sunset at 6 p.m., then that meant the required amount of fasting was twelve hours. They said we should start counting twelve hours from first light in Ireland, and thus I would fast from 2 a.m. to 2 p.m. Others said that we should use the same timings as the people of Mecca: 6 a.m. to 6 p.m., regardless of the sun situation. We decided to give this a try and ended our fast by 6 p.m. However, I felt guilty eating while the sun was still out there. *This is not right*, I thought.

Ramadan turned from being my favourite month to a daunting and confusing time of the year. It felt like it was designed to fit the Middle East, and it was easy for people living there to judge Muslims in Europe for choosing to fast by Mecca's hours. My mother was disappointed to learn that we'd shortened the fasting hours based on a *fatwa*.

'That *fatwa* is not correct,' she told me over the phone. 'It might be a long day now, but when Ramadan eventually comes in winter, you can take advantage of the difference. You'll have the shortest day of fasting!' my mother argued. But what if I didn't still live in Ireland then? It didn't make sense to wait over ten years just to fast for reasonable hours.

Nadia and I kept arguing about Ramadan over text message. She rejected that *fatwa* and criticized me for following it. Although Nadia was breastfeeding at the time and could have used that excuse to stop fasting, she insisted on following the long hours in Istanbul that lasted from around 4 a.m. to 8 p.m. Even Tete was fasting, despite her unstable blood pressure and sugar levels. It was common to endure suffering for a better afterlife reward.

Questioning fasting and trying to justify Ramadan's purpose was something I hadn't done before. I hadn't needed to. Reading online about Ramadan opened the door to other questions I had about religion that I'd never thought of asking myself. I didn't realize that the first domino had fallen.

After the fasting month, my house smelled of *ma'amoul*, the date biscuits that were famously made for celebrating Eid. Housam and I prepared three-dozen gift bags full of sweets and shared them with Patricia's family and Arab friends and colleagues at work.

We took a short break in Dublin to celebrate Eid and had a full schedule of touring the city and visiting its museums. Ireland's history of famine, civil war, the booming economy years of the Celtic Tiger and recession, and how it had managed to recover and advance culturally and politically, gave me hope for Syria. My heart danced when I spotted a famous Irish phrase during a stroll in the Dublin streets: *Céad Míle Fáilte* – one hundred thousand welcomes. It reminded me of the Syrian welcome phrase, only ours was 'one hundred welcomes'. The Irish hospitality was generous.

One day that winter, while waiting for the bus to work, a group of nuns walked past me wearing grey skirts and grey habits. The white cloth underneath the grey looked similar to what women in Syria wear under their hijab to prevent it from slipping. I wondered who had been the first to wear it. Then I wondered why nuns cover their hair, which in turn made me wonder why the rest of the Christian women didn't cover their hair.

My bus almost left without me as the questions grew louder in my mind. I'd seen nuns before in Damascus, but they'd never made me wonder like this. Whose head covering was the right one? I didn't realize back then that I lived in the illusion of a binary religious world where there was no space for any shades of grey. People were either right or wrong, in heaven or hell.

As soon as I reached work, I turned on my computer and started searching online about the origins of head coverings in religion. Before I knew it, I was down a rabbit hole. Despite their differences, Abrahamic religions seemed to agree on one thing: a woman needed to cover up in the presence of God because she was a sin, or impure. However, common strands of Christianity and Judaism didn't expect this of modern women. And why did some argue that modesty is exclusive to women and not men? For years I was taught that God created men with uncontrollable urges and that women should help them avoid doing wrong. The onus is on women to cover up to avoid seducing men. Women should 'satisfy' their husbands; otherwise, it was justified if the man married another woman or cheated.

In the dark rabbit hole, I jumped from one page to the other, comparing religions. I visited pages that I'd never dared to open before, but my mind was addicted already, thirsty for answers. With every page, a myth was destroyed. By the time I reached an article that said hijab was nothing more than a cultural habit born in the desert of Arabia to protect women from the heat and sand, my throat was becoming dry. Moreover, as many Islamic scholars debated, hijab was historically used so men could distinguish the free Muslim woman from the slave. The latter was ordered not to cover up and would be punished if she did so, even if she was a Muslim.

A headache pounded inside my skull. It was almost lunchtime and I hadn't done any work yet, so I closed my web browser with its million open tabs, but I couldn't stop the whirlwind of ideas circling in my brain.

When I reached home, I resumed my search. I wanted to solve this mystery. *I can't stop now.*

'Housam, did you know about all of these debates?' I turned to Housam and asked desperately.

'Yes,' Housam replied calmly.

'How come you never told me about it!'

'Well . . .' Housam looked like he was choosing his words carefully. 'You don't exactly like to discuss those things, remember? I sent you that video you are watching right now during my period of solitude in Lebanon, and you didn't open it.'

A series of situations flashed in my mind. I wished I could go back in time and allow my demons to ask and think, instead of hiding them in the closet.

'How could my hijab just be a cultural habit!' I burst into anger. 'All that heat I endured, thinking of the reward I would receive in the afterlife. How I was setting a good example of an ambitious Muslim girl who doesn't let her hijab get in the way of success!'

Over the following days, my anger grew. It was one thing to say hijab is a social identity, or choose to believe it was God's order in a controversial Quran verse that asks women to cover up, but how did the hijab become associated with honour? How did I believe that I was more protected with a piece of fabric, despite being regularly harassed every time I left the house back then? How come I was in Europe now, the land of 'cheap women' and 'exploiting men', and not one man had looked at me inappropriately? I thought of all the times I was on public transportation, or taking a walk in the winter night, or staying late at the office surrounded by men. Nothing.

I pictured Fulla, the Syrian copy of Barbie who was introduced to the world in a hijab. I remembered all the years I didn't allow Housam to see my hair. Then I thought of Nora, and I wished I had been stronger and said no back then.

As I stood in front of the mirror in the living room, staring at my hair, I couldn't picture it covered any more. Still, I couldn't dare to think of showing it in public. It hit me then that if I decided to take my hijab off, what would I wear during prayer time? If a hijab was unnecessary, then what was the proper outfit for a woman at prayer? But then I thought again. *Why should it matter what I wear when I speak to God?*

That thought led me to read about the origins of praying and fasting and pilgrimage. I became obsessed with finding the one truth about religion that would put my mind and heart at ease, but I never found it.

Religion was woven into every detail of my life. If I took off my hijab and stopped praying, what would become of me? I felt like I had been clenching something tight in my fist for many years, but when I opened it, there was nothing inside.

'What do I do?' I turned to Housam with eyes full of tears.

'You have to stop this madness.' Housam held me in his arms as I sobbed.

'Please, tell me what to do. I can't think any more. I can't focus on anything else. What do I believe in now?'

'I am sorry, but I can't tell you what to do. This is your decision, but I will support it whatever it is.' Housam stroked my hair, and I took a deep breath. 'You don't need to decide anything right now. Let it sink in. Take some time and stop obsessing about it.'

But I couldn't. I was falling. I couldn't go back to what I used to be: I either wore a hijab or not. I either prayed five times a day or not. I needed a label. This grey life was not mine.

I wept until I fell asleep, like an abandoned child, and I wondered why God had left his rules too cryptic for me to understand.

I kept my hat on while I was in limbo, not caring if some hair strands showed. I tried praying at home without a hijab, but it didn't make sense. I threw myself into work to avoid thinking about God, and I wished there was a pause button that I could press on my life until I figured things out. During that time, I started looking at people differently, without the religious labels. It was a much more interesting view.

Despite feeling disconnected from my hijab over the next few weeks, I didn't dare to let it go – not yet. Syrian society made sure to create an illusion of shame that haunted the girls who dared to take it off. That shame haunted their husbands, brothers, and all the men in the family as well; the men who failed to control their women. But knowing my brothers were far away and my father was out of the picture made it somehow less daunting.

In December, I asked Housam if we could get away for a couple of days, so we planned a trip to a coastal town called Clifden that was an hour to the west of Galway. It happened to be around our wedding anniversary. On the bus, I took off my hat and let my long hair fall on my heavy shoulders as I resisted thinking of my mother's disappointed face.

A few months after I came back from that trip, I went to work with my hair over my shoulders for the first time and greeted everyone in the office. I noticed the short, surprised reactions in my colleagues' eyes, but no one commented. The only comments I got were from Arab friends. Between 'Congrats,' and 'Nice haircut,' to break the ice, only one of them seemed upset and couldn't look at me. When I realized that his reaction gave me pleasure instead of bothering me, I knew that I was ready to move on.

However, I wasn't ready to tell my family. I stopped posting pictures online and only shared privately with them pictures of me inside the house. I unfollowed people who disagreed with me every time I tried to have an open discussion about religion on Facebook. Even Fulla the doll was criticized by some Muslims for being 'too fashionable' these days and less 'pure'.

After a while, I stopped posting religious arguments completely. I decided that everyone has to go through their own journey of finding their truth. But when Nadia started an educational activities page for kids, I couldn't help but feel irritated when I noticed how much religious content was woven in.

'This is brainwashing,' I told her one time when she posted the Islamic alphabet worksheet for kids. She didn't appreciate my crude comment and insisted that we should explain religion to kids like we explain maths or physics, and that other religions did the same. I didn't care who else did it. Kids can't comprehend religion at that age. I wished I had had the freedom to explore religion instead of following whatever one was decided on for me. I imagined her daughter, Layal, who appeared in a video on the page wearing the prayer head-covering and reciting the Quran during Ramadan, growing up and choosing a different path from the one her mother chose for her. I imagined Nadia's disappointment just like my mother's – endless.

I unfollowed pages that carried news about disasters in each region of my country, and replaced them with more Irish pages that offered life instead of death. I went with Housam and friends for hikes and felt peaceful, immersed in the natural Irish scenery. I rushed to attend every festival in Galway and I stopped reading the ingredients on every packet as I started tasting different cuisines.

Day after day, I was shedding my skin like a snake, until I decided to close my Facebook account completely and live in one place instead of two. Unconsciously cutting the umbilical cord that connected me to Damascus.

Housam's luck started turning around after nine months in Ireland, when he found a job as a research associate in the Natural Language Processing Unit at the same research centre where I worked. Research visas were much easier to obtain than a work permit and his paperwork was sorted out relatively quickly. Housam managed to combine his studies in English Language with his work as a web developer. He looked alive again and we enjoyed each other's company, commuting back and forth to work together.

Christmas lights started appearing in Galway, bringing joy to the monotonous cold nights. The festival market was our happy spot, which we visited occasionally. Patricia brought us a plastic Christmas tree when she found out we were not planning on travelling home. The idea that we might not celebrate Christmas didn't occur to her. Still, her gesture and her tree filled our living room with a much-needed warm touch. She left a greeting card with a small amount of money as a gift along with the tree, as she did on other holidays like Halloween and Easter. Her generosity was eternal.

In mid-December we went to Christmas dinners with work. I popped crackers and put on the paper crown but still felt uncomfortable when the waiter asked me what I wanted to drink. An Indian colleague asked me once if I would ever try drinking wine. She was a vegetarian, but no one asked her if she would ever consider eating meat. I was still not sure how I felt about alcohol or pork. The two biggest 'no's in Islam. I ordered a Coke and decided to leave this debate for another day. Perhaps living a grey life wasn't bad after all.

As people travelled back home and Galway became empty of familiar faces, I realized how uprooted I was. 'Are you going back home during the holidays?' someone asked once and I froze, realizing for the first time how painful the word 'home' had become. December made sure to remind me of that every year, if I dared to forget.

Assuming Christmas would be celebrated like Eid, we decided to book two days in Dublin to watch Christmas festivals or events like those that used to run during Eid back in Syria. The reality hit us hard when we realized the country closed down during those two days. We ended up wandering the streets of Dublin, empty except for a few international students, and having dinner at Apache Pizza, the only place that was open.

On New Year's Eve, we decided to have dinner in a nice restaurant in Galway. When Housam made the reservation, he thought there would be a countdown or kind of celebration around midnight, but the restaurant informed him that the latest booking was at ten, and they closed at eleven. He booked at ten, and we had a lovely dinner and left as the place closed for a walk in the city centre. We decided to go into a pub to see if there was any live music playing, but it was too packed and loud to be enjoyable. The smell was horrible, the floors were sticky and everyone was visibly and happily drunk. Drinking seemed to be essential to enjoy such a place and time, so we left and decided to go for a walk.

When it was around midnight, we found ourselves next to McDonald's, and I was in the mood for a cup of coffee. Just as we were being served, the staff closed the front doors behind us and started counting down.

'Ten, nine, eight . . .' Yells came from behind the counter as more drunk people knocked on the door, begging to enter.

'That's it, then; we are spending New Year's Eve at McDonald's!' I turned to Housam and smiled.

'McDonald's it is!' He handed me my cup of coffee and raised his in the air – 'Cheers!' – and took a sip, laughing at how the night had descended from a fancy romantic dinner to this.

'Two . . . one . . . HAPPY NEW YEAR!' The crowd cheered while overdressed Housam and I shared a new year's kiss at the McDonald's in the heart of Galway. It was a challenging year that we'd started separately, but I was grateful that we were ending it happily together.

In January, we decided to check our options for meeting up with our families in a country that Housam could enter easily. After some searching, we ended up with Turkey. It required no visas for Syrians and was a country that was easy for Palestinians to get into. So, we made up our minds and packed for Istanbul.

My mother and my baby brother, Majid, who was now studying IT in Saudi Arabia, came to meet me. The cold weather made it convenient to wear a hat and escape the judgement of not wearing a hijab. It was weird to meet my family from the other side of the table next to Housam. We wandered the captivating streets of Istanbul and visited ancient places. My mother carried her anxiety with her. It was her first trip outside Saudi and Syria, and without my father. She was continually checking her watch, worried she would miss a prayer time, or checking her phone, worried my father was calling.

When I went out alone with Majid later in the night, he told me that Mama had changed. 'Since the war in Syria, she's become more religious: praying a lot and reading the Quran constantly. She believes the war is God's punishment for our sins.'

I wasn't much surprised, as my mother tended to blame herself for anything bad that happened. We walked later in the Al-Fatih neighbourhood, a kind of 'Little Syria'. I wondered how many Little Syrias were scattered worldwide and wished there was one in Ireland.

The next day we met Housam's mother, who had flown from Syria to see us. Her health was declining as she missed her previous life, which didn't exist any more. It was hard for Housam to watch her fading but he was helpless, as it was impossible to get her a visa to join us with the current political situation. Walid also joined us later. I hadn't seen him for over three years. When we met, he hugged me tight and I was a little surprised, as we never used to express our feelings for each other.

Nadia and I also reunited, but I wasn't the same person she had met the previous year on the way to Ireland. We avoided talking about religion while she kept staring awkwardly at my hat.

Before leaving Istanbul, I enjoyed eating more Syrian food than I should have, and I almost teared up when I held Arabic books in a new Syrian-owned bookshop. Turkey was the perfect meeting point for the scattered Syrians, separated by sea, land and paper borders.

In the metro, on the way to the airport, Walid asked me if I ever thought of talking to my father. Walid was like my mother, still making excuses for my father's behaviour.

'Your father is dead to me.'

Walid's surprise didn't surprise me.

'I need to move on with my life. He'll never change.' My firm tone made it clear that I didn't want to discuss this any more. I looked away and spotted my reflection in the train window. I looked like a different person.

Chapter 15

Humanitarian

THE FARMERS' MARKET IN Galway was a regular stop that reminded me of the fruit-and-vegetable stalls back in Damascus. Although I had stopped checking the daily news from there, I still missed it intensely. We became friends with some of the people behind the stalls, especially after they found out we were from Syria. The pie lady kept her warm smile, while her partner had a sorrowful look, thinking of everything that Syrians were enduring. The crêpe guy insisted on not taking any money for our order. The bagel guy wanted to discuss politics, while all we wanted was two cream-cheese bagels with *za'atar*, the spice from home that had made me stop at his stall in the first place.

So far, I hadn't seen anything Syrian in Galway – not even anything Lebanese, which was usually more widespread globally. The only falafel place in the city prepared falafels in a different, healthier way. It wasn't bad, but it was not the same. I didn't realize how much I missed the food. I regretted all the times I was picky back home and chose Western cuisine over Syrian. I understood why my father insisted on eating at Syrian or Lebanese restaurants whenever we went out for dinner in Saudi Arabia. I empathized with my mother, who insisted on carrying food in her luggage when she returned from Damascus to Riyadh every summer.

Food looked different here: the courgettes and aubergines were huge, the bread was not thin and flat but crispy and chunky, the breakfast looked like a dinner, spices didn't exist and even the teabag looked weird without a string and a label attached to it. And it wasn't only the food that I missed – the music, the sun, the nights, the language, and the good company. Even the rainfall here was different from that in Syria: it had no sound when it touched the earth, and no odour. I used to hear the rain back in Damascus even if I was sleeping. I'd wake up to the smell of moist earth. The rain in Syria was a festival, a sonata, a reason to dance or fall in love. The rain in Ireland was slow and repetitive, like one tone playing over and over and over.

The farmers' market became a place where our identity was open for discussion. People usually noticed that we were foreigners, even if we didn't talk much. After I took off the hijab, I noticeably managed to avoid that. One time, Housam and I were walking holding hands when we passed by a group of young men hanging out. They smiled at us and one of them said, 'You are the most beautiful non-Irish couple I've seen around.'

The follow-up questions that came after statements like this, exposing my nationality, were unique. At first, I loved satisfying people's curiosity: better they hear it from me than from the media. But sometimes it was overwhelming, and I didn't want to talk about home while waiting for the bus or having a haircut. 'Are you going back? Are you Muslims? You don't look Syrian. What do you think of al-Assad? How do you think it will end?'

Housam was more patient than me. He explained politics and religion and extremism even to those who didn't want to listen. Once, we were blamed for forcing the Irish to travel overseas looking for jobs. Ironically, it came from someone who was not Irish. In general, the Irish were warm and loving. Having their own share of wars and troubles made them more empathetic to the Syrians around them. And for that I was always grateful.

In September 2015, during one of our strolls in the city, we noticed a brown shipping container standing in the middle of a shopping street. Curious to know more, I moved closer to read the sign in front of it.

Eight volunteers had decided to lock themselves inside the container for twenty-four hours with just two bottles of water each, a portable toilet and no food. The art installation, designed by the Giddy Biddy Collective, aimed to raise awareness of the migrant crisis and the struggles endured by migrants to reach a safe haven.

I walked away to hide my tears and my identity. I checked Twitter later to read more and decided to leave a virtual thank-you note for telling my people's story. Luckily, one of the volunteers replied, and that's how I met the kind-hearted Cait Noone.

Cait, a dean at Galway-Mayo Institute of Technology (GMIT) and one of the supporters of the project, invited me to come back and say hi. She described how I could find her, but she could've just described her smile. Cait's smile can be spotted from the end of the world and would make you walk towards her like an insect following the light. She noticed the accumulated tears in my eyes, and she opened her arms to hug me. I didn't resist the generous embrace of a stranger. I needed that hug, but I couldn't understand why. *I didn't go in containers or on boats. I didn't drown. I wasn't kidnapped or tortured or sold for slavery and sex by human traffickers. I am safe. But why am I feeling vulnerable?* Cait became close to us after that day, and that hug was not the last one.

Cait introduced us to the rest of the crew, and a journalist there wanted to do a story about Housam and me. We met with them and talked about the war and the struggles, hoping to raise awareness. It was only after we'd finished and left that we realized how much we had been through. We had never talked about it.

Our story was published later in the *Connacht Tribune*. I don't know if it made much of an impact. Still, when I saw a picture of Housam and me with a full-page article in the newspaper, I realized that our normal life had become a hot story, accompanied by words like 'survive' and 'tragedy' and 'home' and 'hope' and 'new beginnings' and 'gratefulness'. We had become news, despite our efforts to escape it.

Every morning when I scanned the news, Syria would be in the headlines. 'Country X is fed up with the refugees. Country Y is closing its borders in their faces. A boat sank carrying refugees from Syria. A Syrian refugee did something bad. A Syrian refugee did something good.'

Every morning, I read the news. I read it all. I looked at the dead bodies, the exploded remains, the miserable faces at borders, the bodies skeletal from hunger, the weeping mothers and the scared kids.

I would close my web browser, wash my face, drink my coffee and go to work, helpless, hopeless and in denial, fighting the pressing thought that I didn't deserve to survive. I would greet my colleagues and complain about the weather and the overpriced food in the cafeteria and other first-world problems.

Later, in November that year, I found a way to stop feeling helpless. At a tech event in Dublin, I attended an interesting talk about how technology was used to help refugees. The panel included three speakers: one from Unicef, one from an NGO called Techfugees, and another from a humanitarian start-up that focused on developing technological solutions for migration issues. I was ashamed of myself when I realized that those foreigners were helping my people while I did nothing. Up until then, I had thought donations were the only way to help refugees, but little did I know about the other efforts that were being made in that area.

The speakers agreed that not knowing Arabic was a huge challenge for them when trying to reach out to refugees. Hearing this, I knew I had to offer my help.

After the talk, I approached the man from Unicef and thanked him for his efforts towards helping Syrians. In my excitement, I started talking without thinking, while he nodded politely, not sure what it was that I needed.

'I . . . I am a software engineer, and I work in research with Fujitsu. And I know Arabic.' The guy was now listening more carefully. 'If you guys ever need help with the language, I am happy to assist!'

His eyes brightened, and I felt content that my mind and my tongue had managed to coordinate and say the right thing at the right moment. He handed me a business card.

'Send me an email, and I will connect you with our science team.'

I held the card in my hands like it was a million-euro note.

Christopher Fabian, Co-Founder of Unicef Innovation. New York.

Before the end of our second year in Ireland, we figured it was time to move to a bigger and warmer apartment. After months of searching, we managed to find a modern two-bedroom apartment on the west side of the city, in Salthill. It was closer to work and to the endless ocean. Beside it was a campsite, where people chose deliberately to ditch the safety of their houses and spend days and nights in tents.

Packing our things before the move brought me back to packing up my family's house in Damascus and the apartment in Egypt. Another move. But this time, it was by choice. Knowing that gave us a sense of stability. We weren't in survival mode any more; we were now living.

Staring at our empty house as Housam took the last box out reminded me of the day I moved in. This place had hosted our beginnings in Ireland and would always be in our hearts. It was hard to say goodbye to Patricia, but it was time to haunt another place and create new memories.

We hosted a house-warming party and welcomed some friends with homemade dishes and sweets that we took joy in preparing and explaining. When Christmas came around that year, we decided to spend it in Galway with friends who also couldn't travel home. I appreciated the quiet time in our new place and was also busy volunteering with Chris's colleagues.

In our first video call, Ryan and Pablo from Unicef's data science team explained their attempts to use Facebook data to provide support for people on the move. They tasked me with analysing the Arabic social media pages that discussed migration, assessing their value before using this to create a network of users and their locations. The purpose of the project was to attempt to predict the numbers of people on the move, so that humanitarian organizations like Unicef could prepare adequate resources for those people.

To do this I created a dummy Facebook account and searched through content created by Syrians, whether already refugees or trying to be. I started following smugglers and dream-sellers. I didn't consider myself part of this network. I wasn't a refugee, nor did I smuggle others across the sea. I managed to distance myself from this project and get on with the task at hand. At least, I thought I did.

The majority of Syrians were on Facebook; the young and the old, the rich and the poor, the educated and the uneducated. Checking the blue portal became their number one daily activity, as it was the only way to stay in touch with their dispersed families and friends all over the world. Those who were still in Syria had nothing much to do, considering the danger in going outdoors. On the other hand, Syrians who had fled the country were stuck in the asylum application process, which halted their life for years. Unable to work, and often alone, they created a virtual reality on Facebook where they could talk, joke, complain, argue and have company. A mirage in which, once they logged on, they were still at home.

Although Syrians were loyal to Facebook, it let them down. While Facebook opened its arms through the 'Safety Check' button to users worldwide during natural disasters, terrorist attacks or other tragedies, it never activated that feature for people in Syria. In a general statement issued by Alex Schultz, VP of Facebook Growth, he explained:

> *During an ongoing crisis, like war or epidemic, Safety Check in its current form is not that useful for people: because there isn't a clear start or end point and, unfortunately, it's impossible to know when someone is truly 'safe'.*

Even Facebook had given up on us.

*

Early in 2016, I got an invitation through Euraxess to speak at the European Commission in Brussels about the challenges of the refugee crisis, and to share my story, along with two other Syrians. I didn't, at the time, realize how my path was being shaped towards humanitarian work, but I followed my heart.

I also didn't realize before that trip that Ireland was part of the European Union, but not part of the Schengen area that allows free movement. I therefore needed a visa. That required an invitation letter from the conference, a job contract or a letter from my employer proving I was travelling for work and would be back afterwards, a confirmed hotel booking, a non-refundable return flight and an Irish visa valid for at least three months after my intended return date. That was all to get a single-entry visa to Europe. If I wanted to travel again, I had to do the same thing all over.

Although Housam was also invited to attend the conference as a Syrian researcher, his travel document was still not recognized by the same country that had invited him. He had to make a special application to the embassy. After the employees of the embassy discussed his case, they decided to issue him a visa that allowed him to enter Belgium, the Netherlands and Luxembourg only, instead of the regular Schengen visa.

I picked a navy suit for my visit to the European Commission. It was overwhelming to be in a room with everyone talking about the one topic I didn't want to talk about. But I was desperate to do something, anything, to help Syria, to heal Syria. I thought I was over the idea of having a homeland I couldn't return to, but the memories were pushing hard to the surface, and I tried my best to push them back down. I fought the urge to cry whenever someone mentioned a statistic about displaced, dead, drowned or illegal refugees. I tried not to think about how those numbers and percentages represented people I knew and cared about.

I have to be strong, I thought. *I have to represent the resilient Syrian, the one willing to do the impossible to survive.*

Then it was my turn to talk. It was tricky to do this without opening the box of memories. I kept it professional. I did not talk about how I was terrified by the explosions that happened a few metres away from me. I did not mention how I used to go to sleep early, wearing many layers of clothing because it was too cold and too dark to stay awake. I skipped the part about my engagement and marriage during the war. I briefly mentioned my father-in-law's martyrdom, but I definitely did not mention how we saw photos of his body all over social media. How it haunts us still. I never talked about how we didn't dare to dream of having a kid because we were too damaged to raise a child in this unfair world. I skipped many stories, a lot of pain and tears that had no place at that conference. Instead, I talked about timelines and statistics, gave examples of ongoing initiatives and suggested ideas that could be life-changing for many refugees. The conference ended with a lot of applause and I felt good for doing my bit and not falling apart.

On the plane back to the place I called home, I closed my eyes above the clouds and let the pilot do his bit. The flight attendant broadcast a message to the passengers over the tannoy. It wasn't about seatbelts, nor was it about our location or destination. It was about Syria.

'Syrian children are facing a lot of pain and suffering from cold and hunger. Please help us raise funds to support them.' I looked around to see people getting out their wallets and putting money in an envelope with the Unicef logo on it. I was grateful for all the kind hearts on that plane, but heartbroken to hear my country's name mentioned in a donation campaign.

At that moment, all the blocked memories rushed in. The miserable faces, the dead bodies, the explosions, my little cat, my grandmother. My whole life burst from my overloaded memory, and I wept.

~

Up until then, I hadn't told my mother about my decision to take off my hijab. I decided to use my proud moment in Brussels to share the news, hoping to balance out the disappointment. I decided to tell Walid first, who was supportive. I sent him a video of my speech and told him to watch it with her. I wanted her to be proud, to know that it was still me, her daughter. Walid texted me later, saying that she'd cried. She was proud of my speech but hurt that I'd felt the need to hide that from her.

'You think I don't know?' Mama said over the phone later that day. 'You haven't sent any photos of you for the last year. It is all just pictures of grass and water!' My mother couldn't see me, but I felt small, like a child who'd eaten a chocolate and lied about it. She praised my talk, and I let go of a long breath I had been holding for months.

'But what does Housam think about this?'

I realized this was not over yet. Men in the Middle East took the blame for women's 'irrational' behaviours. My father used to say, 'There is no strong woman, but a weak man.'

Stories and gossip overwhelmed Syrian Facebook pages, talking about how women who, upon arriving in Europe, were taking off their hijabs and divorcing their husbands to enjoy the 'fake' freedom that Europe provided for women.

'She integrated' would be used to describe such a woman, and it was never in a positive way. Those stories were told by men who realized their old-fashioned way of treating women as property wasn't accepted in Europe. This was the only reasoning they could come up with when women asked for their rights. Stories about men who changed their lifestyle were rarely mentioned as a bad example. As always, it was mostly women who were judged.

Housam had treated me with equality and respect ever since we'd met. Many Syrian couples adapted to the new cultural changes quietly within their own homes, but the negative stories would create a louder buzz and a quick stereotype about anyone who outwardly dared to change.

I told my mother that this was my decision. She didn't like that answer. Perhaps she expected me to tell her how he was mad at my decision. She wanted to know that someone in my life was still keeping me in check. When she didn't hear that answer, she turned to blaming the Western people who were poisoning my mind. It disturbed me how little faith she had in me and my reasoning. I wished there was a way to show her how people here cared about my personality and actions rather than how I dressed. They didn't measure me by the length of my skirt or the thickness of my stockings. I was disappointed, yet relieved that it was all now out in the open.

Shortly after my speech at the European Commission, the European politicians got fed up with us Syrians and our drama. The increasing numbers of migrant flocks crossing the sea shown on far-right media outlets was enough to convince the world that we were a plague. Soon, a generous offer from the European Union was on the table for Turkey. For six billion euros and a promise of visa-free travel for Turkish citizens, the last open door was shut in our faces.

The disappointment of that news was followed by a chance to make a change through a job opportunity with Unicef in New York. When I first moved to Ireland, I never thought I would soon be considering living somewhere else. I was eager to put down some roots and create a stable home with kids and books and a cat, in a place where I didn't have to worry about leaving them behind suddenly. After everything I'd done to find a home, it felt odd to consider moving again. At the same time, I wasn't sure if the world was safe enough to have kids; if I was safe enough. And yet I couldn't resist the pull of working on a meaningful project that I believed would have an effect on people's lives. My people. Given my visa limitations, I was also offered the flexibility of working remotely with frequent trips to the Big Apple. Eventually, I said yes to the humanitarian world and hoped this step would help me find peace with the global madness.

Another fantastic opportunity came along at the same time. After months of volunteering for Google Developer Groups (GDG), and creating talks and workshops in Galway to empower developers and women in tech, Housam and I got two tickets to attend the annual Google I/O conference in Mountain View, California. We used to watch this annual event, where Google shows off its latest technology to an excited audience, online. Now, we were going to watch it in person on a ten-day trip to the US. Our main destination was Mountain View, but I managed to organize a trip through San Francisco and Los Angeles, ending in NYC before returning home.

One of the advantages of travelling to the US from Ireland was that the security and passport controls were all done on Irish shores, so when the plane arrived in the US it would be treated as a domestic flight.

'You were chosen by the system for a random security check,' the agent at Shannon Airport said while stamping our boarding passes. 'Follow the signs and make sure you are in time for passport control.'

I didn't question the randomness of that first security check, but later, after I started travelling frequently to the US and always getting that extra check, I realized it was never a coincidence.

Our flight was delayed, so we sat in a cafe to kill some time. My phone rang with Sami's name on the display.

'Hey, bro!'

'Hi . . . where are you?'

I told him I was at the airport.

'Oh, I didn't know.'

'I told Mama and thought she would've told you. What's up?'

'Well . . . I am just calling to tell you . . . our father has had a stroke.'

Before that moment, I'd imagined many bad things happening to my father; sometimes I even wished for them. I didn't expect that I would feel this horrible when hearing such news.

'An ambulance took him to the hospital this morning, and he is in a critical condition. I am sorry to be the one to tell you, but I thought you should know. I would want to know.'

Sami hung up, and I pulled myself out of the shock to call my mother.

'Who told you?' My mother was surprised. 'I told your brothers not to say a word because you were travelling today.'

My mother told me about the ambulance and the ICU.

'Don't worry; he will be fine, *inshallah*. The doctor said he was stable.'

'Are you sure? Sami said he is in a critical condition.'

'No, he is better now, but he needs to be monitored. Don't worry. Just pray for him and enjoy your trip.'

I hung up the phone and burst into tears. I wasn't sure how to process all that. *What am I doing in an airport, travelling and having fun, while my father is in the hospital? And why do I even care now?*

I didn't want to proceed with my trip, but I couldn't travel to Saudi Arabia either. The visa work would take for ever, and the chances of getting one were very slim.

I dragged my feet towards the American passport control along with Housam. The officer asked us to step aside and escorted us to a side room.

'You can take a seat over there, ma'am, and you, sir, follow me.'

Housam followed the officer into a room, and I sat thinking this was all just a bad dream. After around ten minutes, Housam returned, whispering quickly that it was a background check and that the officer would match our answers. Housam's voice seemed to be coming from far away, as I was still picturing my father. I couldn't have cared less about the interview, but I followed the orders and took a seat in front of the officer. I stated my name, date of birth, city of birth and all the things he asked that were already listed in my passport, which he was holding in his hands.

'Have you served in the military in your country?'

'No. Women don't serve in the military in Syria.'

The officer looked up from his papers and told me in a cold tone, 'Just answer the question, ma'am.'

The question was ridiculous. That was what I should've said, but

I nodded instead. He then asked me about dates: when did I get married, when did I leave Syria, what was the story behind each stamp in my passport, and finally he asked me to hand over my phone. He started checking my phone calls and text messages.

'Mamitto? Is this your mother?'

'Yes.'

'Who is Sami Aldarra?'

'My brother.'

I wished he would ask me why my family had been calling so I could say, 'My father just had a stroke, and you are being insensitive,' but he didn't. After some time, he looked up, apologized for the interrogation and blamed it on 9/11. He gave me back my phone and let me go back to Housam so we could continue our journey.

As we entered the skies and my phone signal disappeared, leaving me disconnected from my family, I closed my eyes and hoped nothing worse happened while I was stuck up in the air.

After two days and several calls with my mother assuring me that everything was fine and that they'd left the hospital, I found a way to calm down and get back in the mood for adventure.

The US was different from Europe in every way. My knowledge of America was limited to the movies and TV shows I used to watch a lot, but being in the country itself was an eye-opening experience and changed many of my ideas about the US.

I saw people of all kinds. I saw fat and thin, white and black, ridiculously rich and homeless. On the streets I heard Spanish along with many other languages. Diversity was sharp and clear, but why was it hidden in movies?

The next day we visited Google's San Francisco offices for a special networking event for the Google Developer Groups worldwide. Along with other organizers from Ireland, we got to draw the Irish flag on a big whiteboard, representing Ireland. I wished I could raise the Syrian flag as well, but that would never happen with US sanctions preventing Google from operating in Syria. Ironically, a group of Chinese developers spoke about the Chinese government sanctions that prevented Google from operating in China, and how they'd managed to overcome them.

The night was filled with brilliant tech activities and we had lots of fun at the photo booth. Google managed to make the occasion memorable by also offering us accommodation at the luxurious Palace Hotel. We were spoilt for a change, and it felt good.

From San Francisco, we headed to Mountain View, which looked like Riyadh with its palm trees, brands and high roads. Everywhere I looked, there was a billboard with a famous tech company logo. I tried Uber for the first time and was surprised when, during one of my Uber rides, the app showed me a technical interview riddle to solve if I wished to get a job at Uber. Tech was in the air.

After the GDG event, I attended the international Women Techmakers meetup, at which Google hosted female group leaders from all over the world. It was at an outdoor venue decorated elegantly, like a wedding, where I got to meet other inspiring women in tech.

The next day was the big day, when all the developers met to celebrate Google's success. In a big open auditorium, Sundar Pichai, Google's CEO, took to the stage and welcomed us all. As everyone clapped and cheered, my cheeks were hurting from my Cheshire Cat smile. The whole thing felt unreal. I wondered how many Syrians had managed to overcome the sanctions to be there. Being at the launch of the latest technology was a huge personal win. As a Syrian, I was used to being last to get updates, only after someone had found a way to get past international and domestic sanctions. Now, I was the first to know about them.

The event went on for three days, showcasing the giant tech muscles of Google. I got the chance to take one of the many bikes around Google's extensive campus, where everything had the Google colours or logo on it – from pool tables to toothbrushes. It was the first time I saw self-driving cars, but the most special place for me was the Google Android Statues Park that marked the company's mobile operating system's releases.

After Google I/O was wrapped up, we resumed our trip to Los Angeles. Billboards here were advertising the latest TV series instead of tech. We toured Universal Studios, the Walk of Fame, the Oscars stage and the Hollywood sign. We also got the chance to attend the filming of a sitcom and be part of the contagious recorded laughs that always gave me a headache back in Syria. LA was astonishing and fun, yet superficial. I felt underdressed and un-'glamorous' the whole time. It wasn't hard to say goodbye when our trip came to an end.

New York was another beautiful shock. When we first landed, we took an Uber to Central Park. We only had ten hours before our flight back to Ireland and I wanted to explore the city with Housam before I had to travel there for work by myself. We spotted a falafel truck outside the gates of Central Park and treated ourselves to two wraps that tasted nothing like falafel.

After a short snooze in the park, we managed to recharge to go and explore the city's touristy spots. New York made me feel small, but eager to explore more. It wouldn't be too long before I went back again, but this time I would be on my own.

Chapter 16

The Four Seasons of New York – Summer

MY BIOLOGICAL CLOCK WAS still set to Greenwich Mean Time when I woke up with the early sunrise at 5 a.m. I got out of the giant bed and tiptoed to the kitchen to prepare my coffee without waking up Adelle, the nice old lady who owned the apartment. I was not a morning person. I needed some time to wake up mentally before chatting, and she seemed to love that. I had never shared a house before with anyone other than my family, and I didn't enjoy the privacy-deprived life that I had here.

I would have preferred my own place, but I couldn't afford the unreasonable rent. It was my first time using Airbnb, and I still didn't get how people could easily share their homes with strangers. I was lucky to meet a kind one: Adelle, originally from the Philippines, who had lived most of her life in the US. She acted as my mother for the entire three weeks I lived with her. It was remarkable how all mothers – those worrying creatures – shared the same instincts and behaviours no matter where they came from. She was constantly checking on me to see if I needed anything. It was good to have someone looking out for me in this new adventure.

It was still early in the morning, but the streets were already jammed with traffic. I poured my coffee into one of Adelle's mugs and went to sit beside the window in the spacious living room to admire the view of the sunrise over the East River from the eighth floor. I played Fairouz, my morning ritual, on my phone, but her voice didn't fit the backdrop. Maybe only in Syria.

It had been a long time since I had been on such a high floor. The average height of buildings in Galway was two storeys. It made me remember the phenomenon that had spread in Damascus during the first year of the war. While the government was busy quelling the revolution, Damascenes were busy trying to build an extra room on top of their houses, without bothering with permits. This was the people's way to overcome Damascus's overpopulation and extremely high rents. When Syrians met on any occasion, they would joke how Damascus had risen one storey higher above sea level overnight. No one predicted that those extra rooms would be the first thing to be destroyed by missiles over the next few years, and that people would sell their houses and pay everything they had to reach a safe haven or drown trying.

It was scary how those thoughts crept silently into my mind. I pulled myself back to reality and took my eyes off the window, leaving my thoughts to drown in the East River. I couldn't carry them with me on my first day at my new job.

Focus. It is time now.

The humid air was a change from the A/C inside the apartment. Five steps out and I was already sweating. The mixture of my backpack plus the mounting anxiety and July's heat all seemed to work against me. It was still early, so I decided to take a detour to see more of the city on the way. After ten blocks, I finally arrived at Unicef HQ exhausted and dehydrated. The friendly security guy welcomed me and asked me to take a seat in the reception.

Ryan, the friendly face I'd only ever seen on Skype, showed up to collect me. We were finally meeting in person, inside the magnificent Unicef building, and I felt like I needed to stop time to absorb the moment.

New faces welcomed me, new names, new smiles. I shook hands with Pablo, the science team lead and my new manager, still trying to get into reality mode. He took me for a tour that ended at the cafe on the ground floor. Over coffee, he talked about innovation, explained the ongoing projects and showcased a few examples of their previous work. I was trying so hard to keep calm and hide my excitement while listening to him, knowing I would be using my technical skills to change people's lives.

I wanted to work on all of that, right now, and not leave the place until all the tasks were done! I had never felt that I was in the right place as much as I did in that moment.

Later on, I was directed to my desk. On top of it lay a brochure titled 'Welcome to Madness'. The innovation team was multinational, young and casual. No suits. No long meetings. No bureaucracy. It was also refreshing to see several women in leading positions.

Chris showed up later that day and I felt less like a stranger, seeing a familiar face from the tech conference back in Ireland. Energy charged the room as he walked towards me, holding his hand up high. Nervous on my first day and with everyone's eyes on me, I felt it was inappropriate to high-five him. I held out my hand for a handshake, but I ended up shaking his high-five.

Not only were the people of New York diverse, but the cuisines were also limitless. I went out with my team to grab lunch from the delis outside and gathered in the office to share food and jokes. Having a Lebanese restaurant across the road was the best, and a huge improvement on the fake falafel I had had before in Central Park. I also later discovered a perfect lunch spot on the rooftop of the Unicef building, where the view was almost too mesmerizing to go back to work.

As I unwrapped my chicken shawarma sandwich back in the office, someone asked about the situation in Syria and whether it was getting any better.

'It is worse. We never saw it getting this complicated.' I went on about the latest events before I noticed one of my teammates was choking with tears and had stopped eating her sushi. I felt bad for talking about this topic over lunch, and I started apologizing.

'No, no,' the girl coughed. 'I just swallowed a ton of wasabi. Didn't see that there!'

At the end of my first week, the team was planning a trip to a museum, so I joined them to get to know New York and my new workmates. I took the subway for the first time with them, and after they realized I was a 'subway virgin' they started telling horror stories and sharing expert tips.

'If one of the train carriages is empty, don't get in. It is empty for a reason!' Dana, one of my colleagues, said in a warning tone, while the others laughed and started telling drunk-vomiting stories from their time in the city. Dana was one of the few Americans in the team. The majority were a mix from India, Japan, the Philippines and Europe. None from the Middle East.

'Don't walk next to trash bins at night. There are always rats!' Dana went on.

'And beware of pigeons.'

'YES! Those flying rats!'

*

Getting a job in New York was another thing I hid from my family. I told my mother in one of our phone calls about the possibility of a job and that it would be remote, but I never told her I would take it.

'Why would you take a job in the US after all the trouble you and your husband have gone through to settle in Ireland?' Her question was justified, but I knew passion was not a good enough answer. It was exhausting always to have to justify my choices.

To save her from unnecessary stress, I waited a few days in NY before I went out on one of my lunch breaks to record a video in front of the Unicef logo.

'Hellooooo. I am now in New York, in front of the Unicef building. I accepted the job, and I will work remotely, but I need to travel frequently. So, this is my first trip! Everything is fine, and I am renting a place with a nice lady, so don't worry. Love you, Mama.' I waved goodbye and pressed 'send'. My mother's reply popped up shortly on my screen with more exhausting questions.

'How did you travel on your own without Housam? How did you find a place to rent?'

Her overbearing questions always managed to steal part of the joy.

The summer sky in New York looked its best around sunset. Everyone from the office was at a rooftop party that Chris had organized at his place – a yearly tradition, I understood. It was my first trip to Upper Manhattan and I couldn't muster up the courage to take the subway, so I stuck to the bus, which took its time.

When I reached the rooftop, I couldn't keep my eyes off the

magnificent purple-and-pink sky. This city seemed to have a new look every time I glanced at it. My teammates showed up one after the other, some wearing shorts and some in minidresses. My dress was the longest, with socks and flats – closed flats. I realized at that moment how my dress style was still influenced by my hijab days. I'd hidden my body for so long that I didn't know what it looked like any more or what its real size was.

Chris left to welcome a guest who looked older than the rest of the group. When they reached where I was standing, Chris pointed at me.

'Suad, this is my mom, Terese. Mom, this is Suad, the girl I told you about.'

Chris's mother was simple and elegant and easy to smile back at. I had never met a boss's mother – not in Syria, not in Ireland, not anywhere. Chris managed to create a lovely family vibe among his colleagues and I was attracted to that warmth like a magnet.

After a while, the group standing around Terese and me started getting smaller until it was only the two of us. Our small talk turned big when she told me about her Polish parents and their time in the forced labour camps before coming to the US as refugees. She assured me on that rooftop that the world is going to be better. The ugly things going on right now will reach an endpoint eventually. I forced myself to keep smiling. I didn't see that coming any time soon, although I wanted to believe her. I'd taken this job because I wanted to be part of a group that focused on making the world better, but I still had my doubts about the human race.

'It will get better, dear,' Terese said in her calm voice. 'They did all that before.'

Terese's words hugged me. I felt seen without talking. We

exchanged numbers, and she offered to introduce me to New York's museums and parks.

When night came around I checked my watch more than usual, worried about finding my way back through the city. A colleague mentioned she was leaving soon, so I joined her. On the way to the subway station, she told me she was leaving early to catch another party down in the East Village, and I didn't dare tell her I was leaving because I was afraid of the night.

On the train, she showed me on the map above my head where I should get off. I tried to calm my thoughts and avoid strangers' eyes after she left. The subway was like another hidden city, running parallel underneath New York, where the colours were darker, and the people seemed more worn out than the people above it.

I spent the time on my phone. A picture from the gathering popped up on the work WhatsApp group. I zoomed in and out several times, still overthinking the dress code. I tried to remember the last time I had been in shorts. I remembered a pink sleeveless top and shorts that I wore as a little girl. I remembered my mother's hands as she folded up the outfit and buried it in the bottom drawer, the drawer where she kept the things she rarely used. I remembered asking why, why not my drawer, and I remembered her words: 'You can't wear these again – don't you remember what happened the last time you put them on?'

As the train bolted out of a tunnel and the underground lights flickered, I remembered it all at once, like a gasp, like the breath you take after staying underwater for a long time.

I remembered that summer beach trip in Syria when I was little, swimming with my father after my mother and brothers had left for the hotel room, feeling tired and deciding to leave before my father, taking a shower and changing into my pink outfit, waiting for the elevator to take me to the hotel room, a hotel worker suggesting I should take the employees' elevator instead of that faulty one, following him suspiciously, the elevator door closing, his tall body close to my small one, his kisses, his hugs, the number of buttons in the elevator, how many floors left, how angry my father would be.

And he was angry, but not at me. He yelled at the hotel manager after I retold the story I'd already told my mother and which had made her eyes grow in horror. He yelled at my mother for dressing me in those clothes, those shameful clothes.

The train stopped, and so did the flash of memory. My station was announced. I rushed through the train doors and left that memory behind in the darkness of the underground world.

Summers in Syria were too hot to enjoy, as I always wore multiple layers with my hijab, but New York's summer was different. The heat was bearable if I left for work early in the morning and only went home after 5 p.m. when the sun was going down. That's when I liked to stroll down the city streets.

I would sometimes call Housam while I was walking to tell him about all the exciting things I was seeing. I couldn't wait for him to visit and share that new world with me.

The fruit stands spread around the city reminded me of Damascus. I often bought some on my way back home and had it instead of dinner. I learnt how to do my laundry in a shared washing machine and got a yellow metro card, which I only used for buses. I continued avoiding the subway, as it got hotter and more packed than I could bear. At the weekend, I explored the public library. The impressive collection was open to my use once I signed up for a card.

When my feet took me to the famous Strand Bookstore, I felt I had reached book heaven. The sheer range in the US was mind-blowing. There was a book for everything. I was drooling as I browsed, not sure where to start or when I could ever read all of that.

Fifteen minutes down from the Strand there was a small brick-walled eatery with signs in Arabic and a wood-fired oven. My first *za'atar* flatbread, *manoosheh*, arrived shortly. I took a picture before the first bite and posted it on my Instagram: 'This is home.'

There was never a dull moment on Manhattan's streets. Every time I walked around, I stumbled upon something new and amusing. My steps led me one day to the Library Walk, where brass plates held literary quotes from books I had never read. I spent many hours browsing those quotes or sitting in the park by the Library Walk with a book in hand. I was never alone.

Terese became another mother in New York. She invited me to check out MoMA. Her high sense of art and music made me feel embarrassed about how little I could comment when we stood in front of the paintings, but I loved to listen to her. The last part of the museum was the best. An exhibition by Bouchra Khalili showed migration journeys over multiple screens, on each of which there was a map and the two hands of a migrant. We could only hear their voices as they narrated the route they'd taken while marking it with a pen on a yellow map. I pictured the route I took from Damascus to Lebanon to Egypt to Ireland, and now here. That's a piece of art I could stare at for ever.

New York was home to many. During one of my walks, I discovered Chinatown then Little Italy, just metres away from each other. It struck me how a neighbourhood can turn into a country inside another country. All the Chinese signs and food and faces changed to Mediterranean ones and Italian accents. Trucks of dragon fruit and soup dumplings became stands of *cannoli* and gelato. Two worlds coexisted peacefully next to each other without borders, comfortable inside the bigger world of New York.

Open-air cafes and bars were a good change from the dark interior of Galway's pubs. On Fridays, my colleagues – and many of the Unicef staff – hung out at Dug's, a small kiosk with orange metal folding chairs and tables that had a view of the United Nations building standing tall with its many flags. While my friends laughed and enjoyed their drinks, I sipped from my lemonade and smiled, thinking how much this city suited me. I didn't expect to fall for New York. I thought it would be overcrowded and loud and rude, pushing cheap, sugary and fatty food in your face. It was that, but it was so much more. It was diverse and dazzling, and seductively welcoming. Its weather and chaos reminded me somehow of Damascus. Its crowded streets made me feel less lonely, and its noises drowned out the voices inside my head. New York, as a souvenir shop printed on a tote bag, didn't suck that much.

During my last week in the city, while I was getting ready one morning, I received a video from Majid. It was of my father lying in bed. My heart beat faster, alarmed. I hadn't seen that face for four years now.

'What is ten plus ten?' Majid's voice came from behind the camera. My father looked confused. He raised his fingers slowly, trying to count, before he gave up. Majid quizzed him again, but my father was not there any more.

My mother had lied, again!

My father's condition was much worse than what she'd told me two months ago. That man in the video was not my father the accountant, who'd spent the last forty years of his life working with numbers. Feelings of shock and betrayal overwhelmed me. I arrived late to work after talking to my mother, who told me the truth. His stroke had left him with Alzheimer's. I kept my face buried in my laptop for the rest of the day. Whenever I remembered my father's face my eyes welled up, and I went to the toilets to cry it out. By the end of the week, I couldn't wait to go back to my quiet nest in Galway and be with Housam.

~

Spending the rest of the summer in the shade of Galway and with Housam helped me cool down. Having the option to escape and get a change of scene was useful. I set up a desk in the living room and started working around 10 a.m. after Housam left for work. New York didn't wake up until later in the afternoon, so I tried to use that quiet time to focus on my tasks until Ryan logged on and I gave him an update on my progress.

The team also had a robot for remote workers. It was a tablet with two cameras and a speaker on wheels that I could control. This meant I could move around the office and communicate with my colleagues remotely.

Things seemed to work perfectly in the beginning, until I realized the internet connection in the office wasn't great at handling video calls and robots. I had to ask people to repeat themselves many times, and the robot crashed frequently. I couldn't join spontaneous meetings, and important and interesting figures came in and out of the office without me getting the chance to be seen. The worst part was when I started losing my sense of time zones and ended up logging off at 10 p.m. GMT.

It didn't take long before I started feeling isolated working from Galway. Days could pass without being able to talk to anyone. I missed having breaks with my colleagues in NY, grabbing a coffee together or having a casual chat in the elevator. Life back there seemed to move without waiting for anyone, and definitely not for me.

In Saudi Arabia, my mother kept me up to date with my father's condition, but it wasn't getting any better. She also told me that the visa she'd applied for so I could visit had been rejected. The Saudi visa was more complicated than any visa I had obtained so far. The fact that I was born there and had lived there for seventeen years didn't seem to matter at all. Being a Syrian didn't help, either. When my mother told the employee at the foreign affairs office I was Syrian, he waved his hand, dismissing her, without even raising his head.

Majid also applied for a visa to visit me in Ireland, and that was denied as well. My uncle, who knew someone at the Saudi Embassy in Dublin, suggested I go there with all the necessary papers, along with my father's medical report, and talk to them about my visa. I made the visit but nothing came out of it.

In the month since I had returned from New York, stress had become my shadow again. Little things started driving me over the edge. The ticking of the clock began to really agitate me. One night, I reached for the clock hanging on the wall of the living room and smashed it. Housam, who was sitting next to me on the couch, silently picked up the pieces and threw them away.

The next day when he came home from work, he had brought a digital clock to replace the old one. And, in the bedroom, he installed an alarm clock that projected a red beam of light on the ceiling so we could see the time at night. I hugged him, and I cried, and I apologized for whatever was controlling my body. I convinced myself again that it was my hormones and not the unprocessed trauma in my life so far.

I visited a new GP and asked for a solution for my PCOS after the last GP had brushed off the issue and told me it was only a problem if I was trying to conceive. The doctor was more empathetic this time and had a caring look in her eyes that made me drop my guard, let myself feel vulnerable, and cry. I told her about my father and that led quickly to me being Syrian, layering one tragedy on top of the other. She listened and agreed to check my hormone levels, but she also suggested therapy and prescribed temporary antidepressants.

The idea of being mentally ill made me more depressed, and I refused to take them. I wanted to believe that I was a survivor, that my past had no lasting effects on me, that I had left it all behind. But it was still lurking in the recesses of my brain. I chose to ignore my current situation and wait until my hormones were balanced again, when all of this would hopefully go away.

After my blood test showed a spike in certain hormones, and my ovarian scan showed cysts, I was referred to an endocrinologist.

The new doctor asked more questions while filling in forms without looking at me: symptoms, family history of illness, whether I drank, smoked or wanted to have children. It was only when I said the last 'no' that she lifted her head and gave me a puzzled look. I knew I was far from ready to be a mother under the current circumstances. I mumbled about work and travel and Syria and bad timing, but she went back to her papers, saying, 'You'll change your mind later.' Her professional halo melted away and suddenly she looked just like my mother-in-law, telling me I'd regret postponing having children to later in life.

I rejected the suggestion of birth control pills to regulate my hormones because they had made me feel worse when I'd tried them during our first year of marriage. The doctor then suggested a different type of pill to lower my insulin and blood sugar levels, since I was at high risk of diabetes, which was linked to PCOS.

Feeling better about those magical new pills, I left the clinic and noticed the trees outside were starting to lose their colours. It was time to head to New York.

Chapter 17

The Four Seasons
of New York – Autumn

PUMPKIN SPICE LATTE SEEMED to be the official signal that
autumn had arrived in New York.

I took a sip from mine as the train approached. I realized that
adding pumpkin syrup to my coffee was a huge mistake. Why
did everyone like it so much? The subways didn't intimidate me
any more, and I didn't have much of a choice, as it would've
taken hours to get the bus from my new apartment. I wanted to
save some money, so I'd ended up renting a place in Astoria,
Queens, shared with Helena, my tall and stylish Greek flatmate.

Helena's place looked appealing on Airbnb, and she seemed
nice enough over texts. On my day of arrival, she cooked me a
grilled tuna steak with lemon-roasted potatoes. Helena opened
up to me straight away about her personal life while I listened
and nodded and smiled. She talked about family troubles back
home, her ex in the city, and the abortion she'd had to have, while
I was trying not to choke on the sour potatoes. I didn't know
much about abortion besides that it was done secretly in Syria.
I'd been surprised to learn it was not allowed in Ireland.

The bathroom in the apartment was shared. Helena didn't
hide her surprise when she noticed I wore no makeup; she took
her time in the morning and looked like she was straight from a
magazine cover.

The UN buildings were still in the same place I'd left them. I put on my blue badge and merged with the crowds entering the Unicef foyer. When I met the tech team again, I realized they were planning a business trip to the heart of Silicon Valley, a trip that I didn't know about as everyone assumed someone had informed me about it already. It wasn't only the trip that I didn't know about; there were new people I hadn't met and projects I hadn't heard of. People walked in and out of the office, and I wasn't sure who was just visiting or who belonged there. I had many questions but wasn't sure who I should annoy to answer them.

Despite the apologies and good intentions, I felt left out. It was easy to be left out when you worked across the ocean in a different time zone – a slower time zone. Pablo had warned me before my last trip back to Ireland that time moves faster in New York, but I didn't believe it until I experienced it.

I wasn't slow, but New York was faster than me. The city seemed to have its own pace. If New York's life were a video on YouTube, it would look like it was playing at times-two speed. People in this city were loud and confident and overused positive words like 'super' and 'awesome' and 'amazing', and I never could tell if they actually meant them. They spoke and moved and thought faster than humans in other parts of the world. They had meetings in elevators and while walking between cubicles and during smoke or coffee breaks. They sent emails while commuting or queuing for lunch. Speeding up in New York was not a lifestyle; it was a survival instinct. Because most of the team were on a fixed-term consultant contract that lacked any kind of security or benefits besides the daily wage, everyone worked more to prove themselves worthy of a contract renewal.

The trick to keeping up with New York looked easy: coffee during the day to pump up energy and drinks at night to wind back down. Then sleep, reset, and repeat it all over again. The problem was that I only followed the first part of that trick, oblivious to what caffeine did to my already stressed-out body. I couldn't wrap my head around why drinking was so important for bonding or chilling after work. I would've loved to drink tea or coffee, have a big piece of chocolate cake or even smoke shisha, but I would be the one looking out of place. The pressure to drink was there, unsaid, following me like a shadow.

Astoria was quieter than Manhattan. Its buildings were smaller, and its streets were less interesting, except for one: Steinway Street. Ryan had told me before in his clipped British accent about Astoria's mix of migrants, especially Middle Eastern. His fondness for the Middle East had started many years ago when he read a book about my part of the world. Impressed by Syria, he decided to pack a bag after he finished his PhD and spent a year in Damascus learning Arabic, and falling in love with the city and a Syrian girl. During the same year I was trying to find a Master's in the UK, he had gone to Syria. It had taken him five minutes to decide to head to Syria, while my trip was impossible for me, between the overwhelming paperwork and society's views on a girl travelling on her own.

Ryan wasn't the only one who had stories about Syria. Pablo told me about the time he went there and his tour to Palmyra, when he'd met his partner on the tour bus. Ryan's and Pablo's stories about my home brought us closer. Ryan also made sure to mention all the places in New York that he thought might have that link to the home I missed. It was the best gift and I was grateful to have someone like him who understood that deep connection I had with Syria.

The shop displays in Steinway Street showed products from home. Teas, biscuits, cheese and much more, all with Arabic labels. After a few steps up the street, I had forgotten that I was in New York and was transported to a Middle Eastern country with shisha lounges and shawarma restaurants. Most exciting to me was a sweet shop called Al-Sham Sweets & Pastries. It was a small shop with rows of various mouth-watering types of *ma'amool* and baklava and huge circular trays of *kunafa*. It felt like Eid as I ate my favourite treats for the first time since my visit to Istanbul. I even took some to share with my friends at work the next day.

My mother texted me while I was at work to say that another Saudi visa rejection had come in. When I read the text, I felt everything around me disappear. Years after I'd managed to find my freedom, I still felt trapped in a box, in my passport.

I left the office and went to grab a coffee around the corner. On my way back, I noticed a new exhibition in the lobby of the Unicef building, about Syria, my Syria. Quotes and pictures of Syrian children in Al-Zaatari, a refugee camp in Jordan.

'I wish we can all go back to Syria and live a nice normal life again. But I will survive here.'
'I think about how we left our country, why we left and when we'll go back.'
'Syria is the paradise of the earth.'

I read the quotes on my way to the elevator and left the children's photos behind me for the strangers who didn't know Syria.

How come I share the same thoughts with them, even though I am not in a camp?

No matter what button I pressed in that elevator, on every floor at Unicef, in every corridor, there was a piece of the Syrian crisis. A photo of a child in a camp, a map of Syria with different colours and legends, a fundraising campaign. Every now and then, I would get involved in meetings and discussions about the situation in Syria. The besieged, the people on the move, the asylum seekers, those scattered around the world. I joined conversations on how we could help, how to measure the invisible damage, reach the most vulnerable people, integrate the isolated, and how to structure the network of the Syrian diaspora using data. I felt empowered. I thought I was. Privileged to help and make this world a better place. I talked about the refugee crisis during lunch or a coffee break, like it was just another random topic.

As the floor number got higher, I remembered how in one of those meetings, I'd heard a new word: 'displaced'.

Defined by other new words: 'forced to leave'. 'Unable to return'. 'Can't reconnect with family'. 'Lack of community support'. 'Emotional damage'.

Am I displaced? Am I in those statistics? When did I become a victim of war and fit all those criteria? How am I supposed to save the world when everyone thinks I am the one who needs saving?

The dark thoughts invaded again. The elevator doors opened as I reached the highest floor and I left to take the last steps on the stairs to reach the rooftop of Unicef. No photos of Syria there. Just a blue sky, the same sky that covered Syria. Was it really the same one?

*

At the end of the day, I walked out with Pablo, who noticed my upset face.

'I thought you were excited about the Silicon Valley trip. What happened?'

I didn't feel like sharing, so he talked about potential meetings over there and what my contributions could be, but I couldn't focus.

I gave in and told Pablo about that one impossible trip I needed to make, my father's condition and my visa rejection.

'I am so sorry. Have you asked Chris if he could help?' Pablo said in concern.

'Not really. No one knows about this,' I replied.

'It might be worth it. Let me talk to him and see what we can do. Maybe a work visa? I don't know.'

I was touched by Pablo's genuine interest in helping. Before he left, Pablo gave me a hug and the hope that things might magically work out.

My mood shifted after that day. I threw myself into work, and I shared less about my life. I admired how my friends shared stories about their lives and concerns easily, while I hid mine like a treasure. I never realized how heavy they'd become and how much harder it was to breathe with them sitting over my chest.

The only person I felt it was easy to open up to was Terese. I met her again, this time at the farmers' market at Union Square. She was buying some fresh ingredients for her dinner and bought me some to try, but I had stopped cooking in New York, like everyone else did. We had coffee later, and she told me more stories from her past, from the hard days. And I told her stories of my hard days now. Terese was my only comfort in the city, the only one with whom I could stop time and breathe and enjoy the day without feeling like I was being pulled along by a stream. I held on tight to that feeling.

Autumn's trip was planned for longer this time – six weeks – in an attempt to catch up with work while my personal life slipped away. Housam was far away, in place and mind. He was starting an online Master's in Software Engineering – his lifelong dream. Between his job and studies and the five hours' difference between us, we barely found time to talk. He waited for my call, and I waited for his. And when our lines connected, we couldn't say much. My father's situation reminded him of the one he had lost, and his Master's reminded me of the one I couldn't pursue. Our calls became shorter, and the voices became texts, and the topics became anything but us.

I should've noticed how much I'd changed, that my weight and my voice were disappearing. I was buying new clothes every month or two due to a change in size. I didn't realize at the time that my weight loss was not only due to loss of appetite during the summer heat and the extra steps I took to explore the city, but also because of overworking to prove myself in this new position and setting. New York's unlimited fashion options made me feel better about this new development instead of realizing something was wrong. I was tempted to try dresses, short dresses, now that my body was in better shape. Still, I made sure I wore thick black tights underneath that almost looked like leggings. Dresses fitted me perfectly and, for the first time, I loved being a girl; I loved my body.

The trip to the west coast took place at the end of my stay in New York. It included visiting several industry and research giants to pitch collaborations on humanitarian projects where we could benefit from their data or resources. My focus was on social media. I was eager to get my hands on the data these companies had access to, to find useful insights to help the refugees scattered across the blue pages.

Syrian Facebook data was valuable. It contained information about dangerous land and sea routes, approximate numbers of children taking the hardest journey of all, testimonies of harsh situations from people stuck at borders or in refugee camps, calls for aid and medicine in besieged areas inside Syria. In addition to this there were also economic and social indicators, education and unemployment rates, statistics about deaths, conflicts, arrests, torture, kidnappings and lost Syrians, and much more critical data.

I was consuming that dark feed while writing pages full of ideas on how we could use that data for good. I spent weeks digging into pages that reeked of death, staring into refugees' eyes in pictures and reading about their shattered dreams in the comments section. Eventually, that turned into a project pitch.

Before travelling, Pablo told me that he couldn't help with my visa.

'It's OK.' I thanked him for trying, and luckily someone walked over and changed the topic for us. I took a big gulp of my water, swallowed the tears that I didn't cry, and stretched my smile. I always thought that if I kept smiling, my brain would understand that I wasn't sad. It worked that day, at least.

My head was banging when we arrived in San Francisco after missing a coffee dose. I hadn't realized how much coffee I'd been drinking since I'd started my job. One in the morning before leaving, one at work, one after lunch, one in the evening, and sometimes one at night if I stayed to finish some work. Double shots. Double damage.

I went to my room, took painkillers and tried to rest. I couldn't stare at the lights, so I closed the curtains and lay in the dark after turning everything off, but my brain wouldn't switch off.

I joined my team later for dinner and asked if we could stop at a pharmacy on the way to get something that could help me sleep. With Chris and Pablo's assistance, I found a pill to stop the headache and make me sleep. There was a pill for everything in the US.

Despite my headache and not being able to eat much, I was happy to be there with my team instead of seeing the pictures on the WhatsApp group.

The digital clock beside my bed showed the time was 3 a.m. when I opened my eyes. I was very awake and alert, and it was clear my sleeping time was over. I got out of bed, took a shower and tried to kill time in the room, but I was quickly bored. I went to the lobby and found the coffee bar open, so poured myself a cup and sat down to read. George Orwell's *Nineteen Eighty-Four*. I was amazed by how much his dystopian world matched Syria.

When I saw the sunlight growing outside, I went for a walk. I circled the hotel area several times until I glimpsed Pablo smoking at the entrance and looking sharp as usual.

'How's your headache?' he asked.

'All good now!'

'Did you get any sleep?'

'Better than nothing.' I smiled, and he smiled back. We both knew I was lying, but we had a day full of endless meetings. *I can sleep tomorrow.*

I can't remember how many meetings I had that day, but I remember that every time someone showed us a coffee machine, I grabbed a cup. The day was like a long speed-dating event. I was meeting with companies I'd never dreamt of. American companies that would have probably asked me to leave under the US sanctions if they knew I was Syrian. I shook many hands and exchanged business cards with new names. The last meeting was the most important one for me – the blue giant of social media.

Facebook HQ was more like a small town. After passing the security gates, there was a road with buildings on both sides and shops for normal life needs. The famous blue 'like' icon was scattered everywhere like a national flag. I bought a small sticker from the gift shop and a mug to remind me that this trip was not a dream or a hallucination resulting from too much caffeine.

As I entered the building where our meeting was to be held, the image of my father-in-law appeared in my mind, his sleeping face on that deaths page. It must have been here one day, I thought, passing through as a code written on the screens that surrounded me.

With each step I took inside Facebook, more dead Syrian faces started popping up, like holograms. The content of the Syrian pages came back to life in the office in front of me. Young men chanting 'Freedom!' Armed men chasing them in between the employees' desks. Gunfire shattering screens. Missiles turning a meeting room into rubble. Imprisoned figures slowly dying on top of each other. People in black beheading a group of employees having their stand-up meeting. Smugglers pushing overcrowded boats into the sea while Alan Kurdi, the three-year-old Syrian boy, still wearing his little red shirt and navy shorts, lay face-down in the water and drowned. Beside him, an injured boy cried, 'I will tell God everything!' before he passed out next to thousands of other little bodies.

Everyone was loud, fighting, shouting, drowning over and over, stuck for ever as zeros and ones in the blue space. But the keyboards kept tapping, and my team continued walking behind our host, and life continued, as normal as it could be on a sunny day in Silicon Valley.

I wondered if there was a secret room somewhere there with a red button that deleted all that content; that deleted the Syrian tragedy. My heart started pumping rapidly and loudly. *Can they hear it?*

The meeting took place casually in the middle of an open space, surrounded by employees working in their cubicles. I sat in one of the chairs, and after a round of introductions Pablo opened the discussion. I could still hear my heart, but the meeting was too tense to break for a small thing like my heart rate. The people in the meeting were important. The topic was important. This was where I could make a change.

This feeling will go away, I told myself. *I will rest after this. It is the last meeting for today.*

I tried to speak up, but I found myself fighting for breath instead. *Stay calm.* I kept looking between the faces and losing track of what was going on. I said a few sentences, short ones.

This is not going away.

The meeting ended, to be followed up. We walked to the lobby with one of the Facebookers, who chatted with Pablo while Ryan and I walked behind.

'The meeting was good, I think,' Ryan said.

'Yeah.' I was short of words and breath. Ryan noticed.

'My heart is beating really fast. I . . . I can't catch my breath,' I confessed, while holding a hand over my chest as if trying to catch my heart. 'I don't know why. Might be the painkiller I took earlier.'

Ryan asked for the bottle of pills and checked it for any warnings or side effects, but nothing unusual came up. Pablo turned back and saw my face going pale.

'OK. Let's get you to the hotel,' Pablo suggested with an empathetic look. He ordered an Uber and walked outside to wait for it while I followed him with slow steps. Every step felt like a marathon.

'You are starting to worry me. Are you OK?' Pablo said, and I shook my head – no. He grabbed my arm and pressed his fingers over my wrist while looking at his watch. Breathing had never felt that hard. Something was wrong, but I couldn't tell what.

Pablo put his black leather jacket on my shoulders as I started to shiver. My eyelids were closing, and my head felt heavy. *Go to sleep*, my body whispered. I walked with Pablo's help to the sofa in Facebook's reception, while Ryan and the security guy talked about a doctor, an ambulance and insurance. In a few minutes, I found myself surrounded by a group of firemen and attached to several monitors.

'What's your name? What can you feel? How old are you? Are you on any medication?' Their questions came like a flood: strong, fast and repetitive, draining whatever was left of my energy.

'How much did you drink today?'

'She doesn't drink.' Pablo jumped to answer when I took longer to do so, but the fireman holding my arm insisted I answer.

'When was your last period?'

Although I was almost drifting into unconsciousness, I felt too shy to answer. Even in my state, my awareness of shame was so deep-rooted. I tried to remember, and then I realized my next cycle was due.

'Can I lie down, please?' I said desperately. The firefighter helped me lie down on the sofa while keeping an eye on the heart-rate monitor.

'Blood pressure and heartbeat look a bit off the chart, but nothing worrying,' the leader of the group said. 'You are OK. It is probably all in your head. Try to relax.'

I couldn't lift my head any more. *How is this OK?* I felt a bit insulted by his diagnosis, but I was too weak to argue. I'd never felt the urge to shut down and sleep as much as I did at that moment.

An ambulance showed up shortly after and I finally got the chance to lie down and close my eyes. That's all I wanted. Oxygen was flowing gently through a mask into my nostrils. I got injected with fluids, wrapped with a warm blanket and stickered with circles that carried my heartbeat to a monitor. As soon as I arrived at Stanford hospital, I was placed in a wheelchair despite explaining that I felt well enough to walk.

Pablo showed up. He said I was looking better and pointed to the glass window through which I could see Ryan and Chris waiting in the corridor. I smiled weakly and felt grateful. They took turns keeping me company until the doctor saw me. When it was Chris's turn, I felt the most embarrassed, knowing he had dinner plans.

'I am sorry I ruined your evening.'

'You didn't ruin anything. You think I cancelled my plans?' he teased. 'I am still going.'

I laughed, feeling the weight of embarrassment become lighter.

'But I am here to check on you.' His smile changed. 'I know you've been through a lot recently.'

Tears started running down my cheeks. I remembered that Pablo had told him about my father's situation. I felt vulnerable and exposed and appreciative all at once. After Chris left, I was taken into the exam room.

'That looked like an episode of *Grey's Anatomy*,' Pablo joked after I had been examined. Ryan laughed, and I felt better just hearing their voices. When the doctor came in later, he asked if I had any family in the US. I pointed at the two guys and smiled. 'Those guys are my family.'

The doctor went on talking about sleep deprivation, excessive caffeine intake, painkillers and stress. He offered to give me something to help me sleep, and I said yes but wasn't sure how it would work with my return flight in less than twelve hours.

A nurse came and hooked me up to a bag of fluids mixed with sleeping drugs. After a few seconds, my head felt like it was filled with rocks and my body was glued to the bed under me. I tried to talk. I tried to get up, but nothing happened. As I drifted off, I remembered that it was Pablo's birthday and that we had planned to celebrate it after the Facebook meeting – but I had already gone into the dream world.

Chapter 18

The Four Seasons
of New York – Winter

AFTER SOME DAYS OF sick leave back on Irish soil to recover from
the west-coast meltdown, I went back to my remote-working
bubble. It was as if nothing had happened. No one talked about
it, and everyone got on with work.

Housam was chewing his dinner silently in front of me
while I scrolled endlessly on my phone. I don't know when there
became a valley of unspoken words and feelings between
us. I remember coming back from New York broken and lost. I
remember playing that fainting scene in my head a million
times while I pretended to be asleep. I was in Galway, but my
mind was everywhere else. All the things that charmed me
about that little city started bugging me; it was too quiet now,
too peaceful, and too slow and too lonely. Nothing happened
there.

The air between Housam and me was filled with electrical
charge whenever I mentioned a perk of living in New York,
which I did a lot. Our life in Galway became a shadow of my life
in New York: every time we met someone, the conversation
steered instantly towards the sleepless city. In Galway, I became
the New York girl. While in New York, I became the Galway girl.
During my last online meeting, I'd told Pablo to stop calling me
that. He'd laughed, assuming I was joking, before asking why

when he realized I was serious. I didn't explain; I couldn't even if I tried. I didn't know who I was any more.

At a tech event in Galway, I stood away from the crowds during the break, trying to look busy, when someone approached and asked the classic question: 'Where are you from?'

After I answered his question, and all the follow-up ones, he paused for a second and said: 'So, you're telling me you are a Syrian, and you work in the US, and you travel there frequently?'

'Yes.'

'So where do you hide your explosives?' And he laughed, and the people standing around us laughed, and I laughed instead of slapping his face and told him I was an expert in hiding them now.

Later, at night, I told Housam I was sick of all this.

'I don't know why we are still in Galway,' I said to him. 'We barely have anyone here. I made more friends in New York in a few weeks than the two years I spent here.'

'You know we can't leave,' Housam said.

'Why? I can get a US visa and keep renewing it. My passport is working just fine.'

'And my passport is shitty, right?'

'No, it's not. You got the visa, too.'

'Are you serious?' Housam started to get annoyed.

'I just don't have anything here. I have no friends, no family, no work colleagues.' I avoided his question. 'And I can't stop living a normal life just in the hope of getting a decent citizenship some day!'

'What are you saying? You want us to pack and leave? Fine! Let's leave!' Housam was suddenly beyond annoyed at that point. 'Let's move to New York!'

'You know I can't make you drop your residency here. I can't do that to you.' I tried to stay calm.

'What do you want?! You want to live in New York? I will quit tomorrow and move. Stop blaming me for feeling miserable. It's not my fault!'

I knew it was safer for us, at least visa-wise, to stay in Ireland, but I hated not having options. I resented the parallel life I lived. The two SIM cards, the two time zones, the universal power adapter, the endless work events that I missed.

FOMO.

Someone had mentioned that word on the work WhatsApp group when I'd said how much I wished I could join that last event.

Fear Of Missing Out.

But it didn't feel right. FOMO felt like something that would happen to someone who missed a night out or a concert. What's the word for displaced people who miss out on work opportunities and family gatherings due to bureaucracy and paper borders?

Walid's wedding was planned for the following week. Instead of having a visa to Saudi Arabia to be there with him, I had a visa to attend a wedding in India for two of Housam's friends from work whom I knew as well. *Is it FOMO when I think of not being able to be at my brother's wedding? Is it FOMO not to be there after my father's stroke? Is it FOMO missing Damascus and Nadia's laugh and Tete's dishes and Beso's purrs? Is it FOMO missing Housam, who's right here beside me? Is it FOMO missing myself?*

~

The fog added a majestic atmosphere to the Ganges river when we crossed over the bridge in Rishikesh, in the north of India.

People were down there, soaking themselves to atone for sins. Some tourists walked by us wearing hippy clothes. Local children cleared the way for cows that roamed the streets, while bright statues of gods were locked in cages and monks asked for donations. I wondered why poverty and religion always seemed to walk side by side. And I wished to dive into the Ganges, to atone for being Syrian. If only.

The traces of henna left on my hand from the wedding were starting to fade away into a light shade of orange. The intricate lines overlapped with my modern Fitbit watch, looking like they belonged to different times. Like an error you'd spot in a low-budget movie. Despite wearing a watch, I wasn't sure what the time was any more or what time zone mattered now that I was in India. I wore it to keep my heartbeat under control.

After a wedding full of rituals and flowers and fire and music and food, a friend in our group mentioned the New Zealand entertainment company that was organizing dangerous activities like bungee jumps and rope swings in the mountains of northern India. I agreed to join him in a bungee jump. Nothing seemed scary any more. I climbed the high steps before two professionals wrapped me up with ropes and hooks. My friend jumped gracefully with a smile, as if diving into a pool. It was hard to follow his act. I took slow steps to the jumping point and felt my heart filled with rage at this unfair life, enough to blow up the mountain in front of me. I was angry, but it was not the anger that makes you want to yell or break things or clean obsessively or eat carelessly. It was the anger that makes you want to walk over a cliff, and fall.

As I let go, I felt my body fall faster than my thoughts. When I saw the ground getting close, I thought the worst part was over, but the bungee cord bounced me up again, higher than where I first fell from. I wish I'd known that. After some more bounces, gravity did its magic and sent me down. I was still upside down, scared now of slipping from the rope. Two assistants lowered my dangling body to a mattress below. When they quickly unhooked me from my virtual suicide attempt, I realized how I didn't feel any better than before. I couldn't locate my feelings any more.

On our last night in Delhi, Housam and I went to a cafe to talk. Every conversation recently had led to an argument, so we'd just stopped talking. But this time, he talked and so did I. I blamed him; he blamed me. He was hurt. I regretted it. He looked at me, and I looked away. With all the space that had grown between us, I wondered whether I'd married out of love or just to escape my father's prison. I said I didn't want to talk about it any more. He grabbed my hand and said he would never give up on us. I slipped my hand out slowly. I wished he would let go, but I wasn't sure why I wanted to sabotage the only good thing in my life. I wished there had been no rope in that bungee jump and no ground beneath. A void.

~

New York's rooftops were covered in white when I returned to the city a week after India. Brooklyn seemed quieter than Manhattan but livelier than Queens, and I liked that. It was the right amount of life. I'd arranged my trip this time to align with the festive season. Two years of a lonely, bleak Christmas in Galway was more than I could tolerate. Housam had booked to join me later for the holidays.

Working remotely was not remotely working. I asked Pablo

for a meeting in person after hesitating for a long time. No inter-ruptions, no connection breaks. This time I wanted to get a solid plan to make my remote-working life less painful, instead of dragging this problem into my work, which was starting to fall behind as I waited for feedback.

Pablo was having a hectic day but I insisted on having the meeting even if it was the last thing on his agenda. That resulted in sitting across from an exhausted, burnt-out version of Pablo in a formal, dry conversation in which he said he was doing his best and suggested I work harder. I was taken aback by his tone and regretted forcing the meeting. I'd always admired how Pablo pushed me and brought the best out of me, but this now felt like a different kind of pushing, with a wall in front of me that he couldn't see. When we went over all the suggestions I had writ-ten on a piece of paper, I was quiet, thinking how this job would never work out. Working hard wasn't the problem – I'd ended up in an ambulance by doing that. The problems that came with remote working were out of our hands.

The office was empty when we headed back to it. It was Unicef's Christmas party down in the underground hall below the lobby. Pablo insisted I join, so I followed him, planning on leaving as soon as possible. I tried to mingle, but found it hard to smile. Everyone seemed to know each other. I barely knew any-one in the building, and nobody knew me. I was the invisible remote employee.

I left Pablo talking to someone and wandered through people until I ran into a colleague who introduced me to two girls. They were holding red and blue plastic cups and looked a bit drunk. We exchanged names, work titles and floor numbers before the dreaded question came.

'Where are you from?'

As soon as I said 'Syria', one of them threw herself on me and hugged me, while the other looked like she was about to cry. I frowned and tried to smile. I excused myself to get a drink, but one explained that I needed a token to buy anything. I didn't want to bother exchanging money, so I said, 'Never mind.'

'Do you have money? We can lend you some.'

I pretended to look for someone, then left the place and went up to the office feeling offended. *I am not a charity!* The emptiness of the floor gave me a sense of relief – no more awkward conversations. I wanted to sit alone and digest my meeting with Pablo. *This is not working out.* Pablo was fed up, and I was fed up. I was not doing anything besides working, yet I still felt unable to catch up. I was a burden. I felt heavy.

As I sat alone in the empty office, I couldn't stop thinking how everything was wrong. I was wrong. This place was wrong. The party was wrong. The work was wrong. The world was wrong.

~

'Pick a paper from the basket.' Maya stood in the middle of the open-plan office space, holding a basket of folded paper and explaining Secret Santa. 'The name you get is the person you buy a gift for.'

'But what if I don't like that person?' I said. Everyone laughed.

'Suad, c'mon.' Maya rolled her eyes.

'What?' I grinned while pushing my chair back from my desk and walking towards Maya. 'I am serious. It could happen.' I took a peek at the name on the paper I picked, and I was glad it was someone I liked and knew exactly what to gift.

The team's Christmas party took place a few days later. The piles of gifts were set on top of one of the desks, but we didn't have a proper Christmas tree. Instead, Chris opened his laptop and downloaded a picture of a tree, and placed it beside the gifts. Someone hung a thread of lights on the cubicles, and Santa hats and beards were scattered around.

When it was time to announce the gifts, I stood back and didn't reach out for mine. I had a feeling that my name had been dropped or forgotten.

'Merry Christmas.'

Pablo handed me a wrapped gift with my name on it. 'I found it while looking for mine.'

I grabbed it, thinking that even if it was empty, I was glad my name was there. Halfway through unwrapping it, I stopped.

'Wait.' I looked suspiciously at Pablo. 'Are you my Secret Santa?'

'No.' Pablo shrugged. 'Maybe.'

I unwrapped the gift quickly, wondering what his taste in presents would be like. There were two: a small PC chip and a tiny metal puzzle with a picture of the Empire State Building.

'Wow! Thank you.'

'Do you like it?'

'Yeah. It is very . . . what's the word . . . *manly*?' I teased.

'Manly?!' Pablo raised his eyebrows. 'See, this is what you women do. You say you want equality, but when you get something like this, you say it's *manly*.' Pablo went on defending his gifts, and we laughed. For a moment, I forgot that my job was failing me and that I was failing it.

Unlike the official Unicef party, this one seemed more relaxed and intimate, at least for me. I didn't feel like I was standing out. My colleagues said I looked like a happy drunk person, although

I wasn't drinking. For once, I was genuinely delighted not to be the awkward gloomy face in the office.

I put on a Santa hat and danced and took many pictures before the party moved to a karaoke bar nearby. Challenged, I signed up with a friend to do a classic Backstreet Boys song –something I'd always wanted to do, but which didn't fit with my previous identity.

That night was also supposed to be a farewell to Ryan, who was leaving the team after New Year. Our group got smaller as people left, and we ended up sitting at a small round table with six beers and a Coke.

After we'd hurt our vocal cords by singing and shouting, Ryan sat next to me and started talking about his trip to Syria. The fireplace, the power outage, the funny way he tried to speak the language. I laughed a lot before I realized I was in tears. Ryan apologized if his anecdotes were hard to listen to, but I said no and hugged him and thanked him for all the precious memories he'd brought back, before I left the bar. I stood outside to take in some fresh air but my mood was already off. As if I'd woken up from a nice dream to a miserable reality. A few people came and went for a smoke until it was only Pablo and me out there.

'Are you coming back inside?' He threw away his cigarette and turned to head back.

'No.'

I kept my back to the bar and stared at the neon sign flashing on the other side of the street in front of me.

'No?' Pablo changed his direction and turned to look where I was looking. He put his hands in his pockets like I was doing, leaning on the bar's large window.

'You can go back if you want. I'll join you soon.' I smiled, assuring him that I was not upset.

'I know. I am just going to stand and stare at that building over there.' Pablo was already rolling another cigarette. He did what he said. Just stood next to me and blew his smoke away.

'Ryan was telling me about his trip to Damascus,' I sighed. 'I was surprised how much he knew about the intimate little details of living there. I didn't think anyone knew those things that I miss the most but couldn't explain. I don't know if . . .' I took another cold breath filled with Pablo's tobacco. 'I don't know if I'll ever go back, Pablo. I don't know if I'll ever live those details again.' My tears fell anew.

'You *will* go back.' Pablo turned to face me. 'You will live those details again.' He was confident that everything would be fine. He kept desperately assuring me, like he was talking someone down off a ledge.

I kept staring at New York's night while Pablo kept describing a beautiful future. He was the most confident person I knew. Still, he couldn't convince me that I would go back one day.

Housam joined me after he'd finished his own office Christmas rituals. New York's cosy winter brought us a bit closer – the lights, the markets, the events and the snow on top of all that. New York's snow reminded me of home. When it snowed in Damascus, the city became an illusion of a magical place where no ugliness could be seen any more. Housam and I met daily after I finished work, walked in a new direction, and never talked about what had broken and what had healed. He surprised me once with a necklace from the gift shop at the New York Public Library. It was bronze, with a little book-shaped charm with a red leather cover recycled from a real book. It was the best gift.

On New Year's Eve, we headed to Times Square to watch the

iconic ball drop after dinner with friends from work. The police blocked the streets leading to the square, so we walked more than twenty blocks until we found a way to join the crowds. We couldn't reach the heart of Times Square, but we stood a few blocks away where we could glimpse that glittery ball hanging there on the many screens around.

Despite the freezing temperature, the excitement was high. Everyone around us was drunk or dreamy. Housam stood behind me, shielding my body from accidental touches by midnight strangers. Surprisingly, they were easy to talk to and laugh with. As the countdown started, we joined the crowds yelling out the numbers on the screen and taking many dark and blurry photos and videos that we'd never look at again, to document a moment that was too surreal to be true.

'This is a good change from a New Year at McDonald's,' Housam joked and kissed me as people around us shouted 'Happy New Year!' and Mariah Carey started singing. As the crowds began to dissolve, it was possible to get closer to the square. We walked around while music blasted from the many speakers scattered across the place, and the screens touted images of products and shows and young models. I remembered my mother's constant warnings to stay away from the TV screen. *She should see me now.*

The streets were a mess of glitter and confetti and spilt drinks, but people were happy. Sometimes you need to make a big mess to be happy. I walked with Housam holding hands, and we went back to our sublet in Williamsburg to have our own celebration and mark the new year of 2017.

The next day, my dear colleague Mari invited us to her place for a traditional Japanese New Year feast. The warmth of the house in the presence of her family and friends made me realize that I hadn't been to a friend's house in a long time. When one of the guests, who was a professional musician, heard we were from Syria, he mentioned he had a Syrian musician friend.

'I don't know if you know him. His name is Kinan—'

'Kinan Azmeh?!' Housam and I exclaimed at the same time.

'YES!' His eyes widened in excitement.

'Of course we know him!' My mind went straight back to the Opera House in Damascus, where I'd heard him play.

'Well, he has a show next Wednesday, and I am supposed to play with him. Would you like to come?'

'YES!'

I didn't even know Kinan Azmeh was living in New York. It was hard to keep up with the scattered Syrians around the world. Knowing that he lived a few kilometres from us had awoken a tingly feeling of excitement.

Wednesday did not keep us waiting long. Before we knew it, in the heart of New York, in a small crowded pub, we were meeting Kinan briefly before the concert. Maybe it was his familiar Syrian look, his dialect or the warm memories he brought back to us, but meeting Kinan, meeting home within him, made me forget for a moment that I was in New York.

When Kinan took to the stage and started playing with his band, we were transferred to Damascus, to the beautiful times before the war. To when I went to concerts with Nadia or sneaked out with Housam. He was introducing every piece he played with a few sentences telling the background story. That piece was about home and missing home and nostalgia. It was titled with a new Portuguese word he'd learnt: 'Saudade'. The word that is now carved on my heart like a tattoo. *Is that the name of my pain? Is that the name of my disease?*

Kinan said the next piece was about his favourite town in Syria, where he used to go with his family as a kid during summer. 'Jisreen' was the name of the piece – and the town. My heart skipped a beat.

Jisreen was the village in the Damascus suburbs where Housam had bought our future house to settle into as a newly married couple. He'd spent years paying off the loan, crafting its details, supervising the workers while finishing its structure. The dream house remained a dream, since we never had the chance to live there. The war had started and the suburbs turned into a conflict zone. The last thing we'd heard about the house was that a displaced family – a disabled older man with seven daughters – was staying there after their house had been destroyed. Jisreen was not a popular town in Syria and was barely mentioned in the news, so I'd almost forgotten about it. Since we'd left, we'd had to let go of many memories because holding on to them was painful. Holding on to memories from our past life in Syria was like holding on to stones while trying to swim. There was no time to pause and grieve. You assess the damage; you prioritize the pain. One month after we lost access to the house in besieged Jisreen, we lost my father-in-law. You prioritize: a place or a soul? We picked his soul and moved on to the next pain.

When Kinan's clarinet began singing, I felt my heart shatter into pieces at one note, only to be put back together at another. His music was an embrace from home. In seconds my cheeks were wet, and so were Housam's.

The last piece was called 'Wedding'. Kinan dedicated it to all those who had managed to fall in love in the past five years, despite everything that was happening. I reached out for Housam's hand and pressed it gently as I laid my head on his shoulder. I missed us. We couldn't ignore that dedication. We'd never stopped during those five years to catch our breath and be in love, to accept what had happened and live with it instead of sweeping it under the rug. Kinan's music took us home that day. Kinan *was* home.

~

A coincidence led me to Little Syria.

I was standing at the bus stop when I noticed the Arabic letters on the poster next to it. With the exception of the few Arabic words in restaurants and supermarkets, it had been almost four years since I'd seen anything in my native language in a public place.

'Little Syria, NY: An Immigrant Community's Life & Legacy'.

I couldn't believe that somewhere in the city was an exhibition about the previous lives of Syrians now living in New York. I didn't even know there was a Syrian community in Lower Manhattan. The exhibition was held in a more interesting place: Ellis Island, the immigrants' island.

I took the ferry with Housam. Syrian music was flowing out of the entrance door like perfume. The room was filled with photos of important historical Syrian figures who had lived in New York from 1880 up until 1940 and shaped the Syrian community – from merchandisers who imported Syrian products, to journalists and writers who started their own Arabic newspapers.

'What smells remind you of home?'

A sign was displayed in front of two open boxes with a space to smell through. I sniffed *za'atar* in the first box and felt it go straight to my heart. The second one had Arabic coffee seeds mixed with cardamom. I used to find it bitter, but always enjoyed its magical aroma while preparing it for my parents or guests. Many stories were shared over coffee; gossip, and many memories.

Inhabitants of the Little Syria neighbourhood were ironically coming from a country once called 'Greater Syria', a combination of what is now known as Syria, Lebanon, Palestine, Jordan, Iraq, Kuwait and parts of Egypt, Saudi Arabia and Turkey. Greater Syria was split into all those countries after the British and French colonization, and I belonged to modern-day Syria, or what was left of it.

The last part of the exhibition was a documentary called *The Sacred* by Özge Dogan, a Turkish director. It narrated stories and testimonials from people who lived in Little Syria, and how it was destroyed by the Brooklyn Tunnel construction and real estate business, demolishing everyone's homes and scattering them across the island.

I didn't have much interest in documentaries back then, but I sat hypnotized on the chair in front of the screen and listened to the sociology professor Sharon Zukin describing the human need to have a home and the pain of losing one. She said that because everything is changing around us, we instinctively want to stay in one place and put down roots that protect us from moving around. We search for similar groups and classes to build a place familiar to us. But when that place is destroyed and that group is scattered, we lose an important part of ourselves. As I listened to her speak in the empty exhibition room, I felt seen and sad. My wound was a sociological phenomenon. There was vocabulary to explain it. I finally understood that the sickness that plagued me was literally homesickness. The connection to home that I was seeking was elemental, and I wasn't alone.

They say history repeats itself. The documentary, although talking about a former period, was rubbing salt in a recent wound. The Syrian diaspora was expanding. If people felt lost moving from one neighbourhood to the other and losing track of their usual places and faces, how would they feel today, being forced to leave their whole country? Little Syria and Greater Syria had both been lost, and I was still looking for any trace that connected me to them.

I left the exhibition, but it didn't leave me. As I toured the rest of the Ellis Island museum, I felt my pain echoing through each room. Migrants' faces, details of diaspora, parts of stories and struggles. Migrants faced a different kind of injustice; they faced racism, discrimination, minimum wages and unfair working conditions. One room showed the protests that spread against migrants. They were shamelessly reported on in newspapers, one for each nationality or ethnicity: Irish, Italian, Asian, and the list goes on. It was a challenging journey for all these people who had contributed enormously to building this city. This city that was still not sure how it felt towards them.

Inspired by the exhibition, I went on a hunt for the remains of Little Syria. I found myself on Atlantic Avenue in Brooklyn, staring at the window of a shop in disbelief. A rusty sign stood proudly over the shop, despite missing a few Arabic letters.

I entered the shop to ask about the price of the big handmade mosaic box in the middle of the display. The grey-haired man behind the counter smiled, and everything about him looked so familiar. His wrinkles, his smile, his eyes.

'Come in. I will show you more. You are from Syria, right?'

He must have recognized me as I did him, and that only made me more excited.

'Yes! And you?'

'Of course! *Ahla w sahla* – welcome.'

We connected immediately. That was all that we needed to know about each other. He didn't answer my question about the price; instead, he said the classic sentence that every Syrian merchandiser had to say: 'We won't disagree over the price, don't worry about it.'

I almost laughed when he said it. I'd detested that phrase back home and always felt alerted that I was about to get ripped off, but this time it was music to my ears.

Oh, I've missed this.

The guy started pulling boxes in different patterns and sizes from the shelves behind him, while I gazed around the shop. It was full of random Syrian products, from spices to shisha to an Arabic calendar. I kept asking him to show me more of the treasures he had, and he was delighted to present his shop to me. Eventually, he pulled out a big white mailbag with more decorated pieces similar to the ones in the display.

'This was shipped from Damascus. Look at the stamps and address.' He opened the bag like Santa Claus. 'I go there every three months to pick products by myself. I don't trust anyone.'

The address in Arabic stated somewhere in Damascus. My Damascus. I didn't even know that the shops were still in business back there.

'All factories in the suburbs were destroyed or closed. Some took their business to other countries, and some opened smaller ones inside Damascus where it is relatively safer.' My heart twisted a bit. One of the boxes was still wrapped in a newspaper from back home – *Tishreen*, October in the Assyrian calendar. The newspaper was named after the October War in 1973.

My eyes followed the words wrapped around the box, and I bent my head to follow the sentences. I was hungry to read anything printed in Arabic. The headlines were about the current, ongoing war, the unbeatable army's victories, the arrested traitors and the delusional state of security. George Orwell would have been very proud, maybe surprised, to discover how his fictional world of *Nineteen Eighty-Four* had turned into a reality, an ugly one. I would never have stopped for a second to read this back home, but I asked the old man if I could keep the box wrapped in that newspaper, while he insisted on wrapping it in fancy gift paper. I declined softly. 'I want this, please.' I wanted to take a piece of home with me.

Atlantic Avenue had other shops filled with Syrian products, mostly groceries. It was astonishing how food could take me home in a minute without having to worry about visas.

Before Housam left for Ireland, we enjoyed the city as tourists to the max. We attended a *Seinfeld* special at the Beacon Theatre and had a coffee and a piece of cake at the famous cafe where Tom Hanks and Meg Ryan had their first encounter in *You've Got Mail*. As I kissed Housam goodbye, I wished for a miracle that would keep us in New York, near Little Syria and Atlantic Avenue. I wished I didn't have to choose between a passport and a city, between a relationship and a career, home and diaspora.

Being in New York felt like a secret gateway to the home that I couldn't reach, even if it was through food and mosaic boxes and an older man who said, '*Ahla w sahla.*'

*

Soon after Housam left, I started feeling fatigue. A headache and a warmer-than-usual body told me I was about to get sick or get my period. I opened the circle-shaped app on my phone and checked if that was due to happen any time soon. It showed tomorrow. *I knew it.*

A week later, I was still feeling tired and gloomy. Painkillers weren't killing any pain, and my appetite for food was decreasing. I rechecked the mobile app, and it announced that my period would start tomorrow. Every time I opened the app, it showed tomorrow.

I did the maths myself. I was late. Two weeks late. The high ceiling of my room felt closer than ever to my chest.

'That can't be,' Housam tried to reassure me over the phone. 'You are probably tired and sick; that can affect your cycle.'

'I know, but two weeks? I am never that late!'

'Calm down, *habibi*. You are overthinking this. If you're worried, just get a pregnancy test and see for yourself.'

The word 'pregnancy' fell harsh on my ears. I'd only seen those test kits in movies, but I had to know. I grabbed one from the pharmacy and went back to the house to unravel the mystery. My bladder was already empty and my sample was not enough to get a result, so I decided to leave it until later and try to distract myself before I drove myself mad.

Terese invited me to her place and prepared a delicious pumpkin soup, something that I was trying for the first time. She was delighted with the mosaic box I gifted her, and she later showed me her knitting kit and taught me how to cast on my first stitch. I had never had the patience for this hobby, and I used to resent it because it was associated with women, the same way I resented chores or makeup or the colour pink. Terese told me that men knitted as well. She gifted me two knitting needles and a ball of yarn so I could give that relaxing hobby a chance. Terese's kindness encouraged me to open up to her about the possible pregnancy. She eased my worries and offered any help needed, whenever I found out and whatever I decided. After I left her house, I felt my shoulders were lighter.

Later, I met my friends at the East Village for coffee, then walked around the city and explored new books at the Strand, deliberately postponing my return to the apartment to avoid the test waiting for me in the bathroom. I didn't go back until it was 9 p.m. The apartment was empty, but the nauseating smell of my flatmate's seafood dinner was there. My bladder was more than ready this time. It didn't take five minutes, as it specified on the box. It barely took five seconds for a plus sign to show up in the middle of the stick – the sign that would change my life for ever.

The bathroom was small, or maybe it got smaller after I saw the positive sign.

I am going to lose my job.

That was my first thought. *I won't be able to travel any more.* I tried to stop the shivers that went through my body and to think clearly back in my bedroom. I looked at the time on my phone and added five hours to it. Housam must be asleep right now with his phone on airplane mode, as usual. My hands clicked his photo and dialled as a reflex. The thought of waiting eight hours until he woke up made my heart race. I heard two rings before he answered half asleep. Happy to hear his voice, I forgot why I was worried.

'Hi, honey, what's up?' Housam said in a low voice.

I took a deep breath and tried to sound calm. 'I am pregnant.'

'What!?'

'I just did the test. I am pregnant. I am *preg-nant*.' As if I had just heard the words myself, I cried. I didn't want to be practical any more.

'Honey, why are you crying?' Housam's voice was no longer sleepy.

'I am so scared. I don't want to be pregnant.'

Housam was quiet for a few seconds while I sobbed.

'Crying won't help. Stop crying, and we can figure it out,' Housam said softly. I hated it when he said crying wouldn't help. It helped!

'You have options, you know,' he said.

I broke down in tears again. 'This is huge! I can't do this!'

Housam kept trying to calm me down, but I cried until I had worn myself out. I begged him to stay on the phone, terrified that if he hung up I'd be pregnant and alone. His gentle voice brought some safety to my shaken world, and I closed my eyes and temporarily escaped my new reality.

The phone was sleeping next to me on the pillow when I opened my eyes in the morning. Was it a dream? The pregnancy test sitting on my nightstand reminded me it wasn't.

I am pregnant, and there is life in my belly.

Tears started falling again, wetting the pillow. I stayed for an hour in bed, overthinking it all before deciding to get up for work. I couldn't focus on anything in the office and tried secretly to research family planning online, but sitting in an open space meant privacy was rare. I avoided my team. I looked like I'd come from a funeral.

The word 'abortion' felt scary. The pressure of making the

right choice was like cutting the wires on a ticking bomb. If I decided to have an abortion, I had to be quick before returning to Ireland, where abortions were illegal, in two weeks.

I thought being from Syria isolated me from the office, but carrying that secret inside me pushed me into another level of loneliness. Despite my colleagues' acts of kindness and concern, I feared that sharing my secret with anyone would influence my decision. I kept looking at my belly now and then. I couldn't think of myself as a mother, not any more. I remembered blaming my parents for having me, and that was even before a war erupted. My raging relationship with them, and with the world, made me the last person qualified to be a mother. I didn't know how to care or love. Even with Housam, I never understood his ability to love unconditionally, his ways of forgiving and forgetting. I was not meant to be a loving mother. I couldn't keep this baby. It would be unfair to both of us.

The online search led me to Planned Parenthood's website. Two pills, not at the same time, and a heavy period. *How heavy is heavy?* I sneaked out of the office several times to ring the clinic for an appointment before I managed to get an answer. I couldn't risk anyone listening.

The closest appointment was the next Tuesday, in a week; a week of carrying an embryo inside me. I booked the slot and hung up and cried about the overwhelming decision in the Unicef building's outdoor patio area. Despite New York's heavy traffic, I felt stranded on a desert island. I updated Housam with a text, wiped my tears and went back to the office.

Now I had made my choice, I had to face the consequences. The more I read about abortion, the more I panicked. An online forum discussed women's experiences and someone wrote that she'd seen tiny hands and feet afterwards. I was shaken to my bones when I read this. Despite Housam's assurance that it was still in a very early stage – it was barely cells – I couldn't believe him. He decided to book a flight after work on Friday and arrive in New York early on Saturday to be with me for the abortion. I felt guilty for making him take that extra trip, but relieved to have him with me. I needed his arms around me. Housam was my glue.

Terese texted me to check on me, and I updated her in a long message. She gently supported my decision and offered to come with me, but I told her I would be fine. I wasn't fine, but knowing she was there, even via text, made me feel less bad.

I threw myself back into work, knowing that Housam was on the way and my appointment was set up. It was now up to me to be brave enough and go through with it. Everyone around me seemed tense about Trump's inauguration, while I tried as hard as possible to avoid any discussions on the topic. Political talks were nothing but headaches and heartaches. However, politics didn't avoid me.

Trump's infamous ban on Syrians and citizens of other unfortunate nations came in two days before Housam's flight. On 27 January 2017, Trump gave executive orders, effective immediately, to ban people from seven countries, in order to protect Americans from terrorism. One more time, I found myself in a Syrian tragedy. Instead of worrying about my unplanned pregnancy, I had to worry if my husband would arrive, or if I would be able to come back to New York in the spring. The only difference was that this time, I was numb. After years and years of bad news, I didn't expect anything good any more. *What's next? Arrest all Syrians in the US and deport them?* The Muslim ban came to prove my point that this world is too wrong to exist, too damaged to bring another child into it.

Since I needed to take three days off for the procedure, I decided to tell Pablo about my plans. I thought it would look weird to disappear before my trip back to Ireland.

After a very long week, we left work and walked up the street to take our usual route around the block.

'So, tell me. What's going on with you?' Pablo asked.

The words got stuck in my throat. I wished I had a piece of paper so I could write it down instead of saying it. Pablo gave me an encouraging look, and I felt like I was doing a bungee jump all over again.

I told him I was pregnant, and before he could congratulate me with a beaming face, I told him I was having an abortion. The ambulance sirens of New York seemed fitting for that moment. I regretted it immediately when I saw his face turn to shock and confusion.

'I don't want to discuss it,' I said when he asked why. 'I am just letting you know so you can understand why I was acting weird at work and why I'll be absent for three days. I already booked an appointment for next Tuesday. Housam is coming over on Saturday.' I tried to sound as professional as possible. I was done with meltdowns at work.

Pablo talked, but I didn't want to listen. He talked about blessings and gifts and opportunities that might not repeat themselves. I was surprised to hear Pablo speak in that way, more surprised that he cared to debate this personal matter despite my efforts to shut the conversation down. This was not like me opening up about my father's condition, about Syria, about exhaustion on a work trip. I resented always being the helpless girl surrounded by tragedies and in need of intervention. Still, a part of me was curious to know Pablo's unsolicited opinion. I couldn't 'unlisten' to him. After several 'no's and 'why's, I caved in.

'Because I am damaged. Because I am from Syria and I work in New York and live in Galway. Because I never made my parents proud! Because this world is a horrible place!' I blurted it out all at once, like a bullet, realizing only afterwards that I had shared too much, and that a lady standing on the side of the street was now staring at me. I wished I could disappear.

'You are not damaged,' Pablo said sincerely. He focused on the thing he knew best: work. He went on to explain how to adapt my job and travelling to this new change. I tried to find loopholes in his plan, but he had a good answer for everything. The shift in conversation helped take my mind off abortion and its consequences and feel less trapped.

'Think about what would matter in five years from now,' Pablo said. 'It's definitely not going to be a dataset.'

Before we went our separate ways, he asked me to take Monday off to think, but I didn't want to open Pandora's box again.

Housam's passport caused an alert at the passport control section in Dublin Airport. The officer closed his counter and debated with his colleagues what to do with this first case affected by the ban. Luckily, his UN dependant visa allowed him entry.

When I saw him, we stood in the street and embraced in a long, silent hug while people passed us. I was too tired to cry. I felt every inch of my body relax in Housam's presence. The burden seemed less horrifying when split in two.

In the apartment, we opened the discussion. Whenever he

mentioned the A-word, bloody little feet and hands jumped into my mind, and I would start crying. When he talked about keeping it, I would think of all the struggles I had with my parents, all the Syrian children scattered in the camps, and feel that being born was the most unfair thing that could happen to a human.

'You sounded so confident over the phone. Why are you rethinking this?' Housam asked, stroking my hair as I laid my head in his lap. I remembered my conversation with Pablo and felt furious that he'd managed to mess with my head. I confessed to Housam, and he listened carefully before turning the tables again.

'And what do you think about the work options he gave you?'

'I don't know. I guess it is good to know that it is not the end of the world regarding my job. I was surprised he was supportive, to be honest.'

Housam didn't say his opinion. He let me speak my thoughts, and whenever I got overwhelmed with one option, he gave me the other one to consider. We kept doing this until I had a meltdown and couldn't reason any more. He hugged me, and I fell asleep.

We went for a walk in the evening and decided to sit in a cake shop. The cake was too good for such a depressing discussion, but the sugar helped change my mood.

A few bites, then we resumed the debate. This time, I pressured Housam into giving an opinion.

'I think the timing is not right; you know I am in the middle of this Master's and you are figuring things out with your job.' Housam finally gave in.

'But, is that your only problem? Timing?' I said, realizing this for the first time.

'Well, yes. I think having a baby next year would be better timing. We are both swamped right now, don't you think?'

'No! I don't want to have kids after a year. I don't want to have
kids … ever!' I said in shock. Housam's facial expression
changed, and the tiny table between us looked like a bottomless
valley.

'I didn't know that's how you felt,' Housam said.

*How could he not know! Maybe I've never said it out loud, but
the world is still on fire and our circumstances haven't changed –
or have they?* I sat back in my chair and folded my hands, looking
away. A couple took the table next to us, placing a baby seat on
the third chair between our tables. The baby started cooing, waving his little socks in my face. I looked at Housam, and we both
exchanged a look and a nervous laugh. This was the worst possible setting in which to have this conversation!

'If you want to have one next year, then why go through with
the …' I whispered the word 'abortion' even though we were
talking in Arabic. 'What's the difference, now or in a year?'

Housam was surprised by my logic and not sure what to say,
so I kept going. 'I am not going to go through this dramatic
"operation" if we eventually are going to have one next year!'

'OK … so, does this mean … you want to … keep it?'

Housam asked for the bill and we left quickly, as I looked like
I was about to break down. This new update changed the direction of the discussion. I'd thought we were on the same page, but
we weren't.

The next morning, we headed to the subway station to escape
Brooklyn, hoping a change of scene would help the decision.

'Refugees are welcome.'

The three words rose high on the cardboard signs held by strangers on the train to Manhattan. I remembered that there were marches organized against Trump's ban. I was overwhelmed with the kindness of those who decided to spend their Sunday for this cause. I wasn't used to these kinds of signs. I was used to the other ones, the ones that have 'not' in them. The protest felt like a personal message, and I felt guilty for not joining, busy dealing with the unexpected human growing inside me.

We got off at 86th Street and headed to Central Park for a stroll. Housam and I sat by the lake and looked at the kids running around. The sun was warm, as were their laughs. I didn't notice I was smiling along with them. I remembered the familiar giggles from the kids back in Galway while walking on Salthill Beach. The idea of a kid making me smile sounded less strange now than it had back then. I had been eager to live the New York adventure. Six months in, and I was already miserable. More lost than I had ever been, torn apart between two worlds, struggling with remote working and a remote relationship. What if it was this tiny creature that was going to fix it all? Could being a mother be the answer? But what if the baby grew up and resented me for this life? How could I give it the best future?

'What are you thinking?' Housam put his arm around me. I sighed and shared my thoughts.

'Let me process this thought for the next few hours.'

'You know,' Housam smiled, 'when you were crying over the phone and telling me you're pregnant while I was half asleep, I thought for a second it was 2008. I thought we were still in Damascus, and that your family was going to kill me because we weren't married yet!'

I laughed, a bit ashamed of how I'd ruined the news of being a father for him. We left the park after a relaxing walk. I spotted a model in a red dress, jumping while a photographer took quick shots of her. Freezing her moment, legs spread in the air. When we passed by, I noticed she wasn't wearing any underwear. *I will miss this city so much when I am away.*

After we had lunch, we passed a baby shop. I decided to test my feelings and went inside. I looked around for a few seconds before I started panicking.

'I need to get out!' I pointed to the door, laughing nervously as I felt trapped in a maze. I stood in front of the displays of the baby world, and took a deep breath. Being around baby things made my heart warm and nervous at the same time, but it was the good kind of stress, like going on a roller coaster or having a first date.

'I think I want to keep it,' I finally said. 'But for now, let's stay away from those shops!'

On Monday I went to the office, and I worked like it was another day, trying to ignore Pablo's disagreeable face. I wanted to take a little revenge in postponing the news. I felt he'd crossed a line, pushing his opinion while discussing my personal life when I'd made it clear I didn't want to. Now, looking back at that moment, I am grateful that he was there, to doubt my confusion and push me to rethink through the walls I had built around my fears.

At the end of the day, I told Pablo my decision to keep the pregnancy, and his face was beaming again.

'Now, don't expect me to go easy on you just because you are pregnant.'

'I was hoping you would say that.' I was determined to make this work out. I wanted to be the ideal successful pregnant woman, a figure I had never seen in my tech career. I wanted to prove that women didn't need to choose between career and maternity, not realizing I was choosing to go through another battle.

Before the end of the day, I went to the card shop on the corner and bought a card for Housam. They didn't have one that said: 'Sorry for freaking you out, but you're going to be a father'. I bought a 'happy anniversary' card instead. I customized it, scratching out the word 'anniversary' and replacing it with 'new baby', and added: 'to the coolest dad-to-be'.

The infamous Muslim ban changed many things. Kinan was performing a concert outside the US and wasn't allowed to come back to his home in New York. The shop owner at Atlantic Avenue welcomed me with a disturbed face the next time I visited him. He was unable to carry on with his business now he couldn't travel back and forth to Syria. Atlantic Avenue was flaming with protestors. Although my UN visa saved me from all this drama, it didn't make much of a difference. I already felt unwelcome, again, in another country that I'd thought might be a new home. And I couldn't wait to leave.

Chapter 19

The Four Seasons
of New York – Spring

FIRST THING AFTER ARRIVING in Ireland, I went to my GP and told her about my pregnancy. I didn't notice how nervous I was until I ran out of breath at the last sentence. She looked at me in horror. Last time she'd seen me, I was already struggling. Now I was back with an unplanned pregnancy. I assured her I was doing well and ready to do this.

'You know that the medicine you were taking for your PCOS was intended to make you fertile, right?' she hesitantly asked.

'I found out after I got pregnant and researched it online to see if I should keep taking it.' I forced a smile, trying to brush away how furious I had been when I learnt that. 'I am surprised the specialist prescribed it even though I mentioned I didn't want to get pregnant.'

'But you're OK now with the idea?'

'Yes.' I took a deep breath. 'It was a shock in the beginning, but I am OK now.'

When I came back again, I met the nurse with a urine sample for her to test.

'Oh yeah, you're definitely pregnant,' she said casually. A tiny bit of me still thought there might be a slight chance this was all a dream.

For the next five minutes, she explained what would happen

and gave me the appointment dates when I should come in for check-ups. She handed me booklets and brochures with pictures of caring mothers and cute babies on their covers. I couldn't process what she was saying any more. This was not the first time she'd had this conversation, based on the way she was rushing through it. It was my first time, though. I wished she realized that. Maybe she did at some point, because she stopped talking and said, 'You think you are terrified now? Wait till they put that baby in your hands in the delivery room!'

I carried my booklets and thoughts back home. I hadn't told anyone else about my pregnancy, and I wasn't planning to until it became inevitable. I wanted to have some extra time to process it.

Despite the drama of it all, pregnancy suited me. My hormones settled down, and I became a relaxed creature. Housam and I didn't argue any more. He was more caring and I was more appreciative.

'Can you stay pregnant for ever, please?' Housam joked one night. I'd never experienced this feeling before. I was never calm. There was always something irritating me or pushing my buttons.

Deciding to proceed with the pregnancy made me see Ireland as the place to settle in. I didn't feel the urge to go back to New York. I wanted to be in the relaxed nature of Galway, and I agreed with Pablo that I would stay there until I finished my first trimester. But there was one trip I had to make before going back to New York.

My fight to get a visa to Saudi Arabia finally worked out after many attempts and more rejections. The visa was for *Umrah* – the religious visit to Mecca – and it was only valid as long as

Housam accompanied me as my male guardian. The patriarchal world looked very ancient at that point, and after everything I'd been through, I had to accept the rules to visit my family, this time as a wife, not as a daughter. The visa agent told Housam, 'Don't come back to me. This visa process caused me so much trouble and I wish I'd never accepted you in the first place.'

When I put on a black *abaya* again, I felt all the buried memories rush to the surface once more.

Our flight landed in Jeddah, the main terminal for *Umrah* visitors. Airports were not allowed to operate in Mecca and planes couldn't fly over the holy mosque. We decided to stay for one day in Jeddah and then take a flight to Riyadh, where my family lived. Sami was waiting for us at Jeddah Airport, as he was already there for a business trip. It had been five years since I'd hugged him goodbye at Damascus Airport. He looked the same, but many things had changed in our lives. Now he was married to the woman he loved and had two kids who I only knew from photos and videos. *Who can bring back those missed moments?* I wasn't sure if I was permitted to hug him or not at Jeddah Airport, but he hugged me.

Housam reunited with his best friend, who had got married and settled in Jeddah. When we went over for dinner at his place, I saw Housam as a different man. Although he hadn't been in touch with his friends after the trauma he'd been through, they seemed to pick up the conversation from where they'd left it. His friend's wife and I watched two guys laughing about memories we never knew, but their laughs were contagious. Memories from college and road trips and troubles and jobs. That's all they had now: memories. When the night was over, they hugged goodbye, not sure when they would meet again.

The next day we took the plane to Riyadh, where Walid was waiting for us at King Khalid Airport. He was also married now, to a wife I'd never met. He had a new car, and he'd lost lots of weight. We caught up on the way back to our family's house. I forgot how big the city was and how long the rides. I didn't miss that at all.

When our apartment building appeared on the horizon, I felt like a prisoner being brought back to their cell. Housam's presence was a good reminder that I was only there temporarily, and I could leave at any minute.

My mother was behind the door waiting for us. I inhaled her tender motherly scent as we hugged, laughed and cried.

'Go say hi to your father.'

I took a deep breath and walked to the main bedroom where all our arguments had taken place, all his yelling and all my tears. My father was lying in bed covered with a blanket. He was thin, and unshaven. I had never seen him unshaven before. I remembered one time in Damascus when Walid decided to grow a beard and my father forced him to shave it. Having a beard back in the eighties was enough to raise suspicions that one belonged to the Muslim Brotherhood and could lead to all sorts of trouble.

My father's skin was saggy, and the long bones in his arms were visible. The belly that I used to jump over when I was a little girl was gone.

I came closer until he saw me, but I couldn't see him. The tears were blurring my eyes.

'*Marhaba*, Baba.'

I was still nervous about his reaction. Since the day he had told me never to come back home, I had imagined meeting again in many scenarios, but never once like this.

My father looked confused. He said hi back, but I wasn't sure if he knew who I was. My mother stood behind me, fighting her tears, and asked Housam to come in as well. Housam had never met him. He had only received his hatred remotely. Still, he joined us in the bedroom and greeted my father with a smile as if nothing had happened.

'This is your daughter, Suad.' My mother raised her voice, introducing me. 'And this is her husband. He is saying hi.'

My father reached out for Housam's hand and looked him in the eye as he struggled to put a sentence together.

'Are you taking care of her?' my father whispered.

Housam froze for a second, and I felt a pull in my stomach.

'Of course, a'ammi – uncle. *She is in my eyes.*'

My father nodded. My heart was a sky of fireworks. I never thought I'd witness such a moment of peace between the two men in my life, and it was hard to know it was only because of my father's condition. I left the room, threw myself on the first couch and sobbed for the six wasted years of our lives as father and daughter. All for nothing.

My tears kept flowing for a week, pushed by hormones and grief for my father, who was lost but still alive. I wished he was still healthy and angry instead of this. I didn't know if he remembered me or mistook me for his sister, Aunt Sanaa. He never addressed me as his daughter, and he kept asking me about his brothers and sisters as if I were one of them.

My family had had a year to adjust to this new situation and go through all the stages of denial, shock and acceptance. My mother had learnt how to be a nurse, feed him, change his nappies, look after his vitals, and worry about this new situation.

It didn't feel like a good time to share my pregnancy news at first. But after two days I gave up on waiting for the perfect moment and told my mother over dinner before she rushed off again to check on my father.

My mother's rare smile appeared, and she congratulated Housam and me.

'Finally! See how God sent you a baby despite your nonsense decision to postpone. God knows best.' I might have stayed silent and let that comment pass to allow her to enjoy the moment of a miracle, but I couldn't.

'I kept this baby because *I* wanted to.' My mother gasped as I told her about the abortion.

Telling my father was another level of awkwardness. If he thought I was his unmarried sister, how would he react to her being pregnant? My mother insisted, and I told him, but he wasn't there. He looked like he'd forgotten about it before he'd understood it.

My family's house was empty during the day, so it was only Housam and me along with my father. My mother had no help and was used to leaving him alone during her working hours now that she had a job at the university. Although he slept most of the day, I worried about him being alone after I left. What if he needed a glass of water?

I stayed with him when he was up and put on his favourite black-and-white movies. I read paragraphs from his finance books, hoping to bring back anything left in his memory. I saw his eyes become watery; I saw his broken ego when the nurse came in one day to change the dressings on his bedsores. I saw his boredom while staring at the ceiling and his lost look trying to recognize faces and objects around him.

After a week, I got the strength to leave the house and go to the hospital to have my first scan, since I couldn't do it back in Ireland until I was three months pregnant. I was now two months along.

The baby's heartbeat, mine and Housam's played together like a symphony. The heartbeat made all of this real. There *was* something inside me, after all, and it felt marvellous.

After that, Housam and I went to a shopping mall. It was the first time I'd seen women working in shops in Saudi, the same shops that I used to go to and see men behind the counters. Housam was nervous about being in a new world with many new rules for the first time, especially after he found himself standing in the family line to order a coffee instead of the men's line. The two worlds weren't separated as before with barriers and walls – just two lines next to each other.

He was worried he would offend someone if we held hands, or if he spoke when the shop assistant was a woman. I enjoyed a good laugh at him while he imagined how he would end up in prison. Saudi Arabia had changed a lot. The gender segregation was fading, although still there. Most importantly, there were no longer two education ministries and two curriculums. Boys and girls studied the same words now, and the same values.

On 21 March 2017, we celebrated Mother's Day and took many photos. My mother looked sad in all of them. My father's situation had worn her out, and she couldn't help but think of my departure flight, scheduled for the next day. This was not how a family reunion should've been. I had missed so much, and I was going to miss more. I didn't know how long it would be until I saw them again, or if I ever would.

*

My New York spring apartment was located in a fancy high-rise building on Wall Street. I had been lucky enough to find such a place on Airbnb at a reasonable price. My visit was for three weeks, and I was finally ready to share my pregnancy news after reaching my fourth month. My belly was starting to show and it was becoming challenging to button my trousers. It was time to announce.

To make it short and sweet and memorable, I decided to announce it through three-dozen cupcakes decorated with baby-related icons and my due date in icing.

'Good way to avoid a speech!' Pablo teased.

Comments and questions leaked between the hugs and laughs of my colleagues. 'When did you find out?' or 'How are you going to travel now?' or 'Is that why you didn't order a burger from Shake Shack with us the other day?' But one comment caught me by surprise: 'Now you don't need an excuse for not drinking when you go out with us!' It was a joke, but it made me wonder if people would ever accept someone different.

During the time I'd spent in Galway, the science team had expanded. Three researchers had joined after Ryan left, in addition to two visiting researchers. As I passed by the office one day and glanced at the team, I could only see how unfit I was around six scientists with PhDs from prestigious universities, while I didn't have a Master's. My insecurities grew like a beast.

For a new project I was working on, I learnt how to process satellite images to analyse population, temperature and, most importantly, destruction. The last one sparked my interest. There was a big section in the dataset for Syrian satellite images, processed and analysed by a UN agency. 'Before' and 'after' photos measured the amount of destruction that had happened in the country, to determine how much it would cost to rebuild it. I saw pictures of Palmyra before and after. I remembered the first time I saw Housam, on that trip. That time I laughed until my belly ached, and how he lent me his jacket when it became chilly. Palmyra's temples, where we sat down with our friends and sang and listened to the oud echo, were now a pile of dust.

Another satellite image showed a map of Syria split into tiles of red and yellow based on the level of destruction. I knew my family's house was still safe in Al-Mazzeh, but the house Housam had bought in Jisreen was not. We weren't sure what had happened to that area up until then, but when I located it on that map, it was in a red square: severe destruction.

I sent the map to Housam, and he sent me a video of Al-Yarmouk after it was opened again. His cousin had gone to check on his family house. The video showed the house full of sand and barrels. Everything looked almost the same colour. The light was coming from the ceiling where a missile had fallen but failed to explode. A slogan tainted the walls of the living room. His cousin said the house was used as a military base for ISIS due to its central location.

My spring trip was short, as I had to go back and renew my Syrian passport, my Irish visa, and then the American one. I wanted to make a final trip to New York before my third trimester. I wanted to be around my work family when I was heavy and do baby shopping, so I made sure to leave enough time for all the paperwork. Before I took a red-eye flight back to Ireland, I felt my pregnancy sickness was almost gone, so I went for a Shake Shack on my way to the gate. It had been over four months since I'd had one, but I didn't know that Trump's phobia of migrants would make me wait another year before returning to New York.

Chapter 20

A Child Without a Village

IN MAY 2017, HOUSAM and I found out we were having a boy, as my mother-in-law had predicted. Naming the baby turned out to be challenging. Looking for a name that worked in both Arabic and English but wasn't too overused was not easy. We knew the baby would get Irish citizenship since we had been residents for over three years now – a huge relief.

We kept mocking and rejecting each other's suggestions. Not to mention the pressure put on Housam to name him after his late father.

'I would never name him Muhammad,' Housam said firmly. 'My father always told me not to name a child after him.'

'Well, he is dead now. You have to name him after him,' my mother-in-law argued with Housam over the phone. It was not easy to explain to her the consequences of using such a name outside the Middle East and the attachments that came with it.

'How about Kinan?' I suggested. Kinan's concert was a significant moment in our lives, and it turned out I was pregnant at the time, though I hadn't known it. It felt right.

'I don't want Arabic names,' Housam refused.

Despite my attempts to convince him it wasn't very Arabic, it took until we were driving one day and a long truck stopped at the traffic light next to us with the logo KEENAN.

'Huh. I guess Keenan is not only an Arabic name after all?' I said in disbelief.

When we went back home, Housam did a thorough search on the name and found out it had Irish origins. Thus, a perfect name was born.

The US visa situation pushed me to the edge of all the emotions I had experienced over and over: anger, loneliness and frustration at the world's unfairness. I already knew my family and best friends would not be around me during pregnancy and birth. I'd accepted that and tried to focus on the half-full – I thought I still had my work family – but now that was impossible as well.

I took some time to let my anger sink in. I made some decisions that made sense at the time, like leaving the work WhatsApp group and becoming more isolated to protect myself from the pain of being so far away.

'You need to connect with your team. You can't simply disappear.' Pablo was irritated after my withdrawal. How could I explain that pain to him?

Anger wore me down. Even if I tried to distract myself, something managed to slip and remind me of my isolation. Like a quote that was meant to be inspirational: 'If you don't like where you are, move. You are not a tree.' Or a colleague complaining how their visa took three days instead of one. It was like we lived in two worlds, not two time zones, and the difference between the two was hundreds of years. And while they worried about the future, I was still trapped in my past worries.

I decided to take control and try accepting my fate. I made a list of my colleagues' names and thought of a sweet or funny anecdote we shared, and I wrote over twenty postcards, with pictures of different Irish landmarks, to say how much I missed them, that visas would never stop me and that I would be back, reminding myself more than them of this fact.

It was healing, and I found myself smiling through the process. When I finished the twenty-plus cards, I wrapped them all together, addressed them to Mari and waited impatiently for them to arrive. Soon I got smiley photos of my friends along with their cards. Some didn't respond. By the next day, the post-cards' magical effect had disappeared, and I was back to where I was before.

By the third trimester, I started to face the pregnancy reality that I had been avoiding. I hadn't bought any baby-related items yet. I had wanted to postpone that feeling as much as I could. In my seventh month of pregnancy, Housam and I decided to travel to Dublin and do some shopping. We met up with Basel and Nisreen and their little girl after not having seen them for a long time. It was good to have company and get their advice on what baby products to buy. We came back with many boxes, but also a stomach bug that got me admitted to hospital to be hooked up to an IV bag and monitored overnight. Although I was discharged after a day and recovered over a week, that sickness, that feeling of weakness, triggered an inevitable depression.

~

The weekly prenatal health checks with midwives or my GP were the only human contact I was having at that time. The midwife was different every week, but my doctor was the same, and she noticed I got emotional whenever she asked how I was feeling.

She was aware of my complicated and isolated situation. Her face always changed with sorrow when she talked to me, and it made me pity myself. I wanted to hug myself. I wanted to be stronger. But nothing was working. My iron levels were dropping as well, affecting my mood and energy. I had no stomach for work and barely finished my tasks.

'Do you feel like hurting yourself or anyone else?' the midwife asked me once at a scan.

I didn't feel like hurting myself. I had wanted to hurt myself back in Riyadh, and Cairo, and New York and India. The midwife couldn't seem to see all the wounds surfacing from my past.

Did I feel like hurting myself now? I was already hurt.

'You know there is always someone you can talk to,' she suggested. I nodded and cried every time I was told that, but I still didn't believe it. There was no one; there wouldn't be anyone.

On one of those visits to my GP, she suggested therapy again, and I said I would think about it. She mentioned group therapy instead of one-on-one, as that would take some time to arrange. Maybe if other mothers surrounded me, then I would be able to share the burden.

'You don't even need to say anything,' she said. And I decided to give it a try.

The meeting was in a hospital on the other side of the city. I drove there alone, despite Housam's offer to drive and wait for me. I wanted to be alone with my depression.

The room was spacious and hollow. The long windows overlooked a green park surrounding the building. That was the only colour I could see. Maybe there were more colours in the room, but that's how I remember it: dark and empty. It reminded me of

289

the haunted hospital in the horror video game I used to play with my brothers. I took a seat in the circle.

The chairs were filled shortly, and the group leader explained how this would work. 'We come here every week and take turns talking. You don't have to talk if you don't feel like it.'

The round started with one woman giving an update on her improving situation. She no longer felt distant from her two children. I noticed that I was the only one with a big belly popping out from under my blouse and unzipped jacket. I noticed they were all Irish, and they all mentioned their families and friends helping out. Everyone was talking about postnatal depression, while I was still in the perinatal phase.

The thought of how different I was in that group choked me with tears. When everyone finished talking, it was my unspoken turn. Despite the clear statement that I didn't need to speak, I felt the pressure of speaking up with everyone's eyes focused on me.

I am already here, so why not?

'Hi, my name is Suad,' I said, avoiding direct eye contact with anyone. 'I am eight months pregnant. I am Syrian, and I don't think Syrians should have babies.'

The mothers and the group leader tried to hide their tears, but the sniffs echoed in the big room. When I finished talking, the room became quiet; too quiet. Not a word floating. I wished someone would hug me and lie and say everything would be fine, but the session was wrapped up and we were encouraged to come again.

I left the haunted hospital like a patient in the middle of surgery with my wounds fresh and dripping. *This was a mistake.*

I fell behind at work again. I was either on sick leave or not feeling well enough to get much done. Being far away and disconnected deprived me of the social support I ached for. Around the end of my eighth month of pregnancy, I asked for early maternity leave to look after myself. After it was approved, I created a document to hand over all my open projects, and I said goodbye in my last weekly meeting. The internet connection was weak. I only heard a few split words and couldn't see anyone. The line was disconnected with a faraway goodbye, ending my connection to the world in New York that I couldn't reach any more.

During a solo walk along the Salthill promenade, I noticed a sign in front one of the hotels: 'Aqua Yoga Classes for Mothers'. I loved swimming and missed it a lot but wasn't sure about yoga. The first class was offered for free, so I decided it was time to buy a new swimsuit.

Aisling ran the pool in the hotel where the classes took place. She was middle-aged, friendly and caring. The warm water relaxed my muscles as soon as I dipped my toes in. I found myself joining another circle of mothers, but this one felt different. Aisling asked us to introduce ourselves: name, age, how far along in the pregnancy we were and whether we had any specific problems. There were no dramatic confessions, just the usual complaints about backache, sleeping problems, heartburn and other pregnancy issues.

I followed Aisling's steps in the water and listened to her voice guiding us through it. I closed my eyes and placed my hands on my stretched-out belly. *Inhale.* I pictured my baby inside. I smiled despite my overwhelmed heart. *Exhale.* I pictured him splashing the water with joy. He was kicking now. A little tear dropped – a happy tear.

I am tired, so tired, but I love you. I need you here with me. I need you to make this ugly world a better place. I will do my best to protect you and give you a happy life, a happier life than mine.

You deserve happiness.

We deserve happiness.

The yoga class became my regular weekly routine. Being in the water helped me gather myself again and get power from connecting with my baby instead of waiting for support from outside. I started finding pleasure in being a mother-to-be. Whenever I closed my eyes in the water, I could feel the umbilical cord between us. My heart was full. The other expecting mothers were my therapy group, even though we didn't talk outside the water and even though I was, again, the only non-Irish one. But for sixty minutes I had a safe space and the illusion of friends physically around me. The best part was when Aisling announced at the beginning of each class that one of the mothers had gone into labour and had a healthy baby. I looked forward to that day. I wasn't afraid any more.

My GP looked at me like I was crazy when I told her I felt great and I was going back to school part-time. I finally took the first step in starting a Master's in Data Analytics. I decided to move forward with my plans and not postpone for another year, like I'd always had to in the past for financial or visa-related reasons. I needed that degree to feel like I could fit in better at work. Being pregnant would not stand in my way. I was also worried that maternity leave would weaken my technical muscles, so having a Master's to study for during that time sounded perfect.

I planned my first academic term so that I would take only the two mandatory modules, then more in the next term after I had recovered from the birth.

On the first day, I stood in line at the student centre to pick up my student card. Everyone around me was in their twenties, while I was over ten years older and holding a big belly. I enjoyed noticing the awkward glances. I didn't care. I was filled with joy and pride.

At the introduction course where I met the rest of my class, the programme manager welcomed us all and showed us the students' diversity in numbers on one of his slides. Ireland, UK, US, India and Syria. Next to Syria, there was the number one. That was me. I was the older pregnant girl from Syria, and I wanted to laugh about how awkward I must have looked, but instead, I felt special. I stopped fighting how I stood out and looked at it as a uniqueness.

The last month of pregnancy was the longest. It wasn't a myth, after all. I was heavy, with a belly full of stretch marks. False contractions came and went, leaving me wondering how painful the real ones would be. Sleeping was rare, as no position was comfortable. During the last check-in at the hospital on my due date, the midwife told me I would be booked in for induction in ten days.

Housam was patient and loving. His parenting instincts intimidated me. I knew deep down that I would never be as good at it as he was. I knew nothing about children and barely enjoyed their company. He was the kids' favourite in the family. He knew how to make them giggle and amused while I frowned at them for making noise.

'You'll be great. You'll see.'

On 30 September at 2 a.m., my waters broke.

Before I left the house and turned off the lights, I took a look at the empty house and the waiting crib that we had installed last month, and felt my heart beating with my cramps. The next time

I would be back in it, things would be much different. *We will no longer be two. We will be three; we will be a family; we will be home.*

Thirty minutes before the end of September, Keenan arrived through an emergency C-section after twenty-two hours of labour. As I held him to my chest and Housam kissed both our foreheads, I felt the pieces of my broken heart coming together and dark shards replaced with light.

~

When I was twelve years old, my mother took me to her cousin Samar's *mobarakeh*, to celebrate her newborn, in one of the houses in Al-Midan. When we arrived, the house was empty except for my aunt Razan, who met us there. Samar was half sitting, half lying in a large carved wooden bed with four posts at its corners, wearing a pink lace nightgown with a robe on top of it, and holding a sleeping baby up to her chest.

'It was really an easy birth. I'm in no pain,' Samar said.

'Don't ever mention that,' Aunt Razan warned her, then she bent over and whispered to Samar, but I could hear. 'The evil eye doesn't have mercy,' she said in a serious tone. 'Every now and then you should shift your position uncomfortably to show people that you are in pain.'

Samar's house was soon full of women and children. Hot caraway drinks topped with nuts and shredded coconut were circling around on big trays to the guests, who took turns coming over to Samar to kiss her and bless the baby, leaving a small pouch of money or pinning a piece of golden jewellery on her.

Music played, loud and joyful. The kids were playing around

and the fan in the ceiling couldn't run fast enough to cool the place down in a heated Syrian summer.

This is insane, I thought.

When I have a baby, I don't want any of this.

Sadly, my wish was granted.

~

My maternal instincts kicked in faster than I thought. Despite the sleep deprivation, the breastfeeding struggles, and feeling like a stranger in my stretched-out body, my love for Keenan blossomed from the moment our eyes locked. Holding Keenan made me forget any pain that had ever crossed my heart. His peaceful face made me look to the bright future instead of the dark past. Housam's eyes sparkled with life again as he held Keenan in his arms.

Housam filled in for all the villagers that I needed. On the first day at the hospital, when I was desperate for a shower but couldn't move with the stitches and the catheter, he walked me to the shower room and helped me get undressed. I was hormonal and tired and embarrassed about looking and smelling terrible and still bleeding. I tried to reach out for the soap and water, but I couldn't bend or stretch. I sat on the bench in the hospital shower and cried over my fragility.

'You are OK; don't worry. I am here,' Housam said while washing my body, which looked like a crime scene.

Before meeting Housam, I never understood unconditional love; I never had it; I thought of it as a weakness. At that moment in the hospital shower, as I leant on Housam, for the first time, I saw his true and unconditional love.

*

In December, a few months after giving birth, I was invited to a Christmas dinner by a humanitarian organization in Ireland. I took that as an excuse to dress up and see people. The event was held in a luxurious hall with ornate tables covered neatly with white cloths and fancy food. Speeches were given, people clapped, then a famous sportsperson joined us and talked about his time in Syria. A video on a screen showed my country in rubble while he played football with happy kids in shabby clothes and a little girl on crutches. I left the people in suits and dresses and stayed in the toilets for a proper amount of time to make sure the film had ended.

I never understood the need to spend tons of money on conferences and assemblies and celebrities instead of giving the money directly to refugees and other causes. I struggled to watch the way people could distance themselves from the human suffering happening in real time and enjoy a fancy dinner and sometimes trivia quizzes and prizes. I could see the ghosts of the miserable faces of those who had died during the war or while crossing the sea floating in that fancy hall. Life, clearly, was not fair. I was reminded of that fact constantly during my work. The humanitarian world was not my place.

After 2017 ended, my mother-in-law called us, depressed, worried she would die before meeting up with us again. We couldn't obtain a visa for her to visit, so, after some research, I found out that Malaysia was the only safe country that didn't require visas for Syrians. We took a long flight to Kuala Lumpur with our three-month-old Keenan so she could hug her first grandson.

Majid joined us, but my mother couldn't travel and leave my father behind. Sami had become a refugee in France after life in Saudi Arabia didn't work out for him and the situation in Syria remained not safe enough to return. I travelled to visit him and my heart danced when he held Keenan and his kids played with him. I was glad to have a family member a few hours away, even if we were still separated by weeks of visa processing.

When Keenan was five months old, I agreed reluctantly to return to work. I wasn't ready, but I was worried that postponing any longer would make me lose track. I was lucky to find Annette, a kind childminder with a big heart, who later became as close as family to us in Galway. She bonded with Keenan for a few hours daily while I ran between errands. On my first day working remotely again, I quietly cleared my inbox and no one realized I was back to work until the end of the day. The gap between me and my team had grown bigger while I was away. I had missed more events, and they had missed a major change in my life. I was back to being the strange new girl again – maybe I always was.

I visited New York again for a short trip, accompanied by my guys, in the hope of bridging this new gap. I introduced six-month-old Keenan to the city and showed him my favourite spots. He seemed to enjoy the crowds and the noise and the end-less entertainment. I took him to the Unicef building where he moved from arm to arm, spreading smiles everywhere. Before I left New York, I made sure to meet Terese, who held Keenan with the love of a grandmother.

A few months after my return, I finally accepted that this unique job was never going to fit me, especially now that I was officially a remote employee, a mother and a part-time Master's student. This was exactly what had scared me when I found out I was pregnant, except now I wasn't afraid. Keenan's smile made it much easier to let go of things that I couldn't change.

I quit my job and let go of the illusion that my work would

actually save the world, or at least Syria. I wasn't in the right mindset to do such a thing, certainly not while working between two countries when I belonged to neither, and certainly not with a Syrian passport during the Trump era. My wounds were still fresh and I needed to heal before I jumped into humanitarian work again. I left Unicef, New York and my escape of Little Syria, all with a lump in my throat, and decided to focus on my studies and explore my options in Ireland.

Working on my Master's made me feel more in control, despite my thesis still being vague. I knew it would have to do with social impact and be related to Syria. The inspiration came after a taxi driver told me, 'Syrians are terrorists – don't you watch the news?'

I realized after a few words with him that he'd never actually met any Syrians before. Yet he was happy to give us that horrible label. My curiosity was at its maximum. What news was he referring to? When did the word 'Syria' become associated with terrorism? It was then that I decided on my thesis. I wanted to use data analytics techniques to analyse news around refugees in hopes of highlighting xenophobia in the news.

In early 2019, after over five years in Ireland, I was eligible to apply for Irish citizenship through naturalization. Looking at all the stamps in my passport, I remembered all the events related to each one of them. I had dreamt of the day I would have the Irish nationality that would protect me and give me a second homeland. I pictured my scattered friends and family worldwide and the moment that I could finally reunite with each of them without a visa. I couldn't wait.

By autumn, I had graduated with First Class Honours. I held two-year-old Keenan proudly as I put on my graduation gown and held my certificate. My thesis won several awards and was mentioned by TechCrunch as one of twenty-five innovative new projects using tech to help refugees and NGOs. The university president sent me a letter of recognition after my success. Shortly after, I started volunteering with a different humanitarian organization called Techfugees. Founded by Mike Butcher and Joséphine Goube, they are a group of mainly volunteers who believe in the importance of empowering displaced people using technology. They supported my research project for a year and helped me explore ways of scaling it up. Through them, I connected with Dogpatch Labs, the resourceful entrepreneurs' nest in Dublin, through which I got the chance to meet the Dutch royals in a round-table discussion around migration and entrepreneurs.

We moved to Dublin after my Master's, hoping to be closer to friends, tech companies, diverse communities, Middle Eastern food, the airport, and the hustle of a bigger city. Housam found a job as a software engineer in a tech company and I felt it was time to work on me.

~

'I am not OK.'

I told this to my therapist in her damp, chilly room. I told her about a home that burned inside me. That wherever I went, I felt like the odd person out in the group, to the point where I avoided groups completely.

Not-fitting is more painful than loneliness. I realized that in all the shows that I liked to watch, I was the character that stuck out. I was Lane in *Gilmore Girls*, Phoebe in *Friends*, Peggy in *Mad Men*.

I also told her about my traumatizing birth, about Keenan's

299

continuous meltdowns and the long hours we spent alone in the house, Housam at work and no one to visit or have over.

I told her about my mother's continuous questioning about when were we going to come over and why the citizenship was taking so long.

'You've been fighting for a long time, and you have been fighting so many battles,' my therapist said. 'It is OK to take a break.'

She didn't say how. She didn't explain how one can take a break without breaking. Instead, she told me about her trip to Spain, about the sun that I missed so much and how the weather could be affecting my mood.

The hour was over. I had to leave now and pause that pain until the next session. It was December. It was colder outside and darker than when I'd entered, just like me. I shoved the emotion worksheet in my backpack and walked to clear my tears before heading back home.

'Write your emotions down so you can be aware of them as they occur,' the therapist told me before I left. The worksheet was already divided into cells, small cells; smaller than the pain that I wanted to put into words. The pain that wouldn't leave even after four sessions with the therapist.

The window of a coffee shop enticed me to take a look. The place was small and empty and smelled like my favourite addiction.

'What time do you close?' I asked the guy behind the counter.

He looked at the clock hanging on the wall beside him. 'In an hour or so?'

Perfect.

I ordered a flat white and pulled up a chair to sit next to the window so I could watch the life that passed by daily without noticing me. I grabbed my laptop out of my black bag, letting it fall empty over the other chair next to me.

The cursor on the screen was flashing on a white page that I'd created earlier that day. Only one sentence was written over and over.

I don't want to talk about home.
I don't want to talk about home.
I don't want to talk about home.

Epilogue

MY CITIZENSHIP APPLICATION WAS delayed due to Brexit and then the pandemic. It's been 750 days since I applied. Every day, I hold my breath as I nervously check the mailbox, hoping to find the life-altering letter I've been waiting for, my freedom ticket through airports and meaningless borders. I feel trapped, but everyone is trapped now as a new virus flips our destinies one more time. It's easier to say I can't be with my family and friends because of the pandemic than to say it's because I am Syrian.

I force myself to stand on my balcony in Dublin despite the unwelcoming weather. It's quiet and cold most of the time, but I pretend it's somewhere warm and loud, where kids are playing in the streets, music is coming from a car passing by and the sound of a TV is bursting from a neighbour's apartment. I pretend, but the balconies around me remain silent and dark, like graves.

My mother is still stuck in Saudi Arabia, looking after my disabled father, who is stuck in the mind of a ten-year-old boy. She dreams of the day I come back to Saudi Arabia and tells me all about the women who can now drive and sing and live without a male guardian's permission. She dreams about our house in Syria and sends me pictures, sent by our neighbour, of the flowers that are still blooming every spring. She keeps asking me if I pray five times a day; she is probably worried I am going to hell, and I am worried we are already living in it.

My grandmother left this world after the pandemic spread like wildfire in Syria, where life post-war is nothing like life. The financial crisis and even more international sanctions killed whatever managed to survive. I can't picture heaven any more, but I know Tete is in a better place because anywhere is better than Syria today. Sometimes it seems that whoever closed the door on Syria forgot to open a window.

My grandmother died before listening to the last voice message I sent her on WhatsApp; before meeting Keenan; before trying my cooking. With her death dies the last reason for me to go back. I don't think the Syria I once knew and loved is there any more. It has become a memory, a place in a parallel universe that I could only reach with a time machine.

I texted Nadia one day and told her about this book. We had been mostly texting polite messages on birthdays and holidays, with updated pictures of our kids growing bigger. I told Nadia about my overloaded heart in a voice message, and she replied with her overloaded heart through more voice messages. We filled in the gaps for each other on what had happened in our lives during the past few years. I realized then that I wasn't avoiding her due to differences in opinions. Nadia knew my past, my troubled memory, and I wanted to escape that more than anything.

I also texted Omar, my old friend who helped me publish my first essay. He went back to America and settled there with his new family. I told him I was writing again but having trouble unblocking many past events. He sent me a copy of our correspondence that I had lost in switching from one email server to another, and the essays I wrote in Arabic on the Syrian forum that was taken down after the manager disappeared during the war. As I scrolled through my past texts and faced the old me, it hit me how much I've changed.

And I wondered if maybe there is a version of me living back in Syria who still loves the rain; who wears a hijab, speaks Arabic, volunteers with paramedics and spends her time learning to play the piano while her cat purrs on her lap. Perhaps for every Syrian who left the country, there is an alternative version of them resuming the life they had before the war. And as long as those versions of us are still alive, we'll never find peace.

My Syrian friends have changed their names online to look less awkward in their new societies. They are now German, Swedish, Turkish, British, American, like I will be Irish one day and might change my name to Sally. Our kids will have a different journey looking for home. They might never know Syria; they might never speak Arabic and they might never notice something is wrong.

Keenan is now three. People say he has my face, but I am not sure I still have one. We celebrated his first and second and third birthdays with no family around. They missed three cakes, his bald head, his toothless smile and first steps. Keenan thinks his grandparents are magical creatures living in that black rectangle that I keep holding. He thinks his uncle Sami is our friend Suliman, who has the same beard and glasses. Every time I hear bad news from back home or a new dead-children picture pops up on my social media feed, I drop everything and go to check on my kid and hug him tightly.

Keenan's laughter and Housam's warm smile remind me that I am safe and loved. They bring out the best in me. And sometimes, on good days, it feels like it doesn't matter where the three of us are any more.

As long as we are together, we are home.

In June 2021, Day 848, my mailbox wasn't empty. I received my Irish citizenship certification, along with a long letter of congratulations from the Minister of Justice. The end of it says:

Today marks the start of a new chapter in your life, one that you have chosen to share with us, your fellow Irish citizens. We will celebrate your achievements, support you in difficult times and ensure that you always have a place to call home.

Acknowledgements

THIS BOOK IS THE result of a seed my mother planted in my young mind with her stories. My mother, R.N., I don't say thank-you enough, so here it is. Thank you for keeping bridges between us, despite disagreeing with me and despite my reckless attempts to burn them down. We belong to different eras, but I am proud of you and all your achievements, despite your tough times.

My dear brothers, we had our share of troubles, but I know you will always have my back, as I will always have yours. Thank you for spoiling me, each in your own way.

Ioanna Kyvernitou, thank you for being my friend, my first reader and my supporter through desperate times.

My dearest friends: Nadia, Omar, Lara, Nisreen (I deeply wish I could write your real names but we live in days where the word is more dangerous than a gun. You know who you are.) Thank you for your friendship and everything you've done for me over the years.

Doug Young, my wonderful agent, thank you for opening doors for me, for always supporting me and for answering all my questions, big and small, about the publishing industry.

I was lucky enough to have three brilliant editors working on my book at different stages: Fiona Murphy, Sharika Teelwah and Stephanie Duncan. Also Sorcha Judge and the whole Transworld team in Ireland and the UK. Thank you all for guiding me and making this book the best it could be. Special thanks to Mari-anne Issa El-Khoury for capturing in the cover design the captivating details of how one can be torn apart.

I was lucky to know Jan Carson during my writing journey.

ACKNOWLEDGEMENTS

Thank you for the valuable tips, the endless laughs, and for adopting me as a new writer.

Thank you to the Irish Arts Council for a generous bursary that kept me sane in times of financial insecurity. Thank you to Sasha de Buyl, the Cúirt International Festival of Literature, English PEN and Irish PEN for the residency that helped me write the ending of this book. Thanks also to the John Hewitt Society International Summer School.

I was fortunate enough to have mother/sister figures while far from family and in the diaspora. Terese Fabian, Cait Noone, Mary McNally, Liz McCarthy, Patricia Francis, Annette Harri: thank you to the beautiful women who looked after a stranger as if she was their own blood.

Many people contributed in different ways throughout my writing journey. Warmest thanks to Cassia Gaden Gilmartin, Shane Tuohy, Ryan Dennis, Yiannis Doukas, Hannah Trevarthen, Elizabeth Sulis Kim, Daniel Gorman, Harry F. Rey, Neil Hegarty, Kevin Higgins, Stella Calvert-Smith, Justine Solomons, Fiona O'Rourke, Sue Divin, Niall McArdle, Louise Brosset, Josephine Goube, and the Write Now 2020 squad who stuck with me through thick and thin.

Thank you, Dogpatch Labs, Dublin, for being my writing nest during the darkest rainy days.

Housam, my love, I am a risk-taker who jumps with closed eyes only because I know you are there to pick me up if I fall. Thank you for constantly telling me for the past ten years to 'just write!' whenever I told you I wished I was a writer. Thank you for bearing with me through this mad journey. I can't promise it will be the last.

SUAD ALDARRA is a writer and data scientist based in Dublin. She was born in Riyadh, Saudi Arabia, to Syrian parents. In 2003 she moved back to her family home in Syria to study software engineering. After fleeing the war in 2012 she lived in Egypt and the US, before eventually settling in Ireland. In 2021, Suad was awarded the Arts Council of Ireland English Literature bursary. *I Don't Want to Talk About Home* is her debut memoir.